BRIGHT DEEP WATER

Alfred Mehegan in 1924, age 13.
(Author's collection)

BRIGHT DEEP WATER

A Boston Life

David Mehegan

CHINQUAPIN PUBLISHERS

For my children, nieces, and nephews — Beth, Chrisann, Gregory, Jeff, Julie, Katie, Kerry, Lydia, Mark, Nancy, Owen, Sheila — and their children.

Published by Chinquapin Publishers
Norwell, Massachusetts 02061
dmehegan@gmail.bu.edu

Copyeditor: Elizabeth Uhrig
Cover and interior design, typesetting: Janis Owens

ISBN: 978-0-692-87792-0

LIBRARY OF CONGRESS CONTROL NUMBER: 2017940289

PRINTED IN THE UNITED STATES OF AMERICA

This book is set in Electra and Caravan Borders, designed by W.A. Dwiggins

Contents

Foreword

WHY WRITE A BOOK ABOUT A QUIET PERSON, neither saint nor sinner, who lived and died and did not rock the world in any way? That is a fair question about this book, a short biography of my father, Alfred C. Mehegan, and also a love story. To be sure, there have been well-noticed memoirs of unknown persons. I think, for example, of J. R. Ackerley's *My Father and Myself* and Calvin Trillin's *Messages from My Father: A Memoir*. Ackerley's book is often categorized as a pioneering work of gay life, and anything Trillin writes has an eager audience. Whether Al Mehegan's life merits a book depends upon whether quiet lives can be safely ignored or, conversely, whether they merit notice as strands in the fabric of an age.

It is a paradox that most fictional characters (aside from historical fiction, such as Robert Graves's *I, Claudius* and the novels of Hilary Mantel), from Emma Bovary to Willy Loman to the characters of Alice Munro, are ordinary people, and that is what we expect. But nonfiction books are usually centered on the premise that reader interest is limited to fame, wealth, power, celebrity, or notoriety.

My father's life offers none of those attractions. He lived an Irish-American Boston Catholic life in the twentieth century. In that life, full of striving, there was ambition for ordinary things: education, career, marriage, and family. But the waters ahead were mined. There was the Great Depression, as well as the smaller depression in his own spirit. There was war, which did him no physical injury, at least no battle wounds, but diverted his dreams in ways that he could not have anticipated. There was a class barrier. There was a legacy that was no fault of his own, what he called "my poorly started life." There were willful, self-centered parents. Finally, there was drink.

This book, which is not a memoir, though it calls upon memory in places, had its origins in a simple premise. My mother was a large figure in the lives of her twelve grandchildren, all of whom were adults by the time of her death. But they never knew their grandfather, who died when the firstborn was a year old. A family member who died before you were born does not seem quite real, seem to matter in the jigsaw puzzle of your life. Even those we did know who die when we are small children fade in our feelings and memories, and those whom we never knew are no more than hypothetical, like the characters in fiction.

I am the youngest of four children, age seventeen when my father died, and he is still vivid to me more than fifty years later. Sometimes my youngest son would ask about him, and I would answer as best I could. It sounded so odd; he would call him Al—"Tell me about Al," he would say—because he never got to call him Grandpa or Granddad. However I answered him went but little toward realizing my father as a person in his or my other two children's eyes, and I expect this is as true for my nieces and nephews. Often I have wished that my father could have known them, and they him. He did much to make them the kind of people they are, though they are not conscious of that. Such musings led to the idea that a book might be the way to coax him at least partially into reality for their generation. As I turned this idea over in my mind, it occurred to me that if I did not write this story, no one else would, and if I did not write it soon, it might be too late.

So I began, and it was not long before I rediscovered two truths that were part of my work as a newspaper writer. First, in the act of writing, you find out what you know and do not know, and you discover that you know both more and less than you thought beforehand. Like the never-ending bright-colored scarves from the magician's hat, the "more" streams out as you tug at your mind, while the "less" makes you delve into the evidence and ponder more deeply. The process of writing, poring over old files, talking to people, probing old memories, and just thinking when you're away from the work, makes a wholly new story take shape, more complicated and longer than anticipated. What you write in the end often is full of surprises to yourself, with insights and conclusions that you did not foresee. That is what happened here.

Second, I discovered that I know only one way to write a story, mine or somebody else's, which is to tell it as if the reader or listener not only knows nothing to begin with, but is not even sure that she or he cares to know. I could not write solely for my family, those who already have a personal interest. It had to be a story for anyone. That is how this became more of a real book than a letter to my children, grandchildren, nieces, and nephews.

Therefore, what you have ahead of you, if you continue beyond this point, is my best attempt to tell the life story of a person who dreamed and longed to do great things, who studied, worked, went to sea and to war, married, and had children. All that is set against the underlying older story of a marriage of two immature adolescents, their subsequent adventures, and the lifelong repercussions of their actions and characters for their one child. It is also the story of *his* marriage, which was a success but which could not escape altogether the shadows of that old history.

What is the proper attitude for the biographer to take to his subject in order to earn a reader's trust and respect? Must he be satirical, debunking, supercilious? Regard himself as having wisdom superior to that of his subjects, along with retrospection and total power over the material? He can characterize them virtually however he wants—just like a novelist. What is the proper way to use that power? One must begin with the premise that it is not possible to have absolute certainty. One must risk being wholly wrong, or missing the essential truth, as in any work of art.

It was not my intention to write a hagiography, and I do not believe that I have done so. The guiding principle was to include that which serves to reveal my father, which means that other characters, including living family members, might seem underrepresented. I tried to keep in mind that this is his story, not mine or my siblings' or my mother's. She wrote her autobiography, unpublished, as well as shorter profiles of her grandparents, parents, and parents-in-law. My father appears vividly in some of those writings, which makes her the indispensable witness. And though it is, as I said, his story, my mother is the foremost other character, and her costarring role is what makes it a love story.

But here I must take back in part what I have just written: that it is his story and not mine. Of course it is mine, my book—about him, but mine. I have tried to explain how I came to write the book, but not why, not fully. *Why* do we write about our ancestors? To forgive, to punish, to defend, to impeach? To make ourselves young again? I do not know the full answer, which is probably a good thing, if not knowing gives the telling the disquiet of uncertainty.

• • •

I write below that my father did not ever seek attention or put himself forward. The implication of that reserve is that much was necessarily withheld, or at least remained private, and is not known by me and never will be known or recorded. It is therefore likely that this story in some respects is questionable as to accuracy. The reporter's rule is to put in the paper only what one knows to be true. The underlying reality is that what you put in the paper, even when true, is at most a sketch, a fragment. In a newspaper, fortunately, there is always tomorrow and the next day, so that eventually more of the missing can be filled in and early errors corrected. But in a biography there is no tomorrow's edition. Even classics such as Douglas Southall Freeman's *Lee* or Boswell's *Life of Samuel Johnson,* when republished with critical commentaries by others, are usually left alone as to the author's original words. He tells his story, then steps aside. Belletrists, such as Walt Whitman, Marianne Moore, and William Wordsworth, often revised their works, but not so often biographers. I have to tell my story as best I can, then let it go. I can say honestly that I did my best, with what I was able to discover, not to judge, make excuses, or abuse the arrogated power to disclose the thoughts and feelings and motivations of the dead.

At the end of the story, I am left with a sense of mystery and more unanswerable questions. Foremost is the ineffable mystery of character. Why is one person able to extract from himself the barbed hooks of old family pathology while another cannot? How much of injury done to others is attributable to conscious malice and how much to impulsive self-centeredness and lack of imagination? How does one balance reasonable care for one's own interest with duty toward others? Does a sensitive nature make one a better person or only pathetic, too delicate to thrive, to be effective in the world as it is? How does a boy with few adult models forge his own mature, respected adulthood?

Finally, is everything that is sad and painful due only to the random wanderings of chance, with no application across cases, or is there something of use to our own lives that we can learn and draw from such a life as this?

BRIGHT DEEP WATER

Prologue
42.3581° N, 71.0636° W

Butch telephoned me in a tone of excitement. "I was looking around my cellar," he said. "I found something. I didn't even know I still had it. I'll bring it over."

A few minutes later, the red pickup truck stopped in front of my house. Butch got out, holding a small greenish metal object in his hand. He handed it to me. It was one half of a bronze fitting, oxidized green, with remnants of white paint. In form, it was a sturdy U-shaped strip with a ring at one end, about three and a half inches around, with cast-in threaded bolts protruding from the ring.

"It's the old gooseneck from the mast and boom," Butch said. "I must have kept it when I restored the boat."

It would have been attached to the mast of the sloop, bolt end facing aft, with two nuts that were still threaded on. A swivel component, which would have been fastened to the tack end of the boom and allowed it to swing, was missing. Stamped on the back, inside an oval circle, was "A. S. Co. Amesbury, Mass."

"Thanks," I said. "Thanks for bringing it."

I took it inside to my writing room and laid it on the bookcase next to the shells from Eniwetok Atoll, across from my desk, where I could see it while I thought and wrote.

1.

∞∞∞

Immigrants and Children

THE FAMILIAR IRISH TROPE is the dream of long-ago glory crushed and denied by an external power that cannot be defeated, only run away from or evaded with wit, drink, satire, or the consolations of religion. The national culture was full of a combination of vanity, gloom, deprivation, and fatalism. In America there was hope, but many people brought their burdens and impoverishments and habits of thought with them and passed them on to their children. Sometimes their legacy included a sense that the past might foreclose a brighter future.

• • •

"Perhaps I'll make a success of my poorly started life," my father wrote in a shipboard diary, when he was twenty. Not "ill-starred," which would suggest bad luck, but "poorly started," like that of a racehorse stumbling at the starting gate, which puts it behind from the beginning.

My father's friends, and my mother, called him Al, but his family called him Alfred. He was born at home in South Boston. The birth certificate lists 379 K Street, a well-kept wood-frame house built in 1890 that still stands, not far from south-facing Carson Beach. The date was August 1, 1911, and the parents were Esther Donahue Mehegan and Charles Mehegan. He was christened Alfred Joseph Mehegan on August 13 at Gate of Heaven Church at the corner of I (capital letter "I") and East Fourth Streets by Reverend Walter Laubret — not the pastor, presumably a curate — with godparents Charles Bartick and

Catherine Flood on hand. What was then the church is now the parish hall and office across the street from the present, much larger church, completed a year later. It is said that the Carrara marble statues in the new church had to be reordered, as the originals had gone down with the *Titanic.*

Charlie and Esther were eighteen. They had been married in the same church on November 15, 1910, age seventeen. Charlie had a job when he became a father: Alfred's birth certificate lists his profession as "standing fireman." The job had nothing to do with fighting fires. A standing fireman shoveled coal into a steam furnace, usually in a factory or public building, to keep up the steam heat.

Even though early marriage was more common then than it is today, Charlie and Esther's was unusual even for the times, and did not pass unnoticed in the community. When Alfred was a child, probably in adolescence, a neighborhood boy sneered that his parents' marriage had been forced. The boy must have heard it from adults. The imputation that his own existence was a scandalous accident so disturbed Alfred that he went to the church office to look up the marriage and birth certificates and was relieved to find a nine-month interval. Presumably he did not dare to ask his father.

Given his parents' ages, it is hard to imagine that no one tried to talk them out of marrying so young. Perhaps someone did. In an unpublished 2002 recollection of Esther, my mother, Mary Mehegan, wrote that Esther had once told her, "'When we were married my mother had died and so had Charlie's, and I think had they been alive we would have waited.'"[1] Like so much oral history, this is not quite right: Charlie's mother, Rose McManus Mehegan, died the year after the marriage. It is likely, given their ages and personalities, that Esther and Charlie never gave marriage careful thought, but followed an impulse out of physical attraction or desire to escape from parents, or even just a romantic lark. Mae Donahue, Esther's sister-in-law, said to me in a 1987 telephone conversation, "The Donahues were a tight-laced family. She wasn't happy at home. She was very much in love with Charlie Mehegan." Then as now, popular songs spoke of endless love. But Charlie and

Esther had no concept of the long run. When you're seventeen, the long run is the period between now and twenty-one. I heard Esther say once that romance is fine, but you need to have a solid money basis to get married. She was not speaking of Charlie and herself, but their marriage was her first lesson in the point.

Three-seventy-nine K Street was the Donahue house. So it appears that Charlie and Esther were living with her parents, or that she was and they did not yet have a home when the baby was born. However, they did eventually set up housekeeping. Esther told my mother a story of coming home, years after her divorce from Charlie, to visit Alfred, who was then living with his cousins the Mannings. "When she was sitting in the kitchen with him, she saw a pile of chopped wood behind the iron kitchen stove and discovered to her great sadness it was a cherry bedroom set she and Charlie had bought when they were first married."[2]

They came out of a milieu of sadness and loss. All of these Irish families—McManus and Dooley (the grandmothers' maiden names), Donahue and Mehegan—were part of the emigration that followed the famine years, which began in 1845. The bleak bottom of that catastrophe came in the first two or three years, when the potato crop failed entirely. More than a million people died of hunger and disease in those years, and a like number was driven out of the country, to England, Canada, Australia, or America. But even when the worst of the horror had abated, the country people were often in danger of destitution and hunger, and if they could not pay the rent, they were evicted, sometimes forced to emigrate. It was common in the 1860s and thereafter for one or more children of a family to emigrate, get some kind of job abroad, send remittances home to support destitute parents, and, if possible, finance emigration of the family entirely, or one member at a time. Both the Mehegans and the Donahues enacted versions of that history.

Charlie's father, John Charles Mehegan, was born on May 18, 1857, in Innishannon, a hamlet near Bandon in County Cork, in the southwest of Ireland. His baptismal record at St. Mary's Church in Innishannon indicates that he was one of twins; his twin sister, Margaret, lived long enough to be christened but evidently died thereafter. At least two other children, Catherine and Denis, survived childhood. One by one they came to America after the Civil War, Catherine first (the date is uncertain), John about 1880, Denis in 1890. In 1895, Denis filed an affidavit with the district court in Boston swearing to his origin and date of arrival, and expressing his intention to become a citizen. In the boilerplate language of the document, he agreed "to renounce forever all allegiance and fidelity to every foreign Prince, State, Potentate and Sovereignty whatsoever,—more especially to Victoria, Queen of the United Kingdom of Great Britain and Ireland." For an Irish youth, the latter renunciation was not difficult.

Mehegan is an ancient Cork name with several variants: O Mehegan, O Meighan, Meehan, or O Meehan. In Cork there is a ruin grandly called Castle Mehigan. In Ireland and America today it is often spelled that way. In my files I find a typed note dated July 16, 1977, a record of a conversation I had with my father's aunt Mary Mehegan, who died in 1990:

> John Mehegan came to the United States around 1880....
> His sister Catherine had come earlier, alone, and after getting
> established had sent him money to 'come out.' Later he in turn sent
> money for his brother Denis to 'come out.' John got a job driving a
> horse-drawn streetcar in the city of Boston transit system. Aunt Mary
> said he was 'the most wonderful man in the world.' He married Rose
> McManus, and they had four children: Charles in 1894, Mary in
> 1897, Catherine in 1900, and John in 1910. When Rose died, John
> took care of the children as best he could, cooking meals, washing
> dishes, taking care of the house while working for the El—the
> Boston Elevated Railway. He never remarried. Aunt Mary once told
> me that he was a quiet person, who never spoke of his family [in
> Ireland], so she knew nothing of those he had left behind.

Aunt Mary Mehegan, a warm, polite, somewhat shy lady who never married, told me that when she was young and first working, she once said to her father, "Pa, let's take a trip to Ireland and see your hometown." He flatly refused, saying, "There's nothing back there for me"—a clear indication of the poverty he had left behind. He took the oath of U.S. citizenship on October 25, 1887, in U.S. District Court in Boston. His profession is listed as "car driver." At the time of his death, at age seventy, September 23, 1927, he was living in the two-family house at 1115 Adams Street, Dorchester, where Charlie and his second wife, Julia, also lived. Alfred was sixteen when his grandfather died. He must have been a quiet man, for I cannot recall my father saying a word about him.

On Esther's side, the Donahue emigration was more complicated. Daniel Donahoe (early records use this spelling), Esther's grandfather, was born in County Cork in 1830, and Catherine O'Connell, her grandmother, in 1838. They were married about 1853, ages twenty-four and fourteen. Cork was one of the hardest-hit counties in the famine. In these desperate years, they moved to Merthyr Tydfil, Wales, about fifty miles northwest of Cardiff, in the middle of the Glamorganshire coal fields, where Dan found work, probably in the vast Merthyr ironworks. It was not technically emigration, since they remained in the United Kingdom. Their first child, Mary, was born in Merthyr in 1854. Five other children were born there, including John in 1865. When John was born, the family lived at 19 Taff Street, a house that still exists, on a neat narrow lane with two-story row houses, clearly old enough to have been there in the 1860s.

Eldest daughter Mary married Timothy Mascal about 1871. Mascal is a Scottish name; Timothy would have been a Catholic, perhaps from the western Highlands, although the name is found in Ireland also. After two children were born, Timothy died of smallpox, leaving a nineteen- or twenty-year-old widow. Soon after, Mary Mascal left her children with her parents and emigrated to America. In about 1880, her parents, Daniel and Catherine Donahoe, left Wales for Boston. He was fifty and she was forty-three. The iron industry in Glamorganshire was fading. Economic stress had taken them from Cork to Wales, and from Wales to America. They brought with them their children: John, age fifteen; William, age twelve; and Elizabeth, age two. They also brought their grandchildren, Mary and Timothy Leo Mascal, ages eight and six.

By the time of this emigration, Daniel and Catherine's second and third daughters — Margaret, age fourteen, and Catherine, age twelve — were already in America. That suggests that they came with their big sister Mary, who was twenty-six in 1880. Mary Mascal would later be known as Auntie Mary and was, it appears, as much a mother to her younger siblings as to her own children.

An undated (probably late 1980s) letter to me from Mae Donahue said that the Donahues were go-getters to some extent. She wrote, "They had some money, bought homes, went into the laundry business. John, Bill's [and Esther's] father owned a big shipyard in South Boston and was in the boat and laundry business with the family from 379 K Street." I take "ship-yard" to mean boatyard, that is, a boat storage and service yard, perhaps somewhere near where the three yacht clubs are today, east of the L Street Bathhouse on Carson Beach. So Esther was around boats and water very early.

John Donahue married Alice Dooley in Boston about 1892. Their first child, Esther, was born on March 17, 1893, St. Patrick's Day. Later came William, Mary (known as May), and Daniel. Alice died in childbirth in 1905. She was having twins, and while Daniel lived, the second baby died along with the mother. In 1923, years after Esther left home, John Donahue died of diabetes.

• • •

I have sketched two families, a sequence of names and dates and places, and yet I know almost nothing about these people: what they thought or felt, feared or wished for. Nothing about their personalities or morals. They are strangers to me, as great-grandparents and earlier forebears usually are. My father did not know either of his grandmothers. One grandfather died in 1923 and the other in 1927. He knew John Mehegan but probably not John Donahue, at least not well.

Although they came from similar social backgrounds, the marriage of Charlie and Esther Mehegan was under strain from the start. One can see why: She was an entertainer, while he shoveled coal. In her 2002 recollection, my mother wrote, "Esther told me that when she and Charlie were first married they had no money except what he made playing cards."[3] This might have been true; nevertheless, Esther did not take to show business because Charlie couldn't make money. She was in it before she married him.

In a postcard of Nantasket Beach sent to Auntie Mary Mascal at the exclusive Mount Washington Hotel in Bretton Woods, New Hampshire (I'm guessing she was working there in housekeeping; It is hard to imagine that she was a guest at that exclusive resort), dated August 30, 1910, Esther wrote: "Dear Auntie Mascal, am swimming & diving here and May is doing the life saving act. She is quite a performer, yours truly, Esther." So little sister May was also performing, though it is not certain that she continued as long as Esther did. Esther posted similar cards to Auntie Mary in the following weeks from Newburyport and the Rochester Fair in New Hampshire.

The featured swimming act that summer at Nantasket, in the amusement park known as Paragon Park, in the town of Hull, was the Pattee Diving Girls, who later appeared at the Wonderland amusement park at Revere Beach and the Newburyport Fair. The *Newburyport Daily News* for September 12 reports, "The Diving Girls that have been exhibiting all the season at Wonderland [Revere Beach] are all ready to perform as soon as the big tank that has been put down is filled with water." Esther's card from Newburyport was posted the same day: "Dear Auntie Mascal, Am now performing in Newburyport. Esther."

Water shows were a staple carnival and town fair act in the early twentieth century. A water show might have synchronized swimming, riders jumping horses off a diving board, costumed characters (such as King Neptune with a trident) in various skits, and, most impressive, the daredevil high dive off a ladder or tower into a tank. A 1912 postcard for sale on eBay shows the diving tower, which looks like a lighthouse, at Revere Beach.

For a young woman itching to get out from under the control of her father, the attractions of performing would be irresistible, since most other forms of moneymaking were closed. "For some women, swimming offered a means to an income," writes Lisa Bier, author of a history of women's swimming. "Variety shows sometimes included acts in which women would swim underwater or dive into small onstage tanks. The shows were popular because they combined danger, athleticism, and attractive, wet women in a single act."[4] In a 1983 interview published in the Riverside, California, *Press-Enterprise*, ninety-year-old Esther described her early career: "My father said, 'They're crazy, Esther, giving you $50 a week.' They were crazy but they filled the houses all the time."[5]

Esther would dive to the bottom of a tank, where she could be seen by the audience, and, while breathing through a hidden straw, pretend to comb her hair, light a cigarette, sip from a soft-drink bottle, then go to sleep as the band played "Asleep in the Deep." She also did the high dive. The heights of such dives were amazing—sometimes as high as sixty-five feet into a small tank. My mother recalled having seen such a dive, "at least fifty feet," at Paragon Park. She once asked Esther how she could have had the courage to do it. Esther replied that she was always scared, that the only way was not to think but to go as soon as she got to the top. In young womanhood, at least, this appears to have been the way she approached most things: don't think, just plunge ahead.

For a young woman, appearing in a public entertainment of this kind would have been scandalous in the Catholic world of South Boston. A local newspaper account (the name of the newspaper and the date are uncertain) of Pattee's act at Revere Beach reports:

> Manager Pattee, not content with his great success, is adding still more swimmers and divers to a show that now comprises seven of the prettiest girl water performers that ever greeted an audience. La Siren, in her water disrobing act, is giving an act second to none in popularity, and with her twelve dives at every performance, and ten performances daily, is breaking the record for endurance.

Before she was performing for money, Esther was entering swimming races. A 1910 photograph shows her, along with three other teenage South Boston swimmers, holding trophies from winning races.[6] Here, apparently, was Esther's first brush with glamour. My mother wrote that she entered the Boston Light Swim, first held in July 1910, a grueling eight-mile swim from the Charlestown Bridge to Boston Light: "Esther told me that when she came back to the beach a woman approached her, introduced herself as Annette Kellerman and asked her if she would be interested in joining her swimming troupe. Thrilled at the invitation, Esther agreed right away."[7]

• • •

The celebrated Australian swimmer Annette Kellerman came to Boston in 1907 from Chicago, not with a troupe but with her aunt and Jimmy Sullivan, her press agent and later husband, to perform at Wonderland. Soon after arriving, she appeared at the beach to swim in her one-piece form-fitting suit—radically different from the skirt-heavy female "bathing costumes" of the time—and was arrested for indecency. Since newspaper photographs show her being hauled roughly into a police wagon, it was clearly a publicity stunt—probably Jimmy's idea. In court, she argued strenuously that swimming was healthy exercise and a woman could not swim in traditional outfits. The sympathetic judge let her off on the condition that she wear the suit only in the water. The incident gave Kellerman a fantastic burst of notoriety and sparked a public discussion of women's swimwear that marked the beginning of the end of the silly ladies' costumes.

A second, less famous incident happened at the same time. Kellerman was named by an irate wife as the corespondent in a divorce suit against a Mr. Pattee (I have not found the first name). The one biography of Kellerman, *The Original Million Dollar Mermaid: The Annette Kellerman Story*, by Emily Gibson with Barbara Firth, based mainly on Kellerman's own sometimes-vague recollections in old age, reports that Pattee was the owner of a boardinghouse where Kellerman and her aunt stayed.[8] Pattee is an unusual name. Though the book doesn't give the name of the show that Kellerman came to Boston to join, my hunch is that Pattee was not a boardinghouse owner, but her boss, the owner of the diving show where Esther worked in 1910.

There are problems with Esther's account of being hired by Kellerman after the Boston Light Swim. She might have done it later, but according to historical records, Rose Pitonof was the first woman to compete in the swim, in 1910, which would mean that Esther was not in it (or did not finish) that year. Esther could not have entered the next year: She was almost nine months pregnant in July.

Where does this Kellerman story come from? It is possible that Kellerman had seen Esther swim in a race in 1908—she was fifteen that year—spoken to her, and recruited her to the Pattee act. That is, Esther worked not for Kellerman, but with her. Whatever happened, Kellerman left Boston in the fall of 1908 to accept a deal with impresario B. F. Keith to put a water show onstage indoors in New York, and she never returned. So she couldn't have spoken to Esther in 1910. The Keith show was a smash, and Kellerman's fame and career took off. She made several successful aquatic-adventure movies in the silent era, including the 1916 *Daughter of the Gods*, which featured what is believed to be the first-ever nude scene on film —with long hair strategically placed. She got a star on the Hollywood Walk of Fame and in 1952 Esther Williams played her in the biopic *Million Dollar Mermaid*. Jack Carson, second of Esther's three sons from her third marriage, was certain that his mother did swim with the Kellerman act, possibly also the Keith production, although probably not for long.

Whatever happened exactly, the brush with Annette Kellerman was as near to the big-time as Esther would ever come. After she left Boston and before she went to Hollywood, Kellerman's water show was a classy, theater-based vaudeville act, playing in Europe as well as America. Esther never went to Europe. Most of her career was spent where it had started around Boston, in the gritty world of small-town fairs, amusement parks, and traveling carnivals. As early as 1913, she was swimming with the Wortham & Allen Shows, one of the many shows owned by impresario C. A. Wortham. On June 27, 1913, this item appeared in the Duluth, Minnesota, *Herald*, with the headline, "Entire Week of Fun Promised":

The Wortham and Allen shows are said to be the largest, best equipped now touring the country and the Moose have engaged them for a solid week of amusement. The line of attractions that they offer this season are the very best that can be obtained.

The big water show and congress of international diving girls present an aquatic performance of the best and most pretentious [sic] that has ever been offered. Esther Donahue, who holds the Richard K. Fox medal for being the American champion diver and swimmer; Mabel Whittaker, who swam the East river in New York last Easter Sunday; Chubby Whitney, last season with Annette Kellerman; Eva May, the funny woman clown, are some of the principals.[9]

The performance takes place in a specially constructed tank containing many thousands of gallons of water and these young women give a performance that the management says is a "real show."

The wild animal show with lions, leopards, pumas, tigers and bears presents a performance that is the limit of animal Intelligence. Ernestine La Rose, lion trainer; Capt. Dyer and Capt. Cordona are the features.

The famous fire fighting mule, "Maxine," and the Good Night Horse, "Sahara;" a new Pharaoh's daughter with some new illusions; the "cabaret," a select company of singers and dancers; Everett India, Princess Carlita, smallest perfectly formed woman in America; Bobby, the turtle boy; crazy house; dragon's gorge; side shows with freaks and curiosities; the Hindoo wonder workers; carry-us-all and giant Ferris wheel and many other new features go to make up the most complete and best amusement aggregation now traveling.

The shows will all open at 7:30 Monday night and the patrons can rest assured that all the shows are clean and meritorious, as much of the success of the Wortham and Allen shows is attributed to the fact that they present clean shows without exception. The free acts are numerous and of a high class.

Here was twenty-year-old Esther's world in all its nutty, earthy, and extravagant detail, with Bobby the Turtle Boy and Princess Carlita, "the smallest perfectly formed woman in America," a world she enjoyed and felt at home in. She stayed in it, one way or another, for another twenty-five years. Among the telling details in this item, surely written by the show publicist, are that Esther did not use her married name, Mehegan, and that not she but another swimmer, Chubby Whitney (presumably a buoyant performer), is listed as a Kellerman alumna. Why would that not have been said of Esther? Also, the show is "clean and meritorious." This was a common theme in carnival advertisements—"strictly moral," "clean and moral"—since polite society assumed the opposite. As in Meredith Willson's show *The Music Man,* in many conservative communities the carnival represented "trouble, right here in River City."

However she felt about the carny world, there is no doubt that Esther was making money. Apparently, not so Charlie. Her retrospective comment about his card-playing might have been an exaggeration, although she said much the same to my sister Paula. "She told me that she was sending money back," when she was on the road, Paula recalled, "and Charlie was supposed to be taking care of [Alfred], but he was gambling it away." Jack Carson said that in her early performing days, his mother was making fifty dollars a week and sending ten home to Boston. Esther told my mother that one of her uncles "was a steamfitter and it was he who gave Charlie a job and where he learned that business and eventually the plumbing." If true, that he had to accept help from his in-laws while his wife was on the road might have rankled Charlie, given what happened later.

Whatever he earned as an apprentice steamfitter, or steamfitter's helper, whether he gambled it away or not, Charlie's income was less than Esther's, which would have been galling to most young husbands and possibly even made him the butt of taunts among his friends. The 1983 Riverside *Press-Enterprise* story reports, "Even though she had to go on the road alone, Carson [her third married name] said her husband did not say much about it. 'Half the time he was out of work.'"[10]

Clearly Esther was not cut out to be a homebody. When she was out there on the carnival circuit, in the small towns and cities of the

Midwest, Charlie and Alfred were far away, in every sense. Others were closer. For example, there was Esther's boss, Texan Billy Spencer, part owner of the Wortham Show, who ran the water act.

• • •

On March 30, 1914, Esther appeared in court in Kansas City, with a lawyer, and was granted a divorce from Charlie Mehegan. The decree includes this sentence: "Defendant although legally and lawfully summoned herein comes not but makes default." The idea that Charlie would have traveled to Kansas City to defend himself, when Esther could have sued for divorce in Boston, is fantastic. She must have known he would not, and perhaps that was part of the plan. If she had sued in Boston, he might well have testified that she was guilty of neglect or abandonment. She later told my mother that she had divorced him on an impulse—urged to it by girlfriends in the show. She was impulsive, to be sure. But it's hard to believe that she would be so deliberate as to hire a lawyer and go to court on an impulse. There would be court costs and lawyer's fees. It appears there was another impetus, and possibly a funder. Not long after the divorce, she married Billy Spencer, her boss. The divorce decree included this sentence: "It is further ordered and adjudged by the Court that the plaintiff shall have the care, custody, and control of the minor child Alfred J. Mehegan, born of this marriage." Here was the nub of a quarrel that would have bitter, deep, and long-lasting repercussions on my father's life.

On July 24, 1915, a small item appeared in the *Boston Herald* under the headline "Divorced Mother Seeks Custody of Child."

> A writ of habeas corpus has been issued by Judge McLaughlin of the superior court on petition of Esther Spencer of Terrell, Texas, against her former husband, Charles W. Mehegan of Boston, commanding him to produce their child, Alfred J. Mehegan, in court July 28 to show cause why he should not be given over to the custody of his mother.
>
> Mrs. Spencer says in her petition she married Mehegan November 15, 1910, and secured a divorce

from him March 30, 1914, in the circuit court of Jackson County, Mo., in Kansas City. The divorce decree, she says, gave her the custody of their child, Alfred. Pending the trial of the divorce suit, she says, the child was entrusted to the care of Katherine Robinson of Boston by agreement, and she declares the latter agreed to take care of the child till the mother could assume its custody. On March 26 last, she said she received notice from Katherine Robison [sic] to remove the child immediately. At the time, the petitioner says, she was ill at Leavenworth, and could not comply promptly with the notice, so that Katherine Robison surrendered the child to its father, the petitioner's former husband.

The petitioner is now married to William A. Spencer of Terrell, Texas, and has her home there and wants her child.

A second story appeared the next day, with the headline, "Agreement by Parents. Little Alfred J. Mehegan Will Remain in Custody of Agnes Coulter of Revere for Present."

By agreement little Alfred J. Mehegan will remain in the custody of Agnes Coulter of Revere pending further orders of the Superior court in the proceeding brought by his mother, Ethel [sic] Spencer of Terrell, Texas, against his father, Charles W. Mehegan. In divorce proceedings against her husband, Mrs. Mehegan was awarded custody of the child.

The latter was entrusted to the care of Katherine Robinson of this city. When she notified the mother to come for the child she was sick, so Mrs. Robinson turned the child over to the father. The mother, who married Spencer after her divorce, came here to get the child from the father, wishing to take the boy to her home in Texas.

The parties came to an agreement which was signed by both, under which the child will stay with Agnes Coulter and each parent has the right to see it at any reasonable time.

Allowing for the possibility of reporting errors, this account raises questions. The first story says that "by agreement" Alfred, age three and a half, was given to Katherine Robinson to care for "pending the trial of the divorce suit." That means that Esther and Charlie were already estranged at the time of the divorce, sometime before the March 30 decree, and that they had agreed that Katherine Robinson would take care of the child. In other words, Alfred was in foster care before the divorce. Why would Charlie have agreed to that? Perhaps, prior to the divorce decree, there was already an intervention by the city child welfare department that led to the foster placement. Or, if not, presumably Esther did not take Alfred because she was on the road. Perhaps Charlie did not take him because, quite likely unemployed, he had no capacity to care for a toddler by himself. But in that case, why did Katherine Robinson then hand him over to Charlie? Who was Katherine Robinson?

Alfred was in at least three foster homes in early childhood: those of Coulter and Robinson, as mentioned in the *Herald* stories, and one other, which yielded a chilling memory. He was living with the family of a Boston policeman and remembered holding the officer's service revolver and pointing it out the window at passers-by on the sidewalk. He also lived, at least for a time, in South Boston with the large family of Charlie's aunt and uncle, Denis and Susan Manning. Whether he was ill-treated in the foster homes is not known—it is certain that he was not in the Manning home. He never spoke of being abused or neglected. But then, not to accuse anyone of ill-usage or neglect, whatever the facts, was part of his makeup.

In conversation about this history, my brother, Peter, raised a question that I had never thought of. With all that family around, including grandfathers, cousins, various aunts and uncles on both his parents' sides, why was there any need to put "little Alfred" in foster homes? The most plausible explanation is that there was such rancor between the Donahues and the Mehegans that, at least at first, both parties would rather have had the child go to foster care than to the other.

Many years ago I tried to get a copy of the court proceedings on the custody fight but was told that the records of that period had been lost or destroyed. Nevertheless, there are old family stories, told to my mother by Esther, or my father, or his aunts. One account, borne out by the July 25 news story, is that when the case came to court, the judge decided that neither Charlie nor Esther was a fit parent, and that was why Alfred was remanded to foster care. Another was that Esther's little sister, May, age about thirteen, was heartsick over the situation and wanted to take him but was too young to do so. In the 1960s, Esther told Paula that when she sued for custody, Charlie was so bitter that even though he did not really want Alfred, he was determined that she should not have him. Such an attitude would not be surprising. If Esther's performing was not scandal enough in South Boston, the divorce and her brazen attempt to gain custody would have been what the Irish might call "beyond the beyond."

One historical detail of this quarrel seems almost incredible, but given that it came from two sources, it must be true. Sometime after the Boston court's decision, Esther came home and discovered that Alfred was being neglected by a foster parent. Paula recalled: "She told me that she took him. I think she said detectives came after her, sent by the family. It would not be hard to find her—she was in the circus. She said Dad loved being in the circus, everybody thought he was adorable, he used to sit and watch her dive, and clap and clap." It does not seem possible that a small child would be allowed to watch his mother do the high dive; more likely this was one of the tamer water entertainments. As an adult, my father had a memory of circus animals and of seeing his mother dive and of himself running between cars on a carnival train.

There was no recorded story of Esther being arrested, so perhaps the "detectives" were court officers or child welfare constables. In any case, she must have returned with them—she could not have simply turned him over. Whatever exactly happened, it would have been a shock to a three- or four-year-old boy: taken *by* his mother, then taken *from* her.

To be precise, Esther was never in the circus, but in a carnival. A circus was a unified traveling entertainment featuring exotic-animal acts and such daredevil acts as the trapeze and the high wire, all in or above rings—hence the name. A traveling carnival, such as one of C. A. Wortham's, might include a circus as one of its many attractions. The Lackman & Carson Shows (for some reason, carnivals almost always used the plural "shows"), which Esther joined in about 1920, was that type. It had a three-ring circus with trapeze acts, elephants, clowns, a band. Famed lion and tiger tamer Clyde Beatty traveled with the show in the 1930s. Jack Carson remembered a lion cub in a playpen in his parents' Pullman, fed with a baby bottle.

However, as the Duluth *Herald* item makes clear, the carnival was the bigger, surrounding context: It usually had a midway with a Ferris wheel, carousel, and other rides; a freak show featuring the tattooed man, the fat lady, and midgets; games of chance; and some would have a "cooch" act—that is, a mildly risqué "girlie" show. For a time in the 1930s, famous fan dancer Sally Rand appeared with Lackman & Carson. And, of course, it often had a water show, with daredevil divers like Esther Donahue and swimmers in various entertainment routines that included horses, clowns, and synchronized swimming. In a carnival, the various components would usually have been independent operators who signed on for the season.

A typical carnival would follow a grueling travel schedule. The 1923 Morris & Castle Shows, for example, traveled 5,989 miles by train as it played thirty-two cities between April and November, in Michigan, Wisconsin, Illinois, Arkansas, Texas, and Louisiana.[11] All shows spent the off-season in "winter quarters," usually in Florida or elsewhere in the Deep South.

A carnival was a looser and rougher business than a circus. Carnival historian Joe McKennon writes:

> All carnivals would feature diving-girl shows for several years in the teens. Some of these 'water shows' survived the changes of the twenties and were still active on midways in the thirties. . . . By putting the high diver's tank inside an enclosure with seats around the tank, patrons who paid extra could get close-up view of the diver

> hitting the water….By adding shapely young ladies in one-piece bathing suits, that sexual allure that had always been the underlying force on midways was accentuated. Even the wildest of the girl reviews . . . covered up more than those one-piece bathing suits.[12]

The story of Esther, children, courts, and the carnival has a couple of strange and sad echoes. She had a girl child with Bill Spencer, Elizabeth, born January 2, 1916, which means that Esther was close to four months pregnant when she went to court in Boston. Years ago, I spoke with my half aunt Elizabeth Spencer Byars by phone, and when I told her the abduction story, she said, "You're kidding—that almost happened to me."

Esther's second marriage lasted about five years, a little longer than her first. She and Bill Spencer were divorced in November 1919. On March 27, 1920—four months later—again she married the boss, Andrew Carson, partner in the Lackman & Carson Shows.[13]

Whether Esther "married for love" the second and third times, it is easy to see how she might also have had practical reasons, conscious or unconscious: A young woman alone in the carnival life was vulnerable. The shows were always on the move, which meant that local law enforcement could not be counted on in cases of rape or other abuse on the carnival lot. To survive in that world, a woman had to be shrewd and self-reliant— traits Esther possessed in abundance—and a male ally could be important, as much for safety as for love. Besides, it could be a lonely life.

Both Alfred and Elizabeth were taken away, at least for a time, from their natural parents. When Esther and Bill Spencer were divorced, the judge replicated almost exactly the decision of the Boston judge five years earlier: He decided that neither mother nor father was a fit parent and that the carnival was no place for a child. Elizabeth said, "When my mother and dad separated, the court put me with my father's sister, Lizzie, [Elizabeth Kirk and husband, Walter] in Terrell [Texas,] on a room-and-board basis. I was four and the court said I was too young to be in the carnival." However, she had weekend visits with her father when the Wortham Shows was in winter quarters and "a two-week vacation with my mother every one or two years." She was forbidden by her aunt to tell anyone that she was visiting her mother—even that her mother was alive. She had to say that Esther was a family friend. "I was frankly scared to death of her. I was taught that she would kidnap me and make me join the carnival."

Though exaggerated, this threat was rooted in reality. As she had with her first child, so with her second: Esther seems to have thought to get her way by taking the child and absconding. "When I was six or seven," Elizabeth recalled, "both my dad's and her shows were winter-quartered near each other in Fort Worth. My mother was coming to visit and my dad allowed that. I remember being in a car with her and Andy Carson and two other people. We were speeding away from the show. The car stopped and they turned around and went back. My dad was very upset because I was not supposed to be away from the show."

Like her half brother Alfred, whom she would never meet, until she was about seventeen Betty had little contact with her mother. When she was grown, they developed a friendship, though they were as different from each other as were Esther and Alfred. Elizabeth recalled, "My aunt thoroughly disapproved of her"—not the first or last person to take that view of the Southie water nymph.

Esther had no role in Alfred's life as he grew except for a few sad visits and occasional letters. My father remembered Esther visiting him, at about age thirteen, in Boston after Charlie remarried in 1917 and Alfred had gone to live with him and his new wife, Julia Naughton. My mother wrote, "Esther told me later that she remembered that visit, but it was so sad because 'Alfred cried all the time.'" My mother added, "There was no end to the poignancies of these encounters."[14]

After she married Andy Carson, Esther quit swimming and diving, went into the business side of the show, and concentrated on raising three more sons: Andrew Jr. (b. 1921), Jack (b. 1927), and David Carson (b. 1929). In a memoir published in 1997, Andy Jr. wrote that when he was five, his mother took him to Boston to visit her relatives and had him discreetly baptized a Catholic (his father was a strict atheist).[15]

Alfred was sixteen that year, but Esther never introduced her two sons; I feel certain that my father would have remembered if she had. It is odd that she did not. Perhaps Alfred was away during her visit.

Andy Carson Sr. was as tough as Esther, as tough as the carny world demanded. "He ran the carnival like a dictator," Jack wrote in a letter to me, "and would fist-fight any time, especially in a 'Hey Rube' situation." A "Hey Rube" was a brawl initiated by liquored-up local rowdies ("rubes") spoiling for a fight with the carnies. This happened frequently enough that the shout of "Hey Rube!"—a call for help during the attack—was understood by all. According to Jack, his father's sister Lil ran the girlie show, and Esther's brother Dan, whose mother and twin had died in his birth, was a shill for the games of chance. He would appear to win big, creating excitement among the rubes. Then he would go behind the tent, put the money and prizes under the flap, and move on to another booth.

• • •

I do not know what my father knew of these details of Esther's adventures, though he and she remained in at least minimal touch. He probably did know the basic outline. In adulthood, each year on Mother's Day he would telephone the woman who had given him birth and had wanted to keep him, who would occasionally turn up for a short visit but most of the time was far away, somewhere out West, out of reach, out of his life. Although his parents had fought over him at first, to a boy's mind, at least, their treatment of him suggested that neither truly wanted him. The entertainer would appear and disappear in his later life, like a household ghost, never quite present but never irrevocably gone.

2.

∽∾∽

Boyhood

In 1917, CHARLIE MEHEGAN MARRIED Julia Naughton, who was a year younger than he was. He was twenty-four and handsome, as a formal photograph at about age twenty-one shows. As a divorcé, he could not marry in the Church, so the wedding took place before a justice of the peace. He and Julia lived at 749 East Fifth Street, South Boston, part of a two-family house. Now that Charlie had a respectable home life, Alfred went to live with him and his new wife.

The child was a ward of the state (as my mother once characterized it), which meant that Charlie would have had to receive the permission of the court to take custody, two years after the original superior court order. There is neither surviving record nor oral anecdote that Esther contested this move. She was in the carnival far away, with a new marriage and child, and if she had continued the fight, it is doubtful that any court would have sided with her.

Alfred was six in August 1917. On a 1942 U.S. Navy form, he listed 749 Fifth Street as his home from birth until June 1918, omitting the foster homes; he might not have known the addresses, or thought it best not to try to include them. It was as if in his mind his life really began with his father's remarriage.

Julia Naughton had a natural affection for her stepson, having come from an irregular family herself. Both of her parents were Irish immigrants, but her mother was a Catholic and her father was raised in the Church of Ireland, the Irish Episcopal Church. Their marriage had caused a row with his family in Ireland, and when he died, his Irish sisters came over to make sure he was not given a Catholic burial. Their daughter Julia and her sister Mamie had been raised by their mother as Catholics, although Julia became separated from the Church over her marriage. This grieved her deeply, a fact she disclosed to my mother in the late 1940s. Far from a wicked stepmother, Julia was jolly and physically ample, especially in later life. My brother Peter describes her as "an outgoing, rollicking type," and my sister Florence remembers climbing into her lap and snuggling in her generous bosom. Alfred was raised as a Catholic, as was his half sister Mary Rose. In the eyes of the Church, Charlie and Julia were both living in adultery. Nevertheless, in her 1989 autobiography, my mother would write of my father that "though neither Julia nor his father went to church, they insisted that he go, which often happens."[1] Charlie, as we shall see, had good relations with church officials and various local pastors and nuns. The Church did not treat him as a notorious sinner.

This tolerance, given how unbending on sexual or marital irregularities the Church can be even today, might seem surprising. To me, the most likely explanation is that Esther was seen as the malefactor and Charlie as the innocent victim. It was she, after all, who had performed in skimpy swimming costumes in disreputable shows, run away with a traveling carnival, gotten a divorce out West, and married adulterously—a *Protestant*, no less—then had had the cheek to come back and sue for custody, flaunting her scandalous behavior as if it were perfectly acceptable. Given these facts, it is likely that Charlie and Julia's "decent," if technically irregular, marriage was viewed with understanding, if not full acceptance.

In that light, it is not so odd that Alfred and Mary Rose could be raised in the Church without question—children were not punished for the sins of their parents—and perhaps they were supervised in catechism by Aunts Mary and Catherine or other relations. It is also possible that Charlie and Julia themselves did go to Mass at times but did not receive communion, which would not have been permitted under the circumstances. You were not forbidden to *enter* a church, whatever the state of your conscience. Before the Second Vatican Council in the 1960s, at a typical Mass as few as a third of attendees went to communion anyway, so it would not have been remarkable for them to go together or separately and not receive.

Still, there were limits to family piety. I find no record that Alfred attended a parish school, to which Catholic parents were often expected to send their children—my mother encountered this low-level pressure when she did not put my brother and sister into a parish school in Dorchester. My father was quiet about his religious feelings. Yet he went to Mass every week in all the years he was married and once told me, somewhat stiffly, of the importance of "keeping the Faith." I remember his "making a mission," the annual two- or three-night Catholic version of a Southern Baptist revival. He "made his Easter duty"—that is, went to the sacrament of Confession at least once a year. He had a rosary, though I never heard him pray with it; perhaps he did so privately. At his confirmation, a time when a Catholic adolescent boy or girl chooses another middle name to go with that given at birth, he added Charles, his father's name, to Joseph, and preferred it as a middle name: He went by Alfred C. Mehegan for the rest of his life.

In June 1918 the family moved to 43 Pearl Street, Dorchester, in the Savin Hill neighborhood. Alfred attended the Edward Everett School, around the corner on Pleasant Street. Also in 1918, Mary Rose, Charlie and Julia's only child, was born. Despite being half siblings and seven years apart in age, Alfred and Mary Rose were close, and he remained always her protective big brother. When she graduated from Dorchester High School, he wanted her to continue her education. He collected college brochures for her and helped her to apply to Lasell College in nearby Newton. My mother wrote, "He made an appointment for her, and went with her to see the admissions officer, who thought he was her father."[2] This case of mistaken identity was retold with amusement, but the subtext is that her real father either was not interested or could not make the time to be there.

In 1921 they moved back to South Boston, to 845 East Third Street, a three-decker in the City Point neighborhood, near the ocean. Alfred transferred to the Oliver Hazard Perry School on East Seventh Street, where he remained through the eighth grade, to the spring of 1925. He was bright and a good student, which would account for his admittance to Boston Latin School that fall.[3] In August, the family moved to 1115 Adams Street, Dorchester, a neighborhood near the Neponset River (which forms the Boston-Milton border) known as Lower Mills—a more leafy, suburban environment than dense South Boston. Eleven fifteen Adams is a two-and-a-half-story two-family shingled house with a small yard. It became the home for several members of the family: John Mehegan the immigrant, Charlie and Julia and the children, and Charlie's sister Mary. In later years it was owned by Aunt Catherine and her husband, Fred Hanson, and when he died, the downstairs eventually became the dental office of Fred Hanson Jr.

This house would remain Alfred's home address, except when he was at sea, until he was married at age twenty-nine, in 1941. Young people typically in that pre–World War II era did not leave their parents' home until marriage. (My mother recalled her parents in the 1920s discussing in hushed tones a friend's wayward adult daughter, who had actually left home and rented her own apartment.) His room was in the attic space, with a small window overlooking the street. He lived under his father's roof for more than half his life and would work for him when ashore until he was nearly fifty.

• • •

Although the family never again lived in South Boston, the sprawling seaside neighborhood remained an important setting in my father's life. Sometime in the 1920s, the exact year is not clear, Charlie and a partner, John Powers, started a plumbing business, which they named Powers & Mehegan, at 500 East Broadway. "The shop," as it was always called, occupied one half of a single-story building with a concrete facade in Perkins Square, near the corner of Broadway and Dorchester Streets. Powers & Mehegan would never be a big business, but after John Powers left the partnership—the details of the separation are unknown; it is said they quarreled—the firm for decades yielded a good living for

Charlie and his family, and the relatively few men who worked for him full-time.

A central presence in the family's life was Boston Harbor, on three sides of South Boston. Unlike Esther Donahue, the Mehegans were not much into swimming, but they loved to be *on* the water. In the early 1920s, Charlie joined the South Boston Yacht Club, at 1849 Columbia Road, not far from the L Street Bathhouse, where Esther had learned to swim. He served two terms as commodore of the club in the 1930s. As a junior, and then adult, member, Alfred learned to sail and race in and around Boston Harbor. Though he never owned large sailing yachts, in the late 1920s or early 1930s Charlie acquired a twenty-one-foot Alden Indian, a class of lapstrake centerboard sloop. It was a popular design—as many as one hundred were built—raced by clubs all around Massachusetts Bay. My father remembered this boat fondly throughout his life.

Salt water would change his life, as it had his mother's, and lead him far beyond his hometown. The Mehegans and cousin families were active every year in racing in Boston Harbor, and participated in Marblehead's celebrated Race Week every year. Alfred always seemed to be most cheerful, in later life, when on or close to, or even only talking about, the sea.

• • •

We know little about his childhood after the foster years were over; he did not have a fund of boyhood stories, positive or negative. He never spoke, nor did anyone else, of physical abuse in his father's house. He did not suffer neglect or poverty, nor a total lack of love. Besides affection between him and his stepmother, he had a deep bond with Aunts Mary and Catherine. They were more like big sisters than aunts (indeed they were only fourteen and eleven years older than he was, respectively). Aunt Mary told Paula that they would visit him at a foster home and that, in Paula's words, "when they would leave, he would tear the house apart—he did not want them to go."

"Mary thought he was very smart," said Paula. "She was the one who would get him books from the library. Thank God somebody did." He was a reader from an early age. He told my mother that when his parents would tell him to put out the light at night, he would light a candle and keep reading.

He also showed a mild wild streak, or at least high spirits and daring. He told my mother that when he was about twelve or thirteen, he twice ran away from home, the first time staying away for two or three days, living in a chicken coop. The second time, he went to New York and slept on benches in a park, begging for food. She wrote, "He remembered walking across a bridge, possibly the Brooklyn Bridge, when a man came up behind him and asked him for money. He told him he had none and then [the man] started to jostle him over to the railing as if he was going to push him over. He was so frightened that he turned and ran and was lost in the crowd."[4] The story ends there— we don't know how he got home or whether his parents were looking frantically for him in the meantime.

Although we don't know the names of his childhood friends, on Pearl Street in Dorchester or in the South Boston neighborhoods where he lived until he was thirteen, it is clear that many were a tougher breed than he was. Once he was with a gang of boys who took rocks to smash the glass in the outside signs of Protestant churches. My mother wrote, "Al told me he never threw rocks at the signs, though he couldn't imagine why, because all his friends did."[5] Here, as so often in his life, he was resistant to peer pressure. He was his own person, in the family, in any group. But he was not a loner. Later in youth and adulthood, he was popular and gregarious, and loved music and dancing and stylish clothes.

For a boy, the South Boston setting was not always friendly. For one thing, he was relatively small before his growth spurt, which led to an experience he recalled more than once in middle age. He was being chased by several tough boys. He ran into a cellar and somehow barred the door. "I knew I was going to have to come out sooner or later," he said. "I looked around and found a stick," perhaps a broom handle or a shovel. "I came out swinging and beat them off," he said. The moral he drew from this story, expressed to me, was "When you're outnumbered, you don't have to play by the Marquis of Queensberry rules."

This anecdote proved not to be of much use to me when I had bully problems in school (which is when he was prompted to retell it). It is not often practical for a boy to slug his tormentors with a shovel. The story does show, however, that he knew how it felt to be on the weak side, to be alone and cornered. It also exhibits his premise that you could not expect anyone to rescue you; you had to rely on yourself. He would not be going to my school to demand that something be done about the bully—I should deal with him myself. It's the outlook of an orphan or a foundling, which he was not, exactly, but something like it, or perhaps one who felt that his life was provisional and his position insecure.

While there was warmth between him and his stepmother, sisters, and aunts, his relationship with his father was a different story. This relationship struck my mother as sad and strange when she first observed it. She noticed that he had no familiar name for his father, at least not in speech—no Dad or Pa, not even something as formal as Father. This was not true of Mary Rose, who called her father Daddy. In his life that I was a part of, he never spoke ill of his father. He rarely spoke of him at all: no stories, no allusions to feelings or opinions about him. His father was as central a figure in his life as any living father must be. Yet the lack of a familiar name makes it seem as though Charlie was someone Alfred did not really know, almost like a mother's boyfriend or a father who comes home from a long time away at war or in prison. There was always between them a distance, a noticeable reserve.

Age six, when he first went to live with his father, he had little to build a relationship upon. And Charlie was not always an easy man to be close to. In his later years, he lived with Mary Rose; her husband, Jimmy Dillon; and their four children. We would visit them on Thanksgiving or Christmas, as well as at other times. Paula and I both remember him yelling at his grandchildren. "I never liked him," Paula said. "He was grouchy; he yelled at them all the time. I remember thinking, 'Thank God we don't have to live with him.'" Such a temperament would refrigerate the atmosphere between any father and son, especially two with a painful shared history, and who were as well such different people.

And yet, it seems that it was not so between Charlie and everyone. My cousin Jean Dillon, who lived with him all of her life until his death, said that he was not so grouchy. "He was very bossy," she said, "telling you to do that and not to do that, but I always felt that he was good to us." To the world, it seems, Charlie Mehegan was a convivial man with many friends, in and out of business. He cut a dashing figure. Here is my mother's description of him, from a one-page memo she wrote in 2000:

> I never saw him in work clothes. He dressed beautifully, with the highest quality suits, topcoats, overcoats, hats, etc. Impeccable always, he could have stepped out of Louis [an exclusive men's store] on Boylston Street. The first time I saw him at the beach — or it might have been at the Yacht Club — he wore leather thonged sandals, the first I had ever seen on a man.
>
> He was handsome, really, with short gray hair fashionably cut. He had perfect white teeth and very blue eyes. Catherine had those same blue eyes, which was a Mehegan characteristic, apparently, because in the picture of their father John, he seems to have those intense blue eyes too. He was about five feet eight or nine, and slim.
>
> Though unschooled, perhaps not beyond the eighth grade, he was very bright, especially with figures, with a really extraordinary memory.[6]

One of his peculiar habits was to give money to children, including his grandchildren. He always seemed to have cash in his pockets, and when we would see him on holidays or other times, before we could leave he would reach into his pocket and give us each a few dollars. Of course we thought this was great, but my mother thought it was pathetic. She once explained that he knew no other way to express affection. Ginny Dillon, younger sister of Jean, recalled in an email:

I remember Grandpa Charlie as this sharp-dressed, personable, extroverted businessman who always jingled money in his pocket and gave me lots of money, smoked cigars, joked a lot, and had lots of friends. I have a few memories of watching the St. Patrick's Day Parade from his plumbing shop on Broadway in Southie, and going to the yacht club with him, where he was a pretty popular guy. Lots of cocktails and cigars there, along with lots of stories being told to me about Grandpa. To me he just seemed popular and admired.

One might suppose that any boy would want to be like such a father. But in many fundamental ways, the boy Alfred was not and could not be. And this would be held against him by some, to his credit by others. Boyhood was ending, and a gulf would begin to widen between father and son: a set of differences including temperament, education, and life experience.

Charles Mehegan in 1915, age 22.

(Author's collection)

Esther Donahue Carson with her siblings, early 1920s: Esther
between brothers Bill at left and Dan at right; sister May in front.

(Courtesy of David Carson)

Baby Alfred in 1912.

(Author's collection)

Alfred in his Confirmation portrait, about 1924.

(Author's collection)

(*Above*) Esther Donahue, 17, front row second from right, after a South Boston competition. From "Boston's Star Girl Swimmers," Physical Culture magazine, June 1910.

(Courtesy University of Michigan Archives).

(*Left*) The divers and the band at the water-show amphitheater, undated snapshot by Esther.

(Courtesy of David Carson)

Poster for the Wortham & Rice Water Show, 1918. Esther did the high dive
and other acts with Wortham & Allen, a predecessor show, in 1913, and
possibly this one.

(Circus World Museum, Baraboo, Wisconsin)

3.

No Excuse for Deviation

At AGE FOURTEEN, Alfred was accepted to Boston Latin School for the 1925–26 school year. Founded in 1635, Latin School is the oldest public school in America—a year older than Harvard—and has always been Boston's elite high school. (It is actually a combined middle school / high school, beginning at grade seven.) Its alumni comprise an American pantheon, including Benjamin Franklin, John Hancock, Charles Bulfinch, Ralph Waldo Emerson, and in modern times, Bernard Berenson, Joseph P. Kennedy, Theodore White, and Leonard Bernstein. For many a smart poor boy, Latin School was the ladder out of poverty and the working class. In 1911, the dean of Harvard College reported that Latin School had "long been the largest single source of supply," and that "in the previous ten years this school had sent 302 boys."

Admittance to Latin did not require a special examination then, as it does today, but could be granted to pupils "who have been promoted to the seventh or a higher grade of the day elementary schools and who present evidence of scholarship satisfactory to the board of superintendents." Alfred was admitted to class IV-B—IV being the ninth grade, the numbers descending to I, the twelfth grade. The *B* designation did not refer to a lesser level than *A*, but to the number of years at the school; boys who entered at the seventh grade were in the A group, and those entering at ninth grade were B.

Since there had been no education beyond the eighth grade in Alfred's family, it is unlikely that his admission to Latin School was the fulfillment of his father's or stepmother's dream. The idea might have come from a teacher at the Oliver Hazard Perry School or from a parish priest or nun. Or it might have come from Aunt Mary, who had always believed in Alfred and brought him books as a boy. It might even have been his own idea.

For many in the urban Irish-American milieu of that time, in contrast to Jewish society, to aspire to higher education was to put on airs. One of my mother's uncles was offered a full scholarship to St. Mary's School, an elite Catholic high school in the North End of Boston, but didn't take it because, as she once explained to me, none of his friends were going to high school. He became a Boston firefighter. Education for holy orders was the great exception. To go to college for merely secular reasons might provoke the sneering question, "Who do you think you are, Mr. Big Shot? Smarter than the rest of us?" Nevertheless, Charlie and Julia knew what kind of school Latin was and had to have been at least officially supportive. Along with "evidence of scholarship," the 1925 catalog required that applicants "must present a signed statement from their parents or guardians of intention to give them collegiate education."

The Latin School ninth-grade curriculum for 1925 would be a shock to any public high school student today. Here are excerpts:

> English, five periods a week. Reading of some of the books in the lists set by the colleges, with others taken from the authorized supplementary reading and from the school or Public Library. . . .
>
> Latin, six periods a week. Forms, with simple exercises illustrating their use. Oral and written translation of easy Latin into English. Unprepared translation of easy Latin with the help of the teacher. Reading Latin aloud. Oral and written translation of English into Latin.
>
> French, four periods a week. Pronunciation, reading aloud, dictation, oral practice. Grammar: oral and written practice in the forms and use of nouns, pronouns, adjectives, articles, regular verbs

and at least twelve irregular verbs. Translation of simple French into idiomatic English and vice versa. . . .

History, three periods a week. History of the Ancient Orient, of Ancient Greece, and of Ancient Rome. Readings from the myths and legends and biographies of famous men. Instruction in map-drawing, use of the atlas and drill with outline and wall maps....

Mathematics, five periods a week. Algebra. . . . Mensuration [i.e., geometry] as algebraic material.

The tenth grade (III-B) was even more daunting. English again, Latin, French, the student's choice of Greek or German, and mathematics. Latin included "oral, and occasionally written translations into idiomatic English (a.) Of Caesar's *Gallic War*, Books I–IV, and (b.) of at least one oration of Cicero."[1] There was also "physical training," two periods a week.

The Latin School archivist did not have a record of Alfred Mehegan's grades but did find that in his second year, 1926–27, he repeated the IV-B curriculum. In his third year, 1927, he advanced to III-B, so he was making progress. If he had stayed and mastered the work, he would have graduated in 1930, age eighteen, certain of admittance to a good college.

But it didn't happen. The Latin School record book has two columns at the end of each row: "Left"—the date a student left the school—and "Remarks"—the reason for leaving. Often the reason is graduation, in other cases transfer to other schools: "Dorchester," "SBos," "Belmont Hi." In Alfred's case, the date is January 23, 1928. There is one word in the reason column: "Work."

In some respects, one can imagine what happened. He had not done well in the ninth grade, and his classmates had moved a year ahead. And the academics were a challenge; Latin School was meant to be difficult. He probably did well at math, since he was always good at it later in life, and he loved history. But the languages must have been a killer. No one at home could have helped him with his Latin, French, Greek, or German (although that would have been equally true for many kids with immigrant backgrounds). Perhaps he felt disheartened at the difficulty but did not have a mentor, someone to say, "Keep at it! You can do it! You're as smart as anyone in there!" Charlie might have yelled at him about his report cards. He might have been sick over the winter and fallen far behind. It is also possible, considering his later history, that depression was a hindrance.

He never spoke of his failure at Latin School in my memory; indeed, I did not know until I dug into old files that he had gone there. If the program was too much for him, why did he give up on high school altogether? He could have transferred to Dorchester High or one of the Catholic high schools. It was clear then and later that he wanted to go to college. There is an indication in later correspondence (one V-mail letter during World War II) that he had also attended English High School, a less prestigious but well-regarded school, for a while, possibly in the fall of 1928, but it must not have been for long, since he did not graduate.

This setback would have consequences in the following years, not all negative, in peacetime and wartime. It denied certain kinds of experiences to him but granted others that most college boys would never have. Whatever his reason for leaving school, it was not one of the most common at that time—a family's need for extra money. My mother got a job after high school that same year of 1928, hanging up dresses in Filene's Basement for twelve dollars per week, and she turned her pay packet over to her parents, who needed the money. But in Alfred's case, the family was the employer. "Work" was a job at Powers & Mehegan as a plumber's helper, for fifteen dollars weekly. Alfred was apprenticed and would learn the trade of plumbing and steamfitting. His lifelong friend Arthur Penney was apprenticed with him.

He was never ashamed of his subsequent path. He was always proud of his craft, high standards, and skills as a plumber, and later as a bid estimator. He called himself a "mechanic," and explained to me that this word did not simply designate one who fixed cars or other machines, but one who understood and applied technology and mechanical principles. A mechanic was like an artisan, a guildsman. He took pride in excellent work and understood tools and efficient operations. My father once almost got into a fight with a man who disparaged all plumbers as crooks. Still, there might have been defensiveness in this pride. How did it feel to go overnight from translating Cicero to installing toilets? It is clear that he had hoped for better than being a fine mechanic, namely, "a collegiate education." That wish and reach for something better would be repeated in years to come. But first there was a taste of the military.

In the summer of 1929, shortly before he turned eighteen, Alfred signed up as a cadet with the Citizens' Military Training Camp, a ninety-day summer program at Camp Ethan Allen, Vermont, near Burlington. The CMTC was established by the U.S. War Department before World War I to give civilian youth military training, without actual enlistment, so that they might be available if called up in time of war.

• • •

This was Alfred's first experience of a manly regimented setting, and he appears to have enjoyed it. In the CMTC, he was in a cavalry unit, and in an old faded photograph, he stands in the back row of a group labeled "A Troop." It looks like a World War I scene. Officers in the front row are wearing Sam Browne belts and high boots and holding riding crops.

Alfred kept his copy of the *Ethan Allen Patriot*, a paperback yearbook. An excerpt from the *Patriot* "'Troop A' activities":

> July 12th, 1929—The third and fourth platoons rode today, and incidentally, got a little experience cleaning the horses. The program is so arranged that half the troop rides each day during most of the forenoon while the other half does infantry drill. The gold-brickers are already at work finding excuses not to turn out on days when they have dismounted drill.[2]

The entry for July 25 reports, "'A' Troop's scores on the range were available today. Fifty-six men qualified with rifle as sharpshooters, and twenty-five as marksmen. Alan Benner was high man with a score of 98, Mehegan has a close second with 97."[3]

This was Alfred's first use of firearms.

When we were children, he spoke with amusement of this early service in the horse cavalry. He knew there was something funny about it; once he said that you had to give the horse a light kick in the belly before you could properly cinch the saddle. It all sounded like a joke. Dad in the cavalry? I pictured him with Errol Flynn, leading the Seventh Cavalry across the Plains, guidons flapping and bugles blowing. But it was true. There he was in the back row of the brown "class" picture.[4]

The Great Depression was over the horizon, and my mother always said that despite the Jazz Age legend, it was not all happy days until the stock market crash of October 1929. "The twenties didn't roar for us," she once said. "Things were going down for a long time." Still, no one anticipated the cataclysm that was to come. By 1930 it was starting in earnest. That year, Alfred left Powers & Mehegan for "lack of work," as he explained on his navy form years later, which sounds like a delicate way of saying he was laid off. Yet he found a job, "helping a machine operator" at the Skinner Organ Co. in Dorchester. The pay was no better: fifteen dollars weekly.

Skinner Organ was a well-known builder of pipe organs. It merged in 1932 with the Aeolian Co., became Aeolian-Skinner, and eventually went out of business in 1972. The factory was on Sydney Street. Part of it was torn down to clear space for the Southeast Expressway on-ramp from Columbia Road, but the remaining brick building still stands, across the tracks from the JFK/UMass MBTA station. In later life Alfred said of this job only that the constant wheedling and twittering of the pipes being tuned nearly drove him crazy.

He was drawn to the sea by his sailing days in and around Boston Harbor. Sometime in late 1930 or early 1931, fed up with organ pipes, he applied to the Massachusetts Nautical School. He was accepted for the 1931–32 school year. It turned out to be one of the most formative and—at least as he looked back on it—happiest experiences of his life.

The school was founded in 1891 as the Massachusetts Nautical Training School. The word "Training" was dropped later. Today, the Massachusetts Maritime Academy is a four-year college with concentrations in navigation, ship-handling, and engineering. Its degrees lead directly to commissions in the U.S. Merchant Marine and the U.S. Navy. But in the 1930s, it had a far lesser stature and a more limited mission. It was a two-year program, the equivalent of a modern community college.

For Alfred, there were several attractions. First, the school had a real academic program, which could mitigate his lack of a high school diploma, should he want to pursue further education. It was an opportunity to prove that he could succeed as a student. Second, the program included an annual summer cruise to the Mediterranean, which would give him travel experience. Third, it offered training for a professional career, possibly a U.S. Navy commission or eventually a merchant marine captaincy.

He never said how he found out about the Nautical School or whose idea it was for him to go there. The annual cost in 1931 consisted of a clothing fund deposit of $150, a graduation deposit of $50 (refunded upon graduation), and a tuition fee of $50. Tuition increased to $100 in 1933. His father must have paid the fees, since Alfred would not have saved enough from his little jobs.

The training ship was the U.S.S. *Nantucket*, a barentine-rigged steel sailing ship with a coal-fired engine and single screw. Built in 1876 as a U.S. Navy gunboat, its first name was U.S.S. *Ranger*, later changed to *Rockport*. The *Ranger* was built in the waning days of sail, when ship's engines were less reliable than those of trains; the sail rig was meant to be auxiliary. In 1909, the *Rockport* was lent to the Massachusetts Nautical School as a training ship, and in 1918 it was named *Nantucket*. It was scrapped in 1958, long after it had left the academy.

My father always chortled at anyone who identified the *Nantucket* with clipper ships or other graceful birds of the sea. "It was a tub," he said, and indeed while it looks fairly sprightly, painted white, in pictures taken in *Ranger* days, by the 1930s it was painted black. It was boxy, with straight lines and a large stack amidships. Its weight was 1,020 tons displacement, length overall 177 feet, beam 32 feet, and it drew 12 feet, 9 inches. Propulsion came from a single 560-horsepower engine, which drove the ship at a blistering top speed of about 10 knots.[5]

The school year had summer and winter terms. Summer was May through August, including the cruise. Winter was December through March. The Nautical School had no building. *Nantucket* was usually docked at the Boston Navy Yard, near the U.S.S. *Constitution,* and in winter a temporary structure was erected over the deck to create classroom space. Alfred began classes on April 1, 1931. The first term was almost entirely given over to seamanship, with one class in mathematics. His grades, from the Academy archives, in "Practical Seamanship" ranged from 3.4 to 3.6 out of a possible 5.0, and in math he earned a 3.5. In "Conduct" and "Aptitude and Attention to Duty" he scored just under or over 4.0 in each month, and his attendance was a straight 5.0. His final average for the term was 3.97 — twentieth in his class of about 120 students.

Aside from seamanship, that first term had no academic classes other than mathematics, because it was taken up almost entirely by the summer cruise. In those four months the first-year cadets learned not only the rudiments of practical ship-handling, but teamwork and response to command. For any nineteen-year-old, it was the sea and the world seen from the ship, or off the ship, that were the main thrills.

As recorded on an old yellow itinerary card that Alfred saved, the 1931 cruise, with about 120 cadets aboard, covered 11,087 miles. The ship departed Boston on May 14, stopped at Provincetown, then headed due east. Its ports of call included Gibraltar, Palermo, Athens, Istanbul, Milos (Greece), Malta, Algiers, Gibraltar again, and Madeira, returning to Boston September 20. On the way home, the *Nantucket* made an unscheduled stop in Bermuda to drop off a sick sailor who needed hospitalization.

Alfred kept a jaunty, detailed log of the 1931 cruise. Besides the weather and sometimes the progress of the ship, he noted sights from the ship and ashore. Friday, May 29: "Rain with shifting winds. Making just about steerage way under sail." The next day, a note of homesickness appears: "Rain. Still under sail. Canteen open today. Filled up with candy. Racing season opens back home. Would give a year of my life to be aboard *Mohawk* today instead of U.S.S. *Nantucket.*"

June 29, Athens: "We went on liberty this afternoon. I went with an excursion to the various historic points of interest. Acropolis, Arch of Hadrian, Temple of Jupiter, Tower of Winds, Prison of Socrates, Stadium, and the Olympic Area where the Olympic Games were held in 1924." He took pictures, small snaps from a Brownie camera, of jolly shipboard scenes with shipmates and of some of the places seen on liberty. Among the photos is one of him standing proudly in his cadet's uniform in front of what appears to be the Parthenon. He was a long way from Southie and Dorchester.

It is clear from the diary that in his mind, the Nautical School was not just a lark. He was trying to improve himself, get his life on a forward track, and charted his progress, or lack of it. June 30:

> Another month gone by. Have I profited during that period? I wonder. I've become pretty well accustomed [to] the Nantucket routine. I've hardened up considerably, and I think I've learned a bit by sad experience. I've been homesick; I've been tearing mad; I've been contented. I guess this last month has changed my nature a bit in the bargain. —Well, let's look forward to a profitable month of July. *En avant*——

On July 4, *Nantucket* anchored at Istanbul, Turkey. On July 11, en route back to Greece, he wrote:

> Sighted several vessels this morning. We are still in sight of land. The scenery is great. We have our square sails and head sails set. We are constantly squaring the yards around for we are still passing thru the Dardanelles and constantly changing our course. We sighted that fatal spot [Gallipoli] where the Allies tried to land troops during the World War.

August 1, Gibraltar, he wrote, "My birthday—twenty years today. Imagine—I'm getting to be a patriarch."

Nearing home in September, he had a classic sailor's mishap. When approaching land, a ship's officers need to know the depth of the water. He was "heaving the lead"—the sounding lead, a heavy sinker at the end of a line. In that day before sonar, the leadsman would stand on a platform called "the chains," suspended over the water at the bow, swing the lead twice around and let it fly forward at the bottom of the second swing, quickly pull the line taut, then note the mark above the water as the ship passes over the line. Alfred wrote, "Twenty-four hours out of Boston while heaving the lead I got careless and allowed the lead to swing under the chains, and subsequently was knocked into sweet oblivion. When I came to in the sick bay, I was the proud owner of a neatly stitched scalp." He bore the scar on his left forehead, near his hairline, for the rest of his life. It seems miraculous that he didn't fall overboard and drown.

The winter term, December 1931 through March 1932, had a more extensive academic program. Besides seamanship, there was navigation, signals, mathematics, physics, electricity, and engineering. In each of the four months in all of these subjects, Alfred scored lower than 4.0 only three times; at the end of the term, his exam average was 4.50 and total average was 4.36—second in his class. This time, there would be no dropping out to go to work. Nevertheless, even with his academic success, he was sometimes beset with doubt, and a poignant journal entry dated Thursday, February 4, 1932, includes an indirect reference to his early childhood. It also reveals that he had had a particular ambition at Latin School, now out of reach.

> For no good reason at all I've decided to make an entry at this date. I haven't been keeping a log regularly, but tonight I don't feel like studying…. Contrary to opinion one *can* learn something if one tries hard. I'm trying not as hard as I could, but harder than I ever tried in my high school days. For the sake of a foil for my remarks I'll imagine myself to be addressing my guardian angel, my closest

confidante. Do you remember how I used to be at the foot of my class all the time? Remember how I used to be the class clown? No more of that. I'm trying to heed your words of wisdom. Perhaps I'll eventually make a success of my poorly started life, who knows? Perhaps you'll help me—but no, you've been doing your best for almost twenty-one years and I've laughed at your good advice, and consequently instead of being a junior at Tech [that is, MIT] as planned, I'm a lowly Boot on the U.S.S. Nantucket.

On the whole, however, he seemed positive and cheerful. On February 21, he wrote that his girlfriend, Marion, had dumped him for a rival named Ken. He was devastated, though he expressed no rancor toward her or him. Two weeks later, on March 4, he wrote: "For two days I was heartbroken and then my fickle heart pieced itself together as soundly as ever. Now a tiny feeling of relief is creeping over me, for our affair was getting serious, at least from my side and can you imagine me as anyone's husband? I can't quite picture it."

• • •

In 1932, the country was in the free fall of the Great Depression, but for Alfred life seemed secure and fulfilling. He had friends and was learning seamanship and navigation—skills that surely would take him far from the little world of Powers & Mehegan. Best of all, he was looking forward to the second summer cruise.

The voyage began well. *Nantucket* left Boston May 18, stopped briefly in Provincetown, and sailed south to Norfolk, Virginia, then east to Ponta Delgada, Azores; Plymouth, England; Amsterdam; Copenhagen; Göteburg, Sweden; Hull, England; Cádiz, Spain; Gibraltar; Funchal, Madeira. The ship set sail for home in late August.

This year, Alfred's journal contained no daily log but was filled with navigational computations and detailed pencil drawings of mast, sail, and rigging configurations. As he had the year before, he took snapshots ashore, of children in wooden shoes in the Netherlands, of peasants with donkey carts, of a bullfight in Cádiz. There are pictures of him as well, including one with his shipmate Fred Arold (pronounced like Harold), marked on the back "Fred Arold, my pal"; two of Alfred on deck, taking a reading of the sun with a sextant; and two of him looking proudly at the camera, shirtless with muscular chest, with a gang of others hefting shovels. The picture is marked "coaling ship"; that is, loading coal from a lighter alongside.

His favorite story from Europe was the bullfight. He and a group of shipmates had attended the fight in Cádiz and got into trouble by cheering for the bull. The locals did not take kindly to this, and he told of being chased along a beach by Spanish *policía*, who were whacking them with the flats of their swords. Could this have really happened? It sounds improbable now (swords?), but in its details the story took on the stature of legend. Of course, he also told us, when we were small children, that he had once been shipwrecked and tied down on the shore with ropes by tiny little men. Imagine our surprise when we learned the story of *Gulliver's Travels*. What a coincidence!

• • •

The captain of *Nantucket* that year was Clarence A. Abele (1876–1944), U.S. Navy, retired, an 1898 U.S. Naval Academy graduate who had commanded troop ships during World War I. He had never commanded a sailing ship and depended on his senior officers, several of whom had experience under sail. On September 12, the commissioners of the Nautical School received a three-page typed letter from Captain Abele, sent from New London, beginning with this sentence: "I beg to report that the NANTUCKET was overtaken by the recent hurricane on 8 September when 149 miles 113° from Montauk Point"—about 166 miles southeast of Nantucket.

The storm had no name; that convention for hurricanes was still in the future. *Nantucket* left Funchal, Madeira, on August 18, bound for Orient, Long Island, where it would take on coal and go on to Boston. At 0800, August 31, Alfred's log records a fix from a sextant reading, placing the ship at latitude 29° 58' 25", longitude 47° 43' 42"—still in midocean. He was not the navigator, of course, but all the students were taking readings. Later he wrote, "Course & distance from Noon Position August 31 to Montauk Point [Long Island, New York]. . . . Dist. 1363 miles, Course 312°."

He said nothing about a storm. But Abele had been notified by wireless of the progress of a Caribbean hurricane. The officers began to monitor reports of its position. In 1932 this was not easy. There was no radar and no aircraft surveillance of midocean storms. The only way a storm's position and course could be known was by radio reports of ships at sea, or landfalls. Individual ship reports could not plot a storm's exact position, its size and maximum wind speeds, whether it was gaining or losing strength, nor could they calculate or predict course changes. Abele's report continued: "At noon, zone 4 time, 6 September, the ship was 468 miles 116° from Montauk Point. The storm center at 1000 EST [1 a.m.] was in Lat. 28N, Long. 78W, moving north at 10 miles an hour."

In addition to radio reports, ships at sea would use historical charts to estimate the probable movements of storms. The storm was east of the Florida coast, moving a little faster than the ship's usual top speed of about eight knots. Abele wrote, "The September Pilot Chart showed the general course of hurricanes in September as passing out to sea from south of Cape Hatteras. It was decided that the best course was to make speed to the westward to keep on the navigable side of the storm center. Accordingly a third boiler was cut in at 1328." With its single screw, "making speed" in the old gunboat meant zooming along at ten knots, the equivalent of eleven and a half miles per hour. The captain and officers reckoned that the storm would swing clockwise, toward the east, and that the way to avoid it was to outrace it—pass westward to the north of it, after which ship and storm would be headed in opposite directions. At first, it seemed they had made the right choice. But the old tub was just too slow. Abele wrote:

> On 7 September, the weather report at 1000 showed the storm
> center in Lat. 29 N, Long. 75-30 W, and indicated that the storm was
> recurving towards Bermuda. But the 2200 report gave storm center
> in Lat. 30-30 N, Long. 73-30 W, indicating [the] storm was moving

northward again. The barometer now began to fall and indication was that the storm would pass to eastward of the ship. The report of the morning of the 8th plainly indicated that the center would pass to eastward and not far off. The wind had been blowing from the northeast with increasing intensity from 2200 on the 7th and sail was then reduced to the clew of the trysail, and later speed was reduced to 2/3. From then on the wind increased in intensity to a gale. Speed was reduced to 1/3 at 0800 on the 8th and storm trysail and storm spanker was set. Shortly after noon of the 8th the storm reached hurricane proportions.

The eighth was Thursday. Now there was no way to evade the storm, so all sail for headway was furled and replaced by two small triangular sails—a trysail between the fore- and mainmasts, and a spanker at the stern, to try to hold the bow into the wind. The engine was running slowly to try to keep headway.

Huge seas began to batter the ship. The wind was blowing from the northeast, the starboard beam—almost exactly from the right side—and the chart house clinometer, which measures heeling, recorded that the ship was rolling from 30 degrees starboard to 50 degrees port. If straight up is 0 degrees and level sideways is 90, a 50-degree roll is more than halfway down—extremely dangerous to the ship and to the men trying to work and keep control. "It was desired," the report said with notable understatement, "to keep the ship's head up [i.e., headed into the wind] as much as possible as danger was feared if the sea should strike aft." However, the storm sails were not doing the job.

While the ship did not take on much water due to tight battening, at about four p.m. Thursday a great wave hit the starboard side, blew over the bridge, and ripped the motor launch partly off its davits, smashing one end of the boat and pulling out a section of deck planking, which was hastily patched to prevent more water from cascading below. Then, wrote Abele, "The 2d cutter and the whaleboat were carried away and were cut adrift. At 1655 the dinghy was also carried away and was cut adrift." *Nantucket* now had no boats, and the crew of 150, 118 of whom were cadets, would have to live or die with the ship. The radio was knocked out when waves hit the radio shack, so no distress signal was possible. Sometime that afternoon, a one-and-a-half-ton anchor came loose on the deck and began crashing back and forth with the motion of the ship but was safely lashed down. The spanker sail at the stern, doing little good anyway, tore away its fastenings and was taken in.

Though little water was penetrating below decks, the ship was more helpless than ever, and the situation was increasingly dire. The engine could not keep the head up. At this point, the decision was made to shut down the engine, "lie to"—that is, drift—and put out a sea anchor, a sort of canvas drogue on a long line off the bow. Like an anchor on the bottom, a sea anchor is intended to provide drag as the ship is blown by the wind, holding the bow straight into the wind and thereby reducing the side-to-side wallowing. But a sea anchor was not standard equipment for a thousand-ton ship. Alfred's shipmate Fred Arold wrote years later that it was fashioned on the spot from nine-foot wooden spars bolted together crosswise, held in place with lengths of chain, with sail canvas as a balloon. A small anchor was used to hold it open below the surface, something like the trawl doors that hold a fishing dragger's net open as it is pulled across the bottom.

It worked, just barely. The rolling continued, but the severity was reduced, and, Abele reported, the ship "seemed to ride a little more easily." There was no more wave damage. The hurricane-force winds, estimated at 80 to 100 knots at their peak, blew from noon Thursday until about four a.m. Friday. Gradually they diminished, and it became clear that the danger was past. Abele wrote, "From later reports of the storm's course, it appears that the center passed about 80 miles to the eastward of the ship at about 2200 [nine p.m.], 8 September." The incredibly sturdy old tub, manned by an exhausted crew, had blown fifty miles before the wind. When it was deemed safe to do so, the engine was restarted. On Saturday the tenth, *Nantucket* limped into New London, Connecticut, took on coal, and proceeded through the Cape Cod Canal to Boston, arriving on Tuesday, September 13.

• • •

The great storm was a story my father told many times. The ship was heeling over so far, he said, that the yards—the horizontal spars on which the square sails are set—were dipping into the sea. The boats were gone, and everyone knew that there was no way to survive in that ocean. If you went overboard, even if you had something to cling to, the violence of the sea and the wind and spume were so intense that it would be impossible to breathe. Of course we always asked, "Weren't you afraid?" His answer was one I had never heard from anyone who had survived a near-death experience. With the pounding the ship was taking, he and his shipmates were certain that they would die, he said, and their plan, when the ship went down, was to take a deep gulp of seawater right away to speed the drowning. He added, "We were not afraid, because we knew there was no hope." But when the heeling of the ship began to abate, hope returned. Then, he said, when the outcome was again in question, fear returned.

His remembered pessimism is confirmed in a page-one story in the *Boston Herald*, September 12:

Training Ship, Believed Lost, Limps into Port

Storm-wracked and badly in need of repairs, the training ship *Nantucket* of the Massachusetts Nautical School arrived at New London, Conn., from the Madeira Islands yesterday, her officers and cadets declaring that they had given her up as lost during the terrific storm at sea last week….

Because of her age, 60 years, officers of the *Nantucket* admitted yesterday that they were doubtful whether she would survive the terrific battering she took.

There is only one narrative fragment in Alfred's second journal , just after the position computations of August 31:

For twenty-four hours, the [ship] had been mauled and battered by [a] murderous hurricane sweeping up from that womb of storms, the West Indies. She was writhing in the trough, practically helpless.

Up on the seething crest she labored, then that inevitable plate-rending shudder. A sickening roll and the following drop into the trough. Always the question, Will she rise again? The engines were silent, absolutely helpless in the grip of the elements. Headway only served to antagonize the goddess of storms. All hatches and companionways securely battened down, and the crew…

The fragment ends here.

In 1974, an account of the storm was written in the Maritime Academy alumni magazine, *The Bulletin*, by Fred Arold (1913–2007), in which Alfred is a prominent character.[6] Titled "Down Massachusetts Bay We Went A-Sailing," it is written in the first person, and Arold for some reason changed his own name to Harry Green, but not the name of his shipmate, Al Mehegan. Captain Abele is spelled "Able," and two of his officers are the bosun, a German named Harry Brenner, and the watch officer, nicknamed "Sivy."

Arold writes that on September 6 "Green" was wakened from sleep in his hammock by orders to get on deck. As he is getting dressed, his friend Al Mehegan speaks to him.

"Harry, we don't have any lifeboats left. The motor boat is smashed in its cradle and the radio shack is flooded. We couldn't send out an S.O.S if we had to. Chips [Brenner] says we will probably capsize if one of the masts goes." Taking me to one side, then, he pulled a sheath knife from his belt. "When you go on watch at noon, keep your ears open. If I think we've had it, I'll come to the engine room ladder and call. Get up on deck then as fast as you're able. We'll cut the gangway loose with this." He brandished the wicked looking eight-inch blade to show me how fast he could cut the lashing. "We'll get that gangway over the side somehow and tie ourselves to it." I managed a sickly smile at his gutsy plan to survive. That he included me in his plan was the part that made me proud to be his friend.

In Arold's telling, Alfred was the leader of those who had secured the runaway anchor. "We stalked it with lassos," Al says. "I got lucky and looped one fluke, then Thompson ringed the other one. We've got it lashed down in good shape now." Then Al says:

> "You know, there's a big argument goin' on topsides."
> "What's the big argument?" I asked.
> "It's between Sivy and Brenner on one side, Captain Able, the other. Captain says we'll just have to ride her out. Brenner and Sivy want to rig a sea anchor, or a sea kite as Sivy calls it. The Captain says a sea anchor isn't practical on a ship this size. Brenner claims that during the World War, in 1915, Count Von Luckner saved his *See Adler* in a hurricane off South America with one."

The German sailing ship SMS *Seeadler*, commanded by Captain Felix von Luckner, raided Allied commerce in World War I, destroying sixteen ships. It ran aground and was wrecked in Tahiti on August 2, 1917.

Al says, "'Captain's gone to his quarters. I guess he doesn't think it will work, but maybe he hopes it will. I'm off watch, so I'm going to see if I can help.'" After the sea anchor is set, the heeling of the ship declines from 50 to only 30 degrees. "Tremendous seas still towered like gray hills over the stern," Arold writes, "but each time *Nantucket* lifted and the mountain of water slid harmlessly underneath, suddenly we were a ship again. *Nantucket* rode like a gull in a high surf."

Many of these details are unverifiable, and some of the words attributed to Alfred when he first meets "Green" are incredible: "'Oh, yes, I'm Irish all right, and I go to Mass every Sunday,' he said, kind of belligerently." My mother noted on her copy of the Arold account, "He never would have said that!" Perhaps at first he did have a scheme to cut away a gangplank, but an every-man-for-himself plan, abandoning his other shipmates, does not sound like him, and he always said that there was no way they could have survived in that violent sea. In his stories of the storm, he never claimed to have helped secure the runaway anchor.

It is also hard to believe that Arold slept soundly through the smashing of the boats, which happened on the eighth, not the sixth, at the height of the storm.

However, it seems that the dispute between Abele and his officers, or something like it, was real enough. According to Arold, the *Boston Herald* carried a story headlined, "Captain Abele Denies Rift with Officers During Hurricane." A September 11, 1932, *Boston Globe* story reported, "Some of the cadets who came ashore this morning claim the cool head of two veteran seamen, Commander N.E. Merrill and Lieut. N.L. Swertzen, averted a panic among the men, and during the 30 hours these able officers went without sleep to keep up the morale of those on board the training ship."

Arold had the names confused in his memory. There was no Brenner. The Maritime Academy's records for that year list Abele as the commanding officer, Norman E. Merrill as the executive officer, and Nikolai S. Sivertsen (not Swertzen) as the schoolship watch officer. Neither of these men was German. Merrill was himself a graduate of the Massachusetts Nautical School. Sivertsen lived in Boston but was born in Bergen, Norway. It is likely that he, not Merrill, would have known that Luckner had saved *Seeadler* with a sea anchor. That raider was disguised as a Norwegian coal carrier, and its crew members, possibly including some known to Sivertsen, were recruited for their ability to speak Norwegian.

Research into newspaper accounts of the storm, which tore into outer Cape Cod and the Islands, turned up numerous stories, including several about the ordeal of the *Nantucket*. But though I looked through newspapers dating several weeks after the storm, I turned up none about an argument between Abele and his officers. Possibly it was published long after the event. In any case, it is striking that in his report, Captain Abele commends the cadets but does not commend or give any credit to his officers for the survival of the ship, and notable as well that the cadets, in their comments to the press, gave all credit to the officers but none to the captain.

It appears there was another factor in the ship's survival. As *Ranger,* *Rockport,* and *Nantucket,* the ship had always been rigged as a barkentine. That is, the foremast was square rigged, with horizontal spars from which the rectangular sails were suspended, while the main- and mizzenmasts were rigged fore-and-aft, schooner fashion, with sails suspended vertically from the masts. The barkentine configuration can be seen in older photographs of the ship. Before leaving Boston for the 1932 cruise, *Nantucket* was reconfigured as a bark, with both fore- and mainmasts square rigged, and only the mizzenmast fore-and-aft. Presumably this was to make the ship faster under sail. To accommodate this greater mass of sail and balance its effect on the hull, one hundred tons of additional ballast were installed. The *Globe* story reported, "Only for this ballast, the cadets claim, the ship could not have weathered the storm."

• • •

In the winter term of 1932–33, Alfred's academic performance continued to improve. In November he was promoted to "Cadet Petty Officer (Captain of Top-Maintop)." Month by month, in "Conduct" he was marked 5.0 and in "Aptitude and Attention to Duty," he was mostly marked 4.6 or higher. His final standing was 4.33, second in his class. His diploma, dated April 4, 1933, and signed by Captain Abele, records his graduation in "seamanship and navigation" — "with distinction." He was twenty-one.

He always referred to this time of his life as "the Training Ship" — it was "when I was on the Training Ship," never the Nautical School, as if sea duty had been the heart of it. The terms and expressions of his days under sail stayed with him, and he would use them humorously. "All hands on deck!" he would call when he wanted us to rake leaves or help with some other project. "All hands, lay aloft and make sail!" When we were older, the last one in at night was expected to "batten down the hatches." And before lights were out, he would go around to be sure stairs and hallways were clear of any obstructions that would trip one up in the dark; that is, "clear the gangways" to make sure the place was "shipshape in Bristol fashion." Some of these expressions were hilarious; a woman with a wide behind was said, discreetly, to be "an ax-handle and a half across the stern sheets."

. . .

Celestial navigation held a particular fascination; it appealed to his logical and orderly mind. There was something wonderful about figuring out where you were, and where you were going, out on the trackless deep with no signposts and no one to give you the answer. I can easily see why this appealed to him: from a private conversation between oneself and the cosmos, finding one's position and course. His *Nantucket* journals are filled with hand-drawn navigational tables, using various methods, including Dreisenstock, Marcq St. Hilaire, and dead reckoning, to find latitude and longitude. Each has a neat heading: "Compass Azimuth of [symbol for the sun] for deviation August 7, 1932, ship's head 125°," "Marcq St. Hilaire of Moon for longitude August 24, 1932," "Computing Lines of Position by Dreisenstock's Method." and "Dead Reckoning from Navigator's 1200 fix to 1455."

A prize relic was his Bowditch—a copy of *The American Practical Navigator*, by Nathaniel Bowditch, 1930 edition. First published in 1802, this navigator's bible was a heavy book with a weathered brown cloth cover. He said he had used it sometimes as a pillow in hot weather when it was too hot to sleep below decks, which might have been a tall tale, unless he wrapped it in cloth. A *Boston Globe* editorial on March 26, 1940, Bowditch's 167th birthday, included this sentence: "A lad from the Massachusetts Nautical Training ship turned up one evening not long ago hugging proudly to his bosom a yellow calfskin tome which he had purchased on State Street with money earned on a fishing schooner during vacation. 'Here,' said he, 'is my Bowditch.'"

Alfred bought his copy at W. E. Hadlock & Co. Nautical Instruments, 9 Broad Street, Boston, for $2.25. He wrote, "A. C. Mehegan," on the front endpaper, and also in all capitals on the trimmed edge of the pages, so as to be readable when the book was closed. In about 2008, I had the book rebound, carefully preserving the endpapers, and gave it as a gift to my son Owen, who lives in San Francisco. In researching this history, I wrote to Owen to ask him to look at his grandfather's marks on the endpapers and elsewhere in the book. Here is his report:

> On the endplate he drew a compass rose and marked off all the different points; e.g., N, NxW, NNW, NWxN, NW, NWxW, WNW, WNN, W. There are also calculations which appear to be for latitude and longitude. More compass roses on the back endplates, same as the others, it appears. More calculations. Here on a page about finding position by observing bearing and distance to a known object, he has doodled a three-masted ship, with anchor out, on an existing diagram. There is a chapter on compass error, and the last thing in it is this italicized sentence: "There is no excuse for large deviations in a standard or steering compass, and they should not be allowed to exist." He dutifully copied this over, verbatim, right below it. At the beginning of that chapter he wrote, "Study deviation," and underlined it. Here he wrote "A. C. Mehegan, USS Nantucket" on the edge of a page. Lots of jotting down calculations and navigation diagrams as well.

Among the many things he learned in becoming a navigator was the sky-scape of the stars. He pointed them out to us when we were children: Arcturus, Castor and Pollux, Rigel, Sirius, and the constellations Cassiopeia and the Big and Little Dippers, and how to find the North Star from Merak and Dubhe — the Big Dipper's so-called pointing stars. Also the constellations Orion, Andromeda, Spica, and Scorpius — which he called "the Longshoreman's Hook." This to us made him different from other kids' fathers.

He and my brother Peter struggled against each other at times when Peter was in his teens. But Peter remembered, "There was a time, a few years, when we got closer, Dad and me. Maybe it was like that Mark Twain line.[7] We would talk. I remember sitting out on the porch with him on summer nights, and he would talk about the Training Ship, and the stars. He knew all the stars and constellations. It was only a short time, but I was glad that happened."

Although in later life he looked back on the Training Ship as one of the peaks of his life, in the years that followed it did not seem to have worked out so well to the youth who had expected to be "a junior at Tech" instead of "a lowly Boot on the U.S.S. *Nantucket.*" In the third of his journals, well after the last of his calculations, is a long solitary entry dated June 16, 1936, written "for the benefit of my biographer, if one should materialize." Filling several pages in his strong and neat hand, it covers the hard Depression years after graduation through the date of the entry. He wrote of the *Nantucket:*

> Graduation itself was a disappointment to me in one respect. I had really worked hard to gain high marks and had been successful. All thru the two years, or at least after the first six months, my marks were a source of satisfaction to me, and pride to Dad. Imagine, the prize dunce of high school days was second and sometimes first in standing. As graduation drew near it was rumored about that I was to be presented with the prize for the cadet having the highest marks in Navigation & Seamanship. Well, to make a long story short, for some reason or other all the prizes but one were eliminated that year. That prize for the cadet "most likely to become a successful sea captain" went to "Pete" Lapine. At the present moment, Pete is studying commercial art at some college in California. . . . The next three years find me meandering from job to job, always dissatisfied, always unsuccessful.

It seems incredible that an institution of higher learning would peremptorily eliminate its prizes for achievement—unless the prizes carried a cash award and the school was desperately trying to demonstrate tight fiscal management. Indeed, the Nautical School had been under political pressure. A September 28, 1932, *Boston Herald* editorial responded to a plea to save it by an official of the Chamber of Commerce:

We'd like to see his evidence that "public sentiment has been overwhelming in favor of its retention." Legislators have wanted to keep it, for it enables them to help their neighbors' boys. . . . Beacon Hill has not reflected sound public opinion or the best educational judgment on this ocean-going luxury. . . . An impartial group of intelligent men delegated to investigate our schooling establishments and report its findings would probably recommend as a first step that we save the money we are now spending on the *Nantucket*.

Whatever happened to the prizes, the quiet tone of Alfred's musings is consistent with the private dialogue with his guardian angel four years earlier. They reflect a lifelong feature of his character. He could be critical of people in an abstract way. But however disappointed, he never expressed personal envy, rancor, or bitterness. He tended to give others the benefit of the doubt as to their intentions toward him. His instinct was to take personal responsibility for his situation, drive himself to think harder, work harder, do better. This internalizing trait, however admirable, years later would concern my mother, who grew increasingly exasperated at his forbearance over what she saw as unjust treatment at the hands of others.

Notwithstanding his disappointment at his lack of professional progress since graduation, he notes that his academic performance was "a source of satisfaction to me, and pride to Dad." Charlie must have expressed his pride in some way, probably cryptic, unless Alfred heard about it indirectly. It is clear that his father's opinion mattered to him. And speaking privately to himself, at least, here he called his father "Dad."

While it might have seemed to the graduate in April 1933 that a bright maritime career was ahead, a contrary force was in play that he never mentioned as such, not even in the 1936 entry, perhaps because of his reluctance to indulge excuses, or because the term "Great Depression" was not yet in everyday speech. His career started off positively, however. Right after graduation, he went to New York and completed a three-week course in use of the Sperry gyrocompass, a revolutionary advance in navigational direction finding. On May 2 he reported for his first job, on the New York waterfront: one of three quartermasters — charged in part with cargo loading, steering, and navigation — on the S.S. *Pennsylvanian*, a 6,500-ton freighter, under Captain Charles M. Bamforth of the American Hawaiian Line. His salary was fifty dollars per month.

4.

Down to the Sea

ALFRED WAS LUCKY TO HAVE A JOB, though he never said as much in any of his writings. By 1933 the Depression had hit the shipping industry as it had every other part of the economy. During World War I there had been a crash commercial shipbuilding program, thought to be essential to national defense in future time of war. Well after the war ended, hundreds of ships were built with low-cost government loans. But by the end of the 1920s the civilian fleet was hugely overbuilt. Several U.S. steamship companies, including the Dollar Line and the Black Diamond Line (both of whom Alfred would work for), relied on massive federal subsidies for the transport of mail. On the import side, the country was largely self-sufficient in raw materials, energy, agriculture, and heavy industry. As for export, the Asian market was negligible (except for, notoriously, scrap metal to Japan), and the European countries were also in severe depression, having never recovered fully from World War I, and not able to buy much in U.S. goods.

During the Depression, many American ships had no cargoes and no place to go, and hundreds of officers and thousands of men had no work. The great number of experienced senior officers "on the beach"—that is, languishing ashore with no seagoing job—had the additional effect of blocking career advancement for younger men. Though he was able to find jobs, Alfred's chances of working his way up in the profession were slim.[1]

One line that did have jobs was American Hawaiian, Alfred's first employer. Calling itself "the Panama Canal Line," American Hawaiian had hired a number of Massachusetts Nautical graduates. Of the fifty-seven members of the class of 1931, twenty-four were hired by American Hawaiian, including one placed on Alfred's first ship, the *Pennsylvanian*. Most of the ships of the company, which was based at Pier 28 in San Francisco, were named for states: *Arkansan, Dakotan, Montanan, Coloradan, Pennsylvanian*. While its ships traveled to the Far East and Europe, as the slogan suggests the bulk of the company's business from its founding through the start of World War II was in the intercoastal trade. That is, between and along the East and West Coasts, after 1914 via the new Panama Canal. The *Pennsylvanian* was one of the older ships in the fleet, built in 1913. Under the name *Scranton*, it had served as a troop ship in World War I. On its return to commercial service, its old name was restored.

Alfred began a journal on his first day of duty in the port of New York, May 2, 1933, assisting with stowage of pickled hides, flour, and lumber. "I will have a good opportunity to observe stowage methods on this job," he wrote brightly. "I didn't notice the stowage of the flour, but the lumber was planks stowed fore and aft and thwartships both to make a snug fit to wings and overhead." More detailed observations of the loading and the ship itself followed. That night, "My watch partner took me around and explained things to me. I find my duties are similar to those of a Q.M. on the *Nancy* [Nantucket]—and the steering watches aren't as bad as I thought."

The *Pennsylvanian* departed May 3 for Port Newark for more loading. Along the way, it narrowly avoided a collision with a tanker. "The tanker was a converted Hog Island," Alfred wrote.[2] "She was barging down at about 7 knots crossing with right of way. On her starboard hand was a mud bank so she couldn't turn out for us. Our skipper gave her full astern and I'll bet we didn't clear her by five feet." From Newark the ship steamed to Philadelphia. On May 5, Alfred recorded a milestone: "Last night, or rather this morning, I stood my first wheel watch on this vessel. She seems to steer O.K." Possibly he showed his inexperience, given what follows.

"Last night the Skipper gave me a lecture. Do I feel low! He told me that he didn't want me, that he had wanted an ex-cadet who had shipped out— But he said that he'd try me out. 'You can't steer.' 'You won't earn your pay' 'All school-ship men want to be captains in a week, etc, etc.' Boy is he good." The word "good" would appear to be ironic, unless he means something like "He gave it to me good."

Here is young Alfred, full of high hopes on his first maritime job, roughly sneered at by his first captain, a Boston man named Charlie who was almost exactly his father's age (Bamforth's years were 1895 to 1975). The captain tells him, in so many words, "I never wanted you. I don't like your type. You'll never amount to anything." At this distance in time, our reaction to this is to say, "What a jerk; what a boor!" But this apparently was not Alfred's reaction; he did not disparage the captain. He only said, "Do I feel low." Bamforth will "try me out," he wrote, and Alfred meant to prove himself.

For the next five months, besides East Coast cities, he became acquainted with Gulf of Mexico ports (he spoke once, later in life, of the nerve-racking duty of steering up the Mississippi River to the port of New Orleans), as well as West Coast ports. He fell in love with the cities of the Northwest and told us that he had once flipped a coin to decide whether he would stay out there or come back to Boston. Boston won the toss. The end of his employment with American Hawaiian came in October. In his June 16, 1936, journal entry, there is this cryptic explanation: "A row with the second mate led to my resignation."

• • •

The *Pennsylvanian* story has a two-part epilogue, one of which puts the surly Bamforth in a different light. Nine years later, he commanded another American Hawaiian ship, S.S. *Honolulan*. On July 22, 1942, the *Honolulan* was torpedoed by a U-boat about 400 miles south of the Azores islands. Bamforth gave the order to abandon ship. He stayed aboard with the first mate to gather more supplies, but when a second torpedo struck, they jumped over the side and swam to the boats. Then he discovered that one man was missing. He searched the water for the missing man, found him, and got him into the boat. After the ship sank, he navigated the boats toward the Azores, where they were picked up by a British ship. Not a man was lost. In 1944 he was awarded the presidential Merchant Marine Distinguished Service Medal. If my father knew this about his former skipper, he never mentioned it.

As for the *Pennsylvanian*, the old ship toiled on for eleven more years, until in World War II it was again taken over by the War Department, this time for a different mission than that of the first war. In August 1944 it was deliberately sunk, along with many others, off the Normandy beaches, part of a breakwater system for the artificial harbors set up to unload men and equipment after the Allied invasion.

• • •

After leaving the *Pennsylvanian*, Alfred signed on in Jersey City, New Jersey, as an ordinary seaman on the *President Lincoln*, a freighter owned by the Dollar Steamship Line. The name had nothing to do with currency; the company was founded by Scots immigrant Robert Dollar (1844–1932). Under terms of the Merchant Marine Act of 1928, the Dollar Line was among those that survived on U.S. Mail subsidies in the Depression. Even so, it failed by 1938. That Alfred took a job as ordinary seaman, after experience as a quartermaster, shows that he was desperate to get another ship. My mother wrote, "He told me that jobs were hard to find and that he took any job he could get just to get 'off the beach,' as they called it, and back to sea."[3]

He left no details of the *President Lincoln* except, writing in 1936, "I guess home ties were still too strong for I quit there after a couple of months and arrived home quite unexpectedly just before Christmas 1933. No more seagoing for me."

By "unexpectedly" presumably he means his homecoming was not expected by his family. Yet home was hardly sweet—he was back working for his father. "You will remember," he wrote in 1936, "that early 1934 found Boston suffering from a cruel cold spell. Said cold spell kept me employed thawing out frozen pipes in the employ of Powers & Mehegan until I found employment in the Baker Chocolate Mills near my home." He never said what this job was or why he did not stay on at Powers & Mehegan; presumably the new job was unskilled, surely nothing for which he was trained. He always said that for years afterward he could not stand the smell or taste of chocolate. "About March," he wrote in 1936, "my feet became itchy again and I shipped as cadet at $30 per month on the *West Eldara*."

The *West Eldara* was a wreck of a ship owned by Black Diamond Lines, another marginal carrier dependent on federal subsidies. So eager was he to get off the beach — or out of the chocolate factory — that Alfred took the job sight unseen. But when he arrived in Weehawken, New Jersey, on March 20, 1934, and saw the ship, he wrote in his journal:

> So help me, I was stunned at the appearance she made! Without a doubt she was the dirtiest, most uncared for vessel I ever laid eyes on. I was truly sick just glancing about. The cargo gear was worn and frayed, and the various lines and tackles were slack and slovenly. Paintwork was streaked and spattered, and rust and rot showed through everywhere. Even the decks were filthy.

His critical survey of the ship is remarkable in a twenty-two-year-old ordinary seaman; he sounds like a new captain. He softened his judgment in a later comment when he learned that the ship had been tied up, unmaintained, for five weeks. That could at least account for the filthy appearance. Still, he had misgivings.

"Now dog-gone me," he wrote, "I left a fairly decent job ashore without a minute's notice. Also I left my 'honey' with the darndest feeling of regret....To clear matters I will explain that I was undecided about which (of two) girls I liked best, and their particular reactions on the memorable eve just about decided me. Nuff-ced." Whatever had transpired with the two girlfriends, it is clear that stepping away from the dilemma, and his abrupt abandonment of his shoreside job, left him feeling divided and perhaps a little ashamed. After looking over the ship, he made his way to his cabin. At first it didn't seem too bad, or at least he thought he could make it decent enough to live in. But then:

> Oh! The worst has come to pass. I found to my horror that I must share my bunk with a horde of bed-bugs! I wasn't in the bunk ten minutes before I was eaten alive. Know what? I spent the rest of the night on the floor of my room clothed in a slicker and rolled up in my blanket and I nearly froze to death.

As the phrase "Know what?" suggests, in most of these early journal writings, he seemed to be addressing an imagined reader—whether his guardian angel or "future biographer." He craved someone to confide in. He was lonely.

The *West Eldara's* usual run was Philadelphia, Baltimore, Norfolk, Antwerp, Rotterdam, and Boston. On March 23 in Philadelphia, he noticed the S.S. *Oregonian*, an American Hawaiian ship, tied up nearby, went aboard, and discovered two buddies from the *Pennsylvanian*. They chatted for a while before he headed back to his own ship. Eight years later, on September 13, 1942, the *Oregonian* was sunk by Norway-based German torpedo planes during a convoy from Scotland to Russia. Twenty-two crewmen were killed.

For most of the run down the coast and to Europe, his log records weather and minor daily details. Ever the conscientious mariner, on March 22 he wrote, "Philly. I went ashore and got my seaman's passport. I also bought a Nautical Almanac and an Azimuth Tables. After supper I studied a while and found that I've forgotten too much for comfort. Turned in about eight p.m. for I have to go on watch at midnight."

The "passport," which survives, is actually a "Seaman's Protection Certificate" issued by the Bureau of Navigation in the U.S. Department of Commerce, certifying that the holder is a U.S. citizen. It records that Alfred C. Mehegan, age twenty-two, is five feet seven and a half inches tall, with brown hair, "ruddy" complexion, and blue eyes. The youth in the one-and-a-half-inch-inch square photo has thick hair combed straight back and is dressed in a vested suit and tie. He has an intent, serious gaze.

The work was cold and hard. March 23: "Weather overcast and average temperature about 18°. While taking the soundings my fingers were frostbitten several times. Find that soundings are taken just to nearest inch….Had a nap after breakfast. Avoided bed-bug bites by freezing out the room and putting sulphur salve on my uncovered parts."

It was a stormy crossing. On April 17 he wrote, "Nothing much this a.m. Approaching the English Channel, we meet plenty of traffic now. Tonight the *Aquitania* went booming past at about 20 knots. She's a fine looking ship, but her 4 stacks look funny these days." The *Aquitania* was a four-stack Cunard liner of the *Titanic* and *Lusitania* generation, one of the longest-serving liners in history, 1913 to 1949, with three million miles and 450 voyages. Her elegance gave her the name "Ship Beautiful"—in marked contrast, as Alfred could see, to gritty old *West Eldara*.

His last entry for the voyage was on April 27: "Since writing last we have been to Antwerp & Rotterdam. In Antwerp I played the part of a tourist . . . and visited points of interest. In Rotterdam I played the part of a sailor ashore and proceeded to get a wee bit drunk on two occasions. Now we are steaming down the English Channel again bound for Boston."

Although he does not complain of ill treatment in these entries, in the June 16, 1936, entry he looked back at his time on the *West Eldara* and described a formative event.

> I made one round trip and on our next stop at Baltimore, we
> "struck" for higher wages and better conditions. The strike lasted
> about three days, and I spent the final night in the Baltimore
> jail charged with assault on a strike breaker. At my trial the next
> morning, the judge, whose name was Kelley or Murphy or such,
> turned me loose after asking me why a good Mick like myself should
> be getting mixed up with "a bunch of Reds."

In a note from the 1980s placed with his merchant marine papers, my mother added details to his account:

> He told me that conditions on all the merchant ships were indescribable. First when you went aboard you had to de-louse your quarters (and these were officers' quarters) which always included cleaning your bunk of bed bugs. Ship-owners were incredibly greedy and oppressive. When a ship came ashore after the cargo was unloaded you were supposed to get some time off but the captain would inevitably say, at the demand of the owners, of course, "If you want your job, you'll work." Sometimes he would work the entire time the ship was in port, loading and unloading, with no time off at all before sailing time.
>
> Of course the inevitable happened. There were violent strikes all over the coast ports, east and west. Al joined the striking crew on a ship in Baltimore. They had signs and were picketing when they were all arrested. The Communist Party, which hi-jacked every strike in those days, had given them the signs to carry. They even gave out money for food and lodging but Al was wary and wouldn't take it though some of the men did. Even the police sympathized with the owners then because unions were considered to be so radical....
>
> Some of the men went to jail but [the judge] let him go and said "Get out of Baltimore as fast as you can!" Al hopped freights and walked a good part of the way until he got home to Boston.[4]

While strikes were breaking out increasingly on all coasts, among both seamen and dockworkers, Baltimore was an eastern hotbed in 1934. While it is true that the communist-led Marine Workers Industrial Union dominated Baltimore strike-organizing efforts, the noncommunist International Seamen's Union of America was also active. Alfred was no "red" and never would be and still had not, as of his departure from Baltimore, joined any union.

This was, in fact, his second arrest. On his 1942 application for a Navy Reserve commission, he would answer the question about whether he had ever been arrested: "Yes, arrested 1929 using auto without authority, found not guilty in Suffolk Superior Court." But he did not, on that later application, mention the Baltimore affair. It is lucky for him that he never tried to work in academia or the arts after World War II; quite likely in the McCarthy period he would have been blacklisted for his "communist past."

The *West Eldara* met the same fate as the *Oregonian* and Bamforth's *Honolulan*. In September 1942, it was torpedoed by a U-boat off the coast of South America. After the crew abandoned ship, the submarine surfaced and finished it off with shell fire. Presumably the bedbugs went down with the ship.

• • •

Alfred spent the summer and fall of 1934 at home, working for Powers & Mehegan again for eighteen dollars per month and acting as skipper of a racing yacht owned by William Taylor, a South Boston Yacht Club member. "This was a very happy summer for me," he wrote in 1936. "Now surely I wouldn't go back to sea again." But in December, he shipped out, "as A.B. lookout on the S.S. *Manhattan*, American's idea of a super liner."

The *Manhattan* was a 24,000-ton luxury liner owned by United States Lines, but there was no luxury for the lowly lookout. "What misery was in store for me in that crow's nest as we battered our way across the Western Ocean in mid winter," he wrote. "Two trips of peering out into sleet and snow and I was promoted to Quartermaster—helmsman to you! In April I tired of the sea again, and arrived home about Eastertime. My family was glad to see that I intended at last to settle down ashore."

This appears to have been his first real crack at moving up the ranks, and perhaps in time getting his own command. His promotion to quartermaster on an excellent ship carried a salary of seventy dollars a month—not princely, but more than he had been earning thawing out frozen pipes. He had a skilled profession. He might have stuck it out and eventually achieved a command. And yet his ambivalence (and the skepticism in his family) about the seagoing life was evident. Not only were the conditions poor, but it was lonely work. Nevertheless, on May 1, 1935, he shoved off once more, as able-bodied seaman (the bottom rung again) on the S.S. *Katrina Luckenbach*, an 8,000-ton freighter of the Luckenbach line. But one thing was different this time. Two months earlier, in March, he had joined the Eastern and Gulf Sailors Association, an affiliate of the International Seamen's Union. The following year, he joined the National Organization of Masters, Mates and Pilots of America, West Coast Local No. 90. He kept his first union cards throughout his life; they are still in his papers.

Katrina Luckenbach was caught up in labor strife for the next several months, mostly involving work stoppages by dockworkers, in various ports. Alfred seems not to have been directly involved. In August, the quartermaster quit and he was promoted to third mate—another good break. However, in March of the following year, the old third mate was rehired, and Alfred, apparently not willing to go back to an ordinary seaman's job, "wended my weary way home from San Francisco, on the beach again."

This was the end of his merchant career. Still, the sea never ceased to pull at him. In her 1989 autobiography, my mother wrote that her father had worried about Al when they first became a serious couple.

> One day Dad said to me thoughtfully, "The only thing that worries me is that he is a sailor. I'm afraid he will leave you and go back to sea some day." I assured him Al had promised me it would never happen. Dad shook his head and said, "You never lose that urge."
>
> Al told me that that was so true. He said that as we sat looking at the ships outward bound at Castle Island [a South Boston waterfront park adjacent to the main shipping channel], he wanted to be on every one of them, but then he said he knew he would regret it the minute it cleared the harbor.[5]

At the end of his June 1936 entry, he describes a fantasy.

> I have decided to settle down ashore—but in the back of my mind is a germ of an idea; I have just read Ahto Walter's *Racing the Seas*, a story of a young man who solved his problem of restlessness

by sailing the seas in a 30 ft. sloop.[6] I sure would like to do the same, but my present resources amount to about $2.50, and my debts total about $45. Now if I can rescue a millionaire from some terrible fate, or find a small fortune in some manner, I am likely to go to sea again, but as my own captain.

He never did, except in wartime.

His seagoing adventures were a faint reenactment of his mother's career, possibly even an unconscious search for her. Her flight was in the water and his was on it, but both of them "lit out for the territory," one might say, leaving the provincial world of Irish Boston behind, hoping for the new and exciting, coming home for visits but always leaving again. Both of them were drawn to the West Coast. But she, unlike her firstborn, never came home to live again.

The 1936 journal entry is the last of its kind. There were letters later on, but no other secret reflections—at least none that survive. However, a key witness now picks up the story. "The family went to Pemberton again that summer [of 1936]," my mother wrote in 1989. "That was the summer I saw Al for the first time."

Alfred at right, as a 17-year-old cavalry trainee, Fort Ethan Allen, Vermont, summer 1929.

(Author's collection)

Taking a break from loading coal aboard the *Nantucket*.

(Author's collection)

"She was a tub." U.S.S. *Nantucket* off the coast of Portugal, 1936, in post-1932 rigging as a bark. (Courtesy of Massachusetts Maritime Academy Archives)

The runaway anchor in the great hurricane, September 1932. "We stalked it with lassos," Al says. "I got lucky and looped one fluke, then Thompson ringed the other one. We've got it lashed down in good shape now." (Author's collection)

Alfred "shooting the sun" with a sextant, U.S.S. *Nantucket*, 1931 or 1932. (Author's collection)

The cadet in dress uniform, possibly at the Acropolis.

(Author's collection)

SEAMAN'S PROTECTION CERTIFICATE

Cat. No. 1436

No. B 1676

DEPARTMENT OF COMMERCE
BUREAU OF NAVIGATION

I, THOS. WELLS, DEPUTY, Collector of the Customs for the District of PHILADELPHIA, do hereby certify that ALFRED C. MEHEGAN, an AMERICAN SEAMAN, aged 22 years, or thereabouts, of the height of 5 feet, 7 inches, Brown hair, Ruddy complexion, Blue eyes, and a native of Boston Mass., has this day produced to me proof, in the manner directed by law; and I do hereby certify that the said ALFRED C. MEHEGAN is a CITIZEN OF THE UNITED STATES OF AMERICA

In witness whereof, I have hereunto set my hand and Seal of Office this 22 day of March, 19 34

Thomas Wells
DEPUTY
Collector of Customs.

LEFT THUMB PRINT   SEAL   HBA   PHOTOGRAPH

"Seaman's Protection Certificate," a federal identity document issued to Alfred, just before signing on with S.S. *West Eldara*.

(Author's collection)

Alfred's first union card, issued by the International Seaman's Union of America.

(Author's collection)

S.S. *Katrina Luckenbach*, Al's last Merchant Marine ship, about 1936.

(Author's collection)

5.

Love and Law

Mary humphreys mehegan (1911–2002), my mother, was the second child and only daughter of John and Florence Humphreys. John and Florence had met in St. Joseph's parish in Boston's West End, a neighborhood adjoining Beacon Hill, famously destroyed in a 1950s "slum clearance" project. They lived all their married lives in that parish. From 1929 on they lived on West Cedar Street, near Phillips Street, on the working-class "north slope" of Beacon Hill, and thus were not displaced by the wrecking ball. After John died in 1955, my grandmother lived there as a widow until she died in 1964.

Like Charlie Mehegan and Esther Donahue, John and Florence Humphreys had immigrant parents (three from Ireland, one from Nova Scotia). But they were a different kind of family. They were virtual teetotalers, for one thing, whereas drink was ubiquitous in the Mehegan milieu. They were also parish-centered Catholics who remained married for life. Determined to improve himself after being apprenticed in boyhood to an upholsterer, John Humphreys (1875–1955) graduated from Northeastern University Law School — a night school — in 1914. He passed the bar and practiced law, but he could not make a living with it and eventually supported his family as an inspector for the city water department. He was a self-taught intellectual with a gift for numbers and a passion for serious historical and philosophical reading. Florence did not read for pleasure, though she was highly intelligent and shrewd, a sociable free spirit and a natural Irish-American wit. She admired the brains of the man she married, but was not above teasing him. She once said to him, "John, please fix the lock on the kitchen door and try to leave Socrates out of it."

John and Florence's four children were Joe, Mary, John Jr. (known as Jack), and Edward (known as Ned). Jack did not marry, but the other three did and had thirteen children in all. Mary was twenty-nine when she married, having endured needling from her mother and teasing by her brothers that she was in danger of becoming an old maid. In temperament, she was modest and quiet, took after her reflective and bookish father, and though she never went to a four-year college, she was a constant reader, a lover of poetry, music, and art. She was a deeply religious, forward-thinking Catholic intellectual as well as a witty, mild, and extremely empathic person. She was a New Deal Democrat all her life, whereas brothers Joe and Ned became Republicans. She had a clear, economical writing style. Her unpublished profiles of her grandparents and parents, and her autobiography, are sharp chronicles of Irish Boston culture of the late nineteenth and early twentieth centuries. Aside from my father's own fragmentary writings and records, her account of him is the indispensable source.

• • •

They met where she first saw him on the boat, at Pemberton. The town of Hull is a skinny, sandy peninsula about six miles long, protruding into Boston Harbor, with the village of Pemberton at the tip. The ocean side is Nantasket Beach and the west side faces Hull and Hingham Bays. At the beach, from 1905 until it closed in the 1970s, was Paragon Park, an amusement park much like Revere Beach on the North Shore. As mentioned above, Esther Donahue had performed at Paragon in the summer of 1910. The town was served by ferries across the bay from downtown Boston to Pemberton, and Nantasket Pier farther south, near the amusement park and seaside hotels. It was also served by a trolley line. Stops on the line took the names of neighborhoods: Nantasket Junction, Kenberma, Waveland, Allerton, Pemberton Point.

John and Florence Humphreys, sometimes by themselves and sometimes together with siblings and their children, rented summer cottages in Hull almost as soon as they were married, in 1906. A 1916 photo that my mother treasured shows her with two of her brothers and several cousins, parents, uncles and aunts, and one grandfather, all bunched together on the porch of a beach cottage in Kenberma. Over the years, they stayed in different neighborhoods. By the summer of 1936, all the children were grown, but John and Florence still rented a place, and their unmarried children stayed with them when not working or spent time with them on Channel Street in Pemberton. That summer, Julia Mehegan, Alfred's stepmother, and daughter Mary Rose rented a place a few houses away on the same street.

My mother wrote, "Ned [her younger brother] told me that Mary [Rose] Mehegan had an older brother who was in the merchant marine and was apt to disappear on a voyage now and then." He must have been pointed out to her, because she wrote, "I was commuting to Boston by boat and several times when I saw him on the boat I wanted to speak to him but I never did. He used to stand outside right up on the bow no matter what the weather was and I really was attracted to him. I heard him talking to someone one morning and I thought what a nice voice he had." She found out later that he had noticed her, too. He had seen her at the beach and asked her brother Joe, "Who's the new girl?" Joe had replied, "Oh, that's only my sister."

It was a lively summer scene, with dances and parties and boating. That summer of 1936, Mary was staying with her parents at Pemberton and commuting by boat to her secretarial job in Boston. She was working in the law office of Leverett Saltonstall, at the time speaker of the state House of Representatives, later governor and U.S. senator. Al, having left the *Katrina Luckenbach* in the spring, was working, uncontentedly, for his father again. He and Mary were twenty-five. He would not have been at the beach that summer had it not been that Charlie, who did not accompany his wife and daughter to the summer place, did not want Julia and Mary Rose to be there alone at night. He would only agree to their being there on condition that Alfred take the ferry every night after work and stay with them. So you might say that Charlie was responsible for my parents' meeting.

"One evening that summer," my mother wrote, "Ned told me that his whole crowd were going dancing at Fieldston in Marshfield. Al Mehegan was going too but they were short a girl. Would I like to go? Of course I was delighted. So my first date with Al was a blind one. When they picked me up, the car was so crowded I had to sit on his lap, which was an extraordinary introduction, especially for me, to a fellow I had only met for the first time." "Especially for me" is a reference to her shyness.

Fieldston on the Atlantic was a seaside dance hall featuring the top swing bands.

"The night was wonderful," she wrote. "Al was a fabulous dancer and the band was Glen Gray and his Casa Loma Orchestra. It was an absolutely great swing band and I remember the first dance was the 'Casa Loma Stomp.' You know how you usually associate a song with a romantic evening (though there was no romance in the picture yet!) and most people would remember a ballad like 'Stardust,' but ever after Al's and mine was the 'Casa Loma Stomp,' which was about as unromantic as 'Little Brown Jug.' We always laughed about it."

"Casa Loma Stomp" — I listened to it just now online — was an incredibly up-tempo number, like a runaway downhill freight train.[1] It's hard to imagine how anyone could dance to it, unless it was played more slowly in the dance halls.

"But you know," she wrote, "that was the end of it. I never saw him on the boat again nor anywhere in Pemberton. I thought ruefully, 'What I hit I must have made!'"[2]

She *had* made a hit, but he didn't call her again for three years. Why not? My sister Paula recalled recently, "Dad told me that he wanted to finish law school and Mum wasn't someone to be casual with. So he hoped she would still be single when he could be serious. She used to see him at functions, always with different women, more worldly than she."

As so often when one tries to figure out people's motives in the past, this is a puzzle. If he thought so much of her, why would he take a chance that she would not find someone else in three years' time? The subtext, it seems to me, was not only a positive view of her, but a view of himself as not quite good enough. She had polish and manners, nothing like the girls he had known, while he was a rough guy—a high school dropout, a plumber, and a sailor. He would need to improve himself to be worthy of her, to have something to offer.

His last, long journal entry had this line, after the chronicle of his merchant marine career and before his Thoreauvian fantasy of going to sea on his own yacht, like Ahto Walter: "Well, here I am still at home on June 16, 1936. I'm spending a little time getting my name on Civil Service lists." He would find some sort of government job. But something changed his mind. That summer, he applied to Northeastern University Law School.

• • •

Northeastern University in Boston was founded in 1898 as the Evening Institute for Younger Men, in the Huntington Avenue YMCA. Later that year it began to offer courses toward the law degree. It was part of a movement for higher education for working men that was widely supported and promoted by elite educators. The founding of Northeastern Law School was conceived by a committee that included the deans of Harvard and Boston University Law Schools. In the same tradition, in 1909 the Harvard Classics were first published, edited by Harvard president Charles William Eliot. Known as *The Five-Foot Shelf of Books*, this collection of fifty volumes was intended to give working-class men access to the classics, to help them transcend their social limitations. John Humphreys had a set that he almost wore out with reading, and Northeastern was founded to meet that same kind of workingman's ambition and desire. The school grew rapidly after its founding and in 1916 was incorporated as a day university with a range of liberal arts degrees, yet it remained oriented to the uplift of working people. The YMCA connection was not ended until 1948.

My father sought the LLB degree—bachelor of laws. That anyone without a high school diploma could hope to graduate from law school and pass the bar seems fantastic today, but legal education evolved more slowly than medical education. In Abraham Lincoln's day, you studied with a lawyer, using whatever law books you could find or borrow, and were admitted to the bar if you could pass the test. The undergraduate LLB was the standard in the United States until the 1960s and was still granted by Yale University as late as 1970. It was gradually replaced by the JD—Juris Doctor—the graduate law degree that today is required everywhere in the United States.

It always struck me as odd that rather than follow in his father's footsteps, Al followed in those of his father-in-law. There is no record of how Northeastern came into his head after his June journal entry about civil service lists, or whether he knew that Mary's father was a Northeastern Law graduate. She might have told him, or perhaps he heard it from one of her brothers. If he did know, one can imagine that he might have thought it would be a good way to impress her that he was serious. But of course there was a problem: He had never graduated from high school. Even that was not an a priori deal breaker, however. John Humphreys had not graduated from high school either, and Al could produce an even better credential: his academic performance at the Nautical School. His arrest record proved to be no problem. In October, he received a letter from Dean S. Kenneth Skolfield:

> *Dear Mr. Mehegan,*
> I have this morning received a letter from Mr. Hitchcock, Chairman of the Board of Bar Examiners, advising me that the Board have given careful consideration to the matter of your preliminary education and are agreed that you have the full equivalent of a high school education.
>
> I am, therefore, pleased to notify you that we will accept you as a regular student in the School of Law and candidate for the LL.B. degree.

In June, he was thinking vaguely of getting on civil service lists, and four months later he was in law school. It was no lifelong dream; there is no hint in anything that had gone before that he had ever thought of becoming a lawyer. There were no lawyers in his immediate or extended family, and no record of any mentor who urged him to go for it. As for his professional plan, it was vague: He always said that he had hoped to practice some kind of maritime law. My hunch is that law school had less to do with the law than with Mary.

There is a sign that he had misgivings about his plan, even so, while he was in school. On May 17, 1937, a few months into his first year, he applied for a U.S. Navy commission and reported for a physical examination. The navy proved to be less flexible than Northeastern. A letter soon arrived, dated June 15: "You are advised the Bureau of Navigation regrets that your application must be disapproved in view of physical defects," signed W. R. Gherardi, Rear Admiral, USN, Commandant, First Naval District.

He had a slight visual astigmatism. He was also missing nine teeth, most of them molars. It is astounding today to read that as recently as 1937, a thirty-year-old not raised amid poverty or malnutrition could be missing nine teeth. Years later he told my mother that he "had had some molars extracted over the years when he was at sea. He said that if you had a toothache, you went to the nearest dentist to the dock when your ship came in and almost always they extracted the tooth, necessary or not."[3] At that time, four years before the coming of war, such flaws— correctable or not—were enough to eliminate an applicant for a navy commission, notwithstanding impressive qualifications.

A remarkable set of documents was returned to him, along with his entire navy personnel file, when he was formally separated from the Navy Reserve in 1954. It includes a note from the examining physician, J. M. Bachalus, Medical Corps, U.S. Navy, appended to the not-qualified finding, sent to Captain John T. Nelson: "Memo for Captain Nelson: Would you consider waiver of these defects proper procedure?" Nelson replied by hand, on the note: "The right eye is the only real defect. A request for waiver might go through. In such a young man I would hesitate to recommend it. Jtn." So the problem was not the missing teeth, but the vision, even though a later navy physical, in 1942, records that his vision was correctable to 20/20.

Nelson's logic is difficult to understand. Does he mean that with these defects at age twenty-six, Al is bound to develop more defects later on, and not be suitable for the long term? Or that his eyesight is likely to get worse? That they were even discussing a waiver shows that in someone's view his case was a close call. But it went against him.

Newly enrolled in law school, why did he apply for a commission? Was it the pull of the sea, as John Humphreys said? Or was he feeling overwhelmed at the academic demands, as at Latin School? Perhaps he still was not clear what he would make of a law degree. Certainly if he had received the commission, he would have been an excellent suitor in Mary's eyes, and his future would have been clearer.

It is not certain when he began to attend classes. Until recently, Northeastern had quarters rather than semesters, since the school was planned around the cooperative system. Students would study one quarter, then work a quarter for a company partnering with the school, then back to school, etc. The idea was that students would get work experience during their college years. Normally, a Northeastern undergraduate would complete studies in five years rather than the typical four. Although it is possible that as a day student Al could have had a clerical job at a law firm, as a night student who was already working full-time he did not have a co-op job. He finished his law studies with remarkable speed, given that he was working full-time for Powers & Mehegan (now as a plumber, at twenty-five dollars a week) the whole time. Indeed, it appears that he plowed ahead without a break, winter and summer, finishing his degree in less than four years. Accepted in October 1936, he could not have begun classes until January 1937. Yet he graduated in June 1940.

His full-year grades for the first two years were mixed. In 1936–37: Contracts, C; Criminal Law, C; Personal Property, A; Pleading and Procedure, A; Torts, A; for a final average of 85.6. In 1937–38: Contracts, C; Criminal Law, C; Personal Property, A; Pleading, A; Torts, A; Agency,

C; Rights in Land, B; for a final average of 81. His last two years' grades are missing from his papers, and the university archivist could not find them, though she tried at my request. But he was always proud of his record and graduated with a high rank.

In 1989 my mother wrote:

> In early spring of 1939, I was so surprised to get a call from Al asking me if he could see me. I hadn't seen him nor heard anything about him for three whole years, although I must admit I thought of him now and then. It turned out that he had left the merchant marine and enrolled at Northeastern Law School at night and then was actually in his third year. He took me to a Chinese restaurant on Huntington Avenue and there I met all his classmates, or at least those he was friends with. They all sat near one another in classes and were a very close group. There were two boys and two girls, Tom Sheehan, Bud Wholley, Kay Rayner and Miriam McDonald, and they were so friendly to me. In the course of the conversation Miriam told a funny story about a date she had had with Al. She was beautiful. And so bright when they got talking about the law. Not only that but she was younger than I was by about five years. I thought ruefully if she cared for Al I could never compete with her and I had a feeling she did after the next few times I was in her company when the crowd was all together.[4]

She need not have worried. "He kept calling me and we began to single date. All these people were exhausted because they worked during the day (Al was plumbing with his father), went to about three hours of classes every night and then had about three hours of homework after classes. Al had no car but borrowed his father's and we would drive out to Castle Island and park, where he often fell asleep right in the car."[5] A bit of evidence of just how hard he was working is found among the stack of tuition receipts he kept. On January 27, 1939, he made a fifteen-dollar tuition payment (this was a typical amount). Written in pencil on the back of the green receipt is a long vertical column, which includes:

60'-2" galv. pipe
8-2: 45°
2-2" Ys
1-1" TY
1-1" str. TY
1-1" hub
3-2" plugs…
receiving tank
25# lead
oakum
4-12" lags

It is a stock list for a plumbing job.

• • •

My mother described the man she was coming to know.

> Al was a very gentle person, so well-mannered and so deferential
> to me. I hadn't really known what he was like at all from the
> single date so many summers before though I liked him from the
> beginning. He was so interesting too because he had traveled so
> much and had had so many experiences. He would mention them
> casually now and then. I had met Julia at Pemberton and of course I
> knew Mary [Rose] because of her friendship with Ned.

As she came to know him better, she was struck that he did not, in
his manner or personality, resemble his family. "I could not reconcile
Al with that family," she wrote. "He was just nothing like them at all."
She might have added that he also did not look much like them. He
resembled his mother's family, which I discovered when I first met his
half brother Jack Carson in the late 1990s. The Donahue favor, alas,
would be held against him.

Soon she learned his complicated early history. She wrote that in

May of 1939, he had taken her to a movie "at the Fenway Theater, which was on Massachusetts Avenue, and when we came out he told me he wanted to make a telephone call to send Mother's Day greetings to his mother who lived in California. I was dumbfounded. Then he told me about Julia being his stepmother, that his parents were divorced and that he hadn't seen his mother since he was thirteen."[6] Possibly this refers to Esther's last Boston visit during his childhood.

My mother added, "I thought he was such a wonderful person to remember her and he did every Mother's Day for the rest of his life. It was extraordinary, because many a son in a normal situation might have forgotten to do that. I thought it told so much about him."

She learned as well that, in addition to the turmoil of his early childhood, his present family life was also unhappy, though not in any obvious way.

> Julia, Al's stepmother, was a warm and loving person. She often asked Al to bring me to dinner at their house on Adams Street. Al's father would be there and his sister Mary, but gradually I began to feel there was something peculiar about it all. Julia would never sit down with us, though she would chat with us from the kitchen or when she was serving. But if Al's father got a phone call she would simply say 'telephone' and he would get up and take the call. Taking me home the first night I was there, Al explained that [Charlie and Julia] had had a violent argument years before and hadn't spoken to each other ever since but continued to live together. It eventually stretched to the incredible period of eighteen years, and Julia told Al once she couldn't remember what the original argument was about. It was the most tragic arrangement I could ever imagine and Al told me it was one of the reasons he was always happy to go to sea.[7]

Then, another bothersome fact entered Al and Mary's life story. It's not a remarkable fact, and though she calls her discovery of it "a harbinger," she did not know that at the time. He invited her to a dance at the South Boston Yacht Club, where Charlie Mehegan was now commodore.

Tom Sheehan came too, with another girl. It was a lovely summer evening with a full moon and as we were going in, the door burst open and a body came hurtling down the steps. I was terrified but it seems the man had simply been bounced out for improper behavior. Al was terribly embarrassed and apologized to me, but afterward he and Tom had a good laugh at it, especially when Al said, "There's nothing like trying to impress a girl and have someone punch out a drunk right in front of her."

When we went in there was a loud band and all of these tough, bleached blond women dancing around with their dates, most of whom were half drunk. Several of the women rushed over to him and threw their arms around him, calling him "Alfred."…Again I thought he was so unlike them he might have come from another planet.

There was an open bar and as the evening wore on, Al and Tom began to drink more and more. I was very unhappy about it and finally dancing with him I asked, "Please don't drink any more." He seemed so surprised and then said, "Nobody ever asked me not to drink before. I won't have any more." And he didn't. Somebody cut in and as I passed him he passed me a note asking me to go out on the outside deck. (I still have it. It's on a green receipt for a fee at Northeastern, in the tin box in my dresser.) So we went outside and it was a gorgeous moonlit night right on the harbor. We talked a little about liquor and he told me that he had been drinking since he was about eighteen, sometimes heavily. When I asked him what his father had ever said about it, he said, "Nothing. All he ever said to me was, 'If a person is going to drink they are going to drink.'" But he didn't blame his father, though I thought it was so sad that he apparently had no relationship with him.

It was evident as time went on that he cared deeply for his father but their relationship was so strange that he actually had no name for him. He didn't call him "Dad" or "Pop" or anything. I never heard of that in my life before nor have ever heard of it since.[9] I gradually came to believe that his father, incredible as it seemed, didn't care for Al as a father would normally do. Much, much later when I met his mother she told me that when Al's father had gotten his custody in their divorce when Al was two she was convinced he didn't really want Al at all, but just didn't want her to have him.[10] So Al had a terribly tragic background, but I didn't know that then.[11]

Here is where my mother's resentment of her father-in-law, for which she would have ample reason in time, first appears. She had had little experience of a distant father-son relationship, given that her father's with his children—perhaps especially with her—was warm and close. Nobody ever will know how Charlie felt about Alfred, but there were signs, early and late, that he did have some concern about his welfare, however stiffly they treated each other in person. Another fact might have increased the awkwardness, perhaps even a sense of rivalry, between them: They were so close in age. When Alfred was a first-year cadet on the *Nantucket*, Charlie was only thirty-seven. Charlie's younger brother John, a Boston police officer, was my father's uncle and yet was only nine months older.

Al and Mary went to a dance that Halloween, and in the car he asked her not to date anyone else. "You know I'm deadly serious about you," he said. She wrote, "I was overwhelmed with delight. Of course he didn't know that he was the *only* one I was dating. I can remember being in the office walking down the hall and thinking, 'I must remember to take one step after another and land or I will be airborne.'"[12]

> One night, Al borrowed his father's car and we drove to a restaurant on Sea Street [in Quincy, just south of Boston]. It was the Fox and Hounds then, but has had many names since, though the building is still there. There was a booth we always sat in on the right side and it was there he asked me to marry him. Of course I said yes. In my heart of hearts I had hoped he would ask me eventually, though I never really thought it would happen. For one thing, I was terribly old. I was twenty-nine and though I didn't tell him then, I had discovered to my dismay that he was six months or so younger than I was. He laughed so when I told him later of my fears.[13]

Soon after, he surprised her with a silver and yellow-topaz ring from the Parenti Sisters, a store she had always loved and had shown to him. The shop, at 97 Newbury Street, was owned by Delfina Parenti and Zoe Parenti Borghi, Florentine immigrants whose original handmade jewelry is highly collectible.

Mary wrote, "He apologized for its not being a diamond even though it was an engagement ring, because he could not afford to buy me a diamond then, but I loved it, much preferring it to a diamond."[14] She wrote to her friend Rita Greene (who years later returned the letter to her), January 25, 1940: "One reason that I wanted to write you, Rita, was to tell you of my being engaged. Did you ever hear *anything* so astonishing? I'm terribly in love with him—Al Mehegan is his name and he is *everything* I've ever wanted."

His senior year was a killer, with work and exams. She saw him only once a week that spring of 1940. He would visit her at her family home, at 76 West Cedar Street.

> He would come to see me after class at 9:30 in the evening. He would just stay for an hour or so and take the El from Charles Street home. Living in the city as I did, on the weekends we would walk all over the city. There was a Childs Restaurant on Boylston Street and we would often go there. But mostly we window-shopped, which sounds pretty tame I know but it doesn't matter what you do when you are in love as long as you are together. Al loved shoes and he knew all the men's shoe stores. On the weekends we often went to a concert or to a museum, things that he had never done before. He had no cultural experiences at all growing up, but he loved all those things that I loved, experiencing them for the first time.[15]

He graduated in June. A pristine ticket to commencement, perhaps an unused extra, survives. "Northeastern University Commencement Exercises, Tuesday Evening, June 18, 1940 at 8 o'clock. Boston Arena. 238 St. Botolph Street, Boston." Mary wrote, "I had never been to such a huge indoor graduation, but Northeastern had so many colleges, including several night schools, that they filled the entire floor of the Arena. I'm not completely clear now but I don't think his parents went or any of his family because I remember sitting with Tom's mother and his sister."[16]

How is it possible that on such a proud occasion—the first college degree in the family—his father and stepmother and sister were not present? It would seem they had more important things to do, or perhaps didn't want him to get a big head. That would be so Irish. Esther must have known of his graduation, if he had called her as usual on Mother's Day, a few weeks before. Perhaps she congratulated him. That Christmas, he did buy Mary a diamond. "I didn't want one," she remembered:

> but he just wanted to buy it for me, so I agreed. I thought his family might have made comments, though he wasn't one at all who moved because of what anyone thought—another quality that endeared him to me. So one Saturday, we went to Long's on Summer Street, where I had seen some lovely rings in the window. Al only had $100 and when we went inside, looking in a case, the salesgirl asked, "What price range were you interested in?"' and when Al said, "$100," she waved us toward another counter and said, "Oh, you want the costume jewelry." It was very funny, we thought afterwards, because we both were so offended we walked right out and you know, I have never gone in there since.[17]

Eventually they found a diamond they liked, at A. Kopelman and Sons, at 451-453 Washington Street. The Kopelman receipt is dated December 18: "Ladies Platinum Diamond Ring, $75." "It was little," she wrote, "but I felt it was like the Hope Diamond."[18]

My mother's comment that "he wasn't one at all who moved because of what anyone thought" testifies to a distinctive trait that my siblings and I would come to know well. He could be more than stubborn; he could be immovable when it came to doing what he thought was right.

They had intended to marry in the fall, but the worsening situation in Europe and fears for what it might mean for their future caused them, as it did many people, to move the date up, to March 11, 1941. It was Lent—normally not a permissible time for a Catholic wedding, but the Church had relaxed some of its rules to accommodate the times.

The wedding was at St. Joseph's church on Chambers Street in the West End, her parish church, where she had been christened and where her parents had been married in 1906. Al's pre-wedding to-do list, a vertical column on the front of an envelope, includes: "Hotel, transportation, flowers, honeymoon, shirts, call home in re supper and car, cash check, license, shoes, tailor." Each item is neatly crossed off. It might seem remarkable that all these small pieces of paper would have survived, but both of my parents saved all manner of small documents and mementos, especially my mother.

Not all Lenten restrictions were eased. There was still a somber mood in churches, with statues and crucifixes shrouded in violet, and there could be no music or flowers. As if to add to the somberness, it snowed, intensely at times, for much of that day.

"When we got to the church, my heart sank because it was dark and cold," my mother wrote. "The altar looked so bare, without flowers or lighted candles, that I could have cried. We were in the sacristy when Father Mullarkey came in and turned on all the lights, which made it so much warmer, and he was a big hearty friendly man, which helped. With no music and St. Joseph's being such an old church, you could hear the floorboards creaking as people came up the aisle."[19] The ceremony was brief, and fifty years later she wrote that, strangely enough, she could remember little of it. The small reception was at the Lincolnshire Hotel at 25 Charles Street, near Beacon Street. Their wedding night was at the Sheraton Hotel at 91 Bay State Road, which later become a Boston University dormitory.

She was totally inexperienced sexually and worried about it, while he clearly had at least some experience. She wrote that he was generous and patient, and never made her feel awkward or inadequate. She recalled, "I was to know then, and in so many other events of our married life, that Al had a strength of character, an inner goodness, that must have been part of his natural endowment, because he had had such a rough life, a broken life really. He hadn't learned that from anyone. It was a pure gift and I always marveled when it showed itself in small and serious matters as life went on. The Church would have called it 'grace,' I suppose."[20]

For these few weeks, they could almost block out the looming terrors in the world outside. But that world was hovering near, in the form of Local Board 32 of the Selective Service system.

6.

Dark Horizon

Had there been no war, their lives would have been different. This of course could be said of hundreds of millions of little people like them, many of them slaughtered in fighting or mass murder. At least Al and Mary survived. The war in Europe began in September 1939, with the first crushing German onslaught the following spring—just before Al's graduation. The America First movement, whose vocal and eminent spokesman was Charles Lindbergh, was vehemently opposed to American intervention and remained hugely powerful. Mary and Al were thinking about their lives together, but the scent of the approaching storm was unmistakable. In September 1940, the draft was reinstated, along with the offer of a one-year army enlistment, after which one's military obligation would be considered satisfied. To Al, who registered for the draft in October, the one-year offer was tempting. It was still possible to imagine that the United States might avoid full involvement in the war. But some foresaw the real future.

"I knew a boy at the Community Fund [where she worked, the predecessor of the United Way]," my mother wrote, "Todd Van Eyck, and I told him Al was talking about taking that one-year enlistment to get it over with. Todd said, 'He is crazy. Mark my words, we are going to be in this war up to our eyeballs.' But America couldn't face that then, especially Al and I in the middle of a romance."[1] Still, they knew that if war were to come, or come closer, he was bound to be caught up in it.

That summer of 1940, he had signed up for a bar review course, intending to take the exam in the fall. But he fell ill with severe stomach pain, could barely eat, and lost a lot of weight. It was never explained—a doctor ruled out an ulcer. My mother's theory in retrospect was that he was exhausted from three and a half years of grueling work and study. Perhaps so, but exhaustion would not explain the gastric pain. By the fall he was feeling better but had had to skip the review course and so decided to postpone taking the bar exam until the following year. Before long, the exam would be the least of his worries.

He cast about for ideas for a job to which his law degree might apply and fired off queries in all directions. He received a form letter dated September 12:

> Dear Mr. Mehegan,
> This receipt is acknowledgement of your application for appointment to a position in the Federal Bureau of Investigation, United States Department of Justice.
> You are advised that arrangements have been made to afford you the necessary examination in connection with our application. You will be further advised as to the time and place for this examination. All expenses in connection therewith are to be borne by you and this letter should not be construed as a probable offer of appointment.
> Very truly yours,
> John Edgar Hoover
> Director

My mother found this letter decades later and wrote on it, "I never knew he did this. He tried everything." If he ever took the FBI test, there is no record of it. That same month, he talked to a family friend who was a boarding officer in the Bureau of Marine Inspection and Navigation, part of the U.S. Department of Commerce. The friend thought that Al's knowledge of ships would qualify him for the same position. Al applied and got the appointment, at a salary of $1,400 a year. It was a shipboard job, for which he was well qualified, on ships in port. The drawback was that it was only a one-year appointment. But it would give him a kind of marine law-enforcement experience, which could not but be helpful in a legal career. The job title was "ship personnel inspector." Duties included inspection of incoming ships to ensure compliance with a recently revised federal code for equipment. The printed rules and regulations to be enforced, "Laws Governing Marine Inspection," as well as other publications, are among his papers. His main duty was to interview captains and muster (i.e., inspect) the crews, to ensure that the papers of the men on board agreed with the crew manifest. He would go out on the harbor pilot boat and meet the vessels offshore, then accompany them to their berths.

While all this was going on, including preparations for the wedding, he was attending night classes at Boston Trade School—a city high school—for a certificate in plumbing. He had worked for his father's firm on and off for years but evidently never had any formal training toward a state license. His certificate, dated March 27, 1941, notes that "for the term of 1940–41," he had "an attendance of 55 evenings." He must have slept little.

In early January 1941, he began looking for another job, knowing that his inspector position would end in September. He wrote to South Boston congressman John W. McCormack, majority leader, and later Speaker, of the U.S. House of Representatives (and, like everyone else of importance in South Boston, or so it seemed, a friend of Charlie's), asking for help. "I am particularly interested in marine personnel work," he wrote, "particularly where it is affected by marine legislation. For this type of work I have unusual qualifications." On January 18, McCormack replied: "I have received your letter and have written to the Commander of the Bureau of Marine Inspection to see if you can be given some other position with that Bureau. When I have a reply, I will advise you. I certainly hope you will be successful in securing another assignment."

But not even John McCormack was powerful enough to work his will with the bureaucracy. He sent Alfred a copy of a letter, dated January 22, from R. S. Field, director of the Bureau of Marine Inspection:

My dear Congressman,

All positions in this Bureau must be filled through Civil Service channels. When it was found necessary to appoint a number of Ship Personnel Inspectors in this service, the Civil Service Commission, due to the urgency of the work to be performed and to the absence of a sufficient number of qualified eligibles on their register, authorized the filling of these positions temporarily without reference to the competitive provision of the Civil Service rules and regulations. However, persons so appointed did not acquire eligibility for transfer or appointment to other Civil Service positions.

In view of the fact that Mr. Mehegan does not have a Civil Service status, I am sorry to inform you that he cannot be considered for another position in this Bureau. Insofar as his present appointment is concerned, there is no indication at this time that it will be terminated in the immediate future.

Al was not simply worried about termination. He had assumed that the boarding officer position—clearly "urgent," according to Field's letter—would exempt him from the draft but learned that it would not. His exposure to the prospect of being drafted was distressing, not because he was reluctant to serve, but because, in his mind, to be taken as a private in the army, at age twenty-nine, with his education and maritime experience, would be a waste of his capability. If the United States were to enter the war, he wanted to serve in the way he knew best: at sea.

On February 19, he wrote to the commandant of the First Naval District, based in Boston, explaining that he had been rejected for a navy commission in 1937 because of defects of eyes and teeth. He noted that the defects had been corrected—he had dentures and eyeglasses—and asked to reapply for at least a Merchant Marine Naval Reserve commission, adding, "As my local draft board will soon take action on my case, I would appreciate a prompt reply." On February 24, the assistant district personnel officer coolly replied, "The physical standards for appointment in the Naval Reserve have not changed, but are in fact being strictly adhered to, and if you were found to be physically disqualified in 1937 it is probable that this would be the same result at this time."

Aside from the physical problems, my mother wrote, he had learned of an unwritten disqualification—essentially a class distinction: "A degree from night school, as his was, was not accepted as a degree from a day college might have been."[2] The navy's view was that Northeastern Law School was not a real college, which would have come as a surprise to the Harvard and Boston University deans who had promoted its founding. Another college graduate that spring, one John F. Kennedy, received a full navy commission. He had no seagoing experience— unless one counts trips as a passenger on fancy ocean liners—but his father was ambassador to the Court of St. James. And he was a Harvard man.

An indication of the simultaneity of wedding preparations and the draft crisis is that Al's pre-wedding to-do list, mentioned above, was made on the back of the envelope containing the rejection letter from the navy personnel officer, postmarked February 24, addressed to him at 408 Atlantic Avenue, the address of the Bureau of Marine Inspection and Navigation.

He was ordered to report for a draft physical March 3. A few days later—just before his wedding day—he received a draft card in the mail. He had been classified I-A—"Available. Fit for general military service." The classification was not wrong; he was still single as of the time it was made. After he was married, he could apply for reclassification as III-A—"Deferred because of dependents"—but he might not succeed, because Mary was still working, now as a secretary for the Red Feather Agencies, the predecessor of the United Way. Furthermore, he would have to prove that the marriage was not a sham. That would not be difficult, and indeed they did secure letters to that effect, including one from her former pastor, Father Leo McCann, who wrote, "I desire to attest to the fact, that there was a definite intention of marriage, and engagement, existing between Alfred Mehegan and Mary Humphreys prior to July 1940. . . . Often during the past two summers I had discussed with this couple their plans for the future." Al had, as well, the receipts for the Parenti Sisters engagement ring and the Kopelman diamond.

It is not clear if he applied for reclassification as III-A, but in any event it did not happen. What he wanted was a naval defense job—if not a commission, something maritime related that would be considered essential and would justify a II-A, "Men necessary in their civilian capacity." Selective Service was calling men by age, with the youngest first, so at twenty-nine he would probably have time before his name came up. His shipping-inspector job, though it gave no deferment, would also probably put his name well down the list when it came to the draft board's order of call-up. But there was no doubt that once his job ended in September, he would be taken.

The uncertainty overshadowed the new marriage and any plans they might have made. There was no honeymoon; they stayed home, and both soon went back to work. They had rented a two-room basement apartment in a Victorian house, with a shared bath, at 6 Wilbur Street, in Uphams Corner, Dorchester. The apartment was a dump without even a kitchen sink, and Mary discovered that the landlady snooped inside while they were at work.

One Saturday soon after they were married, they got a visit from Philip Mallard, a *Nantucket* shipmate who had been a year ahead of Al. He had stayed in the merchant marine and now was a captain. "He was handsome and covered with gold braid," my mother wrote.

> He came especially to get Al to join a ship in the merchant fleet as they were desperate for qualified officers, but also because the money was fantastic. Phil was single. Al was sorely tempted because the ships going overseas were protected by U.S. destroyers, but the danger was still great. German submarines even that early were attacking some of the convoys. It was then that we began to fear that war was inevitable for us....There were passionate arguments on both sides, but I think the most important thing that contributed to

the shift in our thinking was that we heard Ed Murrow's broadcast from London every night. In the background were the terrifying sounds of screaming German bombers, the bombs falling, the sirens of the air raid signals, and we knew that was where our frontier was. I remember how persuasive Phil was. He told Al he was crazy, [that if he were to take Mallard's recommendation] he would surely wind up with his own ship. But Al decided he would [keep trying to] make the Navy, despite the money.[3]

Mallard had a civilian position, but Al, as he made clear in his application for a commission, wanted at least a merchant marine naval reserve commission; that is, to serve as part of the naval armed guard aboard convoyed vessels.

To that end, he hatched a plan. He came home one day in mid-April and told Mary that he had signed on as an AB—an "able bodied" ordinary seaman—on the S.S. *Mobilgas*, a gasoline tanker running coastwise between Texas and Portland, Maine, with stops in Boston and New York. Mary was devastated. They had been married six weeks. The ship would make only one-week runs, he told her, so their times apart would be brief. On April 22 he got a telegram: "REPORT TO STEAMSHIP MOBILGAS AS ABLE SEAMAN APRIL 23RD 9 AM." Mary borrowed her brother's car and drove him to the ship, which was unloading at the Town River Terminal in Quincy. It was less than a mile from the Fox & Hounds, where he had asked her to marry him two years before.

"I didn't know how I was going to tell my family," she wrote, "especially Dad, who had warned me about marrying a sailor. But he was very understanding, although he did say quietly, 'I knew he would.'"[4] After she told her parents on the twenty-fourth, she sent Al a shore-to-ship radiogram on April 25: "HEALTHY BUT DESOLATED. FAMILY APPROVES YOUR DECISION. CAREFUL. MARY." She wrote several letters to him on the *Mobilgas*, which he kept. In one, she wrote, "I sent your mother in Los Angeles this telegram: 'Greetings and best wishes for a happy Mother's Day. Love, Alfred.' I hope that was all right and not presumptuous of me." Esther Carson and her two younger sons, David and Jack, lived at 6336 South Hoover, Los Angeles. Andrew Jr. was in the army, stationed in the Philippines.

On the day he left, Al wrote to his draft board, not to ask for reclassification but to explain that when he had tried in February to apply for a reserve commission:

> I was told that they couldn't use me. However, at that last interview I was told that if I'd go back to sea on my license, and thereby show some recent navigation experience, I would be considered for a Merchant Marine Naval Reserve Commission. My past experience as a merchant officer would then count. Captain McNeely of the Socony Vacuum Oil Co offered me this opportunity to go back to sea. I am to sail as Able Seaman for a few trips in order to get my sea legs back. When I am ready he has promised to put me on.[5]

The rest of this letter, which appears to be a handwritten copy, is missing. Presumably it went on to say that McNeely had promised to endorse his fitness for a naval reserve commission. It is clear that he intended to apply. In an employment history he compiled around this time, he wrote that he had resigned from the Bureau of Marine Inspection "to return to sea for the purpose of acquiring some recent sea experience in order to apply for a commission in the Naval Reserve."

If he got the commission, he wouldn't be on a fighting ship, but he would be navy, not merchant marine like Mallard, and not an army private. Notwithstanding McNeely's encouragement, there was no guarantee that the navy would accept him, and no promise that the Local Board 32 would wait. However, on May 7 he was reclassified II-A, "Men necessary in their civilian capacity."

The *Mobilgas* was a new ship, built in 1937, a 10,000-ton, 156-foot tanker. After a few runs, the ship's northern terminus was changed from Portland to New York, and Mary made several trips there to meet Al when it came in. They stayed at the Commodore Hotel, alongside

Grand Central Terminal. At home, she was frantic with worry, knowing that American ships had already been sunk by U-boats near the coast. She might not have known, but Al probably did, that a torpedoed gasoline tanker would likely explode like a huge bomb.

While he was away, she found a better place to live, an apartment above a garage alongside a suburban house at 630 Adams Street, East Milton, just south of Boston. They always remembered it affectionately. It is the earliest home my brother Peter and sister Florence can remember.

Increasingly restive on the *Mobilgas*, where his skills and knowledge were wasted, Al learned of an opportunity as a deck officer on another ship, the U.S. JMP *General Richard Arnold*. On April 30, he wrote to the Harbor Defense quartermaster of Long Island Sound to apply for the job. An assistant quartermaster replied May 7, to 630 Adams Street, "If you are still interested in the position of Boatswain at $1620 per annum, which is a probational, indefinite position, please report to this office. The government boat [that is, the *General Arnold*] leaves New London daily at 7:30 a.m. for Fort H.G. Wright." He got the job, but again, it was temporary—six months from May 26, 1941. Though his job title was boatswain, he actually served as first mate.

The *General Arnold* was, oddly enough, an army vessel that sailed between New London, Connecticut, and Fort H. G. Wright on Long Island. "JMP" stood for "Junior Mine Planter." Though technically designed to lay mines, JMPs were obsolete for that function and were more often used for river or harbor transportation. They were slightly smaller than standard mine planters. Tiny *General Richard Arnold*, 98 feet long and 179 tons, was built in 1909 and looked more like a tugboat than an ocean-worthy ship. Its captain was John Sorensen, a Norwegian immigrant. Al came to like and respect him greatly for his skill and attention to duty. He saved a pile of Captain Sorensen's navigational notes on Long Island Sound, which remain in his papers. Perhaps he was reminded of Nikolai Sivertsen, the Norwegian watch officer of the *Nantucket* who had helped talk the captain into trying the sea anchor.

In July, Mary discovered she was pregnant. "Al was terribly excited about the prospect of having a baby," she wrote, "because no one wanted a family more than he did, probably because his own had been such a strange one."[6] He was not like those who do not want children because their own childhoods were unhappy and they cannot imagine that they could succeed where their parents had failed. She resigned her job at the Community Fund. Now they had stronger grounds for a III-A draft deferment, but Al was still intent upon either navy service or a II-A. He was sure that the draft would eventually take married men, and he was correct.

That summer he learned that the Boston Navy Yard was desperate for pipefitters to work on warships. He had the skills, applied for a job, and was hired. On July 15, he wrote to the Fort Wright quartermaster, "Please accept my resignation as Boatswain on the U.S. *General Arnold*. I realize that the vessel is now short-handed, having lost the services of the deckhand on July 15. Therefore, if you are not able to replace at least one of the two men left short, I am willing to return for one more watch." He did not want to leave Captain Sorensen in the lurch. But his resignation was accepted.

The *Mobilgas* survived the war, had a long career with many names and owners, and was scrapped in 1959. But U.S. JMP *General Richard Arnold* had a sadder fate, unrelated to the war. Six months after Al left the ship, on January 8, it was sent out from the Portsmouth Navy Yard in New Hampshire in a roaring gale, on an emergency mission to aid *L-88*, another mine-layer dead in the water twenty miles southeast of the Isles of Shoals. Companion vessels turned back because of the conditions, but little *General Arnold* plowed on, like the Little Engine That Could. It reached the powerless ship, drifting amid heavy seas. Lines were put aboard and the two small ships were lashed together and taken under tow by another, larger ship that reached the scene. But suddenly the *General Arnold* sprang a leak and quickly began to settle. A seam had let go, and *L-88* barely had time to cut the lines between them before the *General Arnold* foundered and sank. Ten men drowned in the freezing water, as the helpless *L-88* looked on, before the tow ship could get to them.

My parents never knew the full story. My mother wrote that "Al always had an affection for that small ship and much later in the war he read to his dismay that it had foundered in a North Atlantic convoy and all hands were lost. He hoped fervently that Captain Sorensen and the crew he knew weren't on it but he never did find out."[7] In fact, the only survivor was the captain, who was plucked from the water by the crew of the *L-88*. But his name was William H. Chasteen. He must have succeeded John Sorensen when the ship was reassigned to New Hampshire.[8]

• • •

Al's Navy Yard work, he wrote in the work history, included "installing compressed air lines to gun turrets, smoke screen and depth charge release gear." He would be home, and have a defense-related job. However, the disadvantage of the job was that it would not get him into the navy. Of course, he could have volunteered as an ordinary sailor, but that would be only slightly better than being a private in the army. He often worked the night shift, and Mary sometimes stayed with her parents in Pemberton. The Boston Navy Yard was humming, and new shipyards were springing up on all coasts. One was in Hingham, across Hingham Bay from Pemberton, and she was comforted at night to see sparks flying from welding torches as new ships took shape.

One Sunday afternoon in early December, she turned on the radio to get the weather report and learned of the Japanese attack on Pearl Harbor. Within days, the United States was at war with Japan, Italy, and Germany. "I remember looking out the window at the sunny street," she wrote, "with its normal traffic passing by, and thinking, 'Everything is changed. Life will never be the same.'"[9]

7.

ᔕᕼᕼᔕ

Secret Agent

ONE OF THE IRONIES of Al Mehegan's life is that one so honest and transparent would begin his military service with an assignment practicing deceit.

In January of 1942, Mary's brother Joe heard from a friend that the navy was setting up a counterintelligence service in East Coast ports. In Boston, my mother wrote, "they wanted someone who knew the Port of Boston intimately, especially the waterfront, because there had been reports of people pumping American sailors to find out sailing times, especially in the bars when the sailors might have been drinking. Everywhere then on posters there were warnings like 'Zip Your Lips' and 'Loose Lips Sink Ships.'" Joe thought of Al and gave Mary an unlisted number for him to call if he was interested.

He was very much interested. He applied, was given a glowing recommendation by the shipping commissioner, took another navy physical, and again failed it. However, by now the navy's crack personnel system had heard about the war.

February 20, 1942

Dear Mr. Mehegan,
In spite of the fact that you were not found physically qualified for service in the Intelligence Branch, United States Naval Reserve, it is

suggested that you return to this office for the purpose of completing additional papers in connection with your application.

It is possible that a waiver of the physical defect may be requested if you are found qualified in all other respects.

> *Very truly yours,*
> *F. M. Forbes*
> *Lt. USNR*

Possible—not a sure thing. In truth they needed and wanted him, badly, but there was a problem. His appointment, were it to happen, would have to be secret. Mary would know, but no one else, and she would know nothing of his assignments. And there was another problem. He already held a defense-essential job, working on warships, which he would have to resign, but he could not explain why. Normally this would be impossible. My mother wrote:

> You could not resign from a defense industry during the war
> without the most serious reason. His superiors at the Navy Yard
> were furious. The personnel manager virtually called him a traitor.
> They could not be told why he was leaving, and implied that he had
> pulled strings to get out. It was very hard on Al, who never would
> have done such a thing. But then the Navy stepped in, fortunately,
> without telling them he was going with Naval Intelligence, so [the
> Navy Yard] had to indicate officially that he was "discharged without
> prejudice."[1]

This awkwardness over the secrecy hit close to home at times. My mother wrote, "One of his cousins who worked at the Navy Yard would wait for him after Mass and ask him, 'Where are you working now, Al?' But he never found out because Al successfully avoided him at church each time."[2]

He was hired on March 26, as a civilian, even though he would be an operative for the director of Naval Intelligence within the First Naval District. His salary was $233.33 a month. My mother always called it

O.N.I.—Office of Naval Intelligence—but that name in so many words does not appear on any of Al's correspondence. In official letters, the department is called N.I.S.—Naval Intelligence Service. The D.I.O., noted at the top of most letters, was the District Intelligence Officer, to whom Al reported. Al's code name was M-26, the date of his appointment. (He kiddingly called Mary M-27.) He was directed to rent a post office box, which he did (Box 111, East Milton), at which he would receive pay and instructions. The first paycheck, for two weeks' work, was $116. His reports were to be sent to P.O. Box 535, Main Post Office, Boston.

The service issued a uniform of sorts. When he left the Intelligence Office later, he was given a receipt for the return of:

One pair leather gloves and Jungle Cloth outfit consisting of
Trousers
Jacket
Helmet
One rain outfit consisting of trousers and hood

Jungle cloth was a kind of navy-issue khaki. The jacket was short and sheepskin lined. The helmet is a puzzle: What sort of helmet would be worn by a man posing as a waterfront habitué? Most of the time, his activities consisted of listening, watching, and reporting. A set of guidelines dated April 29, 1942, instructed him to "take special note and report on any of the following circumstances":

1. Workers, or persons who frequent the waterfront, and who in your opinion, have pro-Nazi or Pro-Fascist sympathies. Also report any acts, associations or utterances on the part of these persons that would indicate such sympathies.

2. Persons who may be spreading Axis propaganda such as "We are fighting England's battles for her," "This isn't our war," etc. Many persons of Irish ancestry have strong anti-British feelings and can still be 100% loyal to the United States and in full support of our

war efforts. However, if these persons express strong anti-British feelings that border on Axis-issued propaganda, report them that so that we may make an inquiry to determine whether they are Axis agents.

3. Any attempts to start organizations or new unions among waterfront workers, also any labor agitators or persons attempting to cause dissension amongst these workers. We do not wish to interfere or become involved in the activities of any duly authorized or legitimate labor unions. However, it is possible that certain Axis agents or other subversive elements may attempt to get control of existing labor unions or to start new organizations. They would then be in a position to seriously hamper our war effort through strikes and labor troubles.

4. Any rumors that may come to your attention wherein the loading or discharging of cargo has been held up and delayed by gross negligence, on the part of stevedores or longshoremen, causing damage to winches or other ship's equipment.

The list goes on to include any damage or pilferage: "Be especially vigilant to detect and determine any circumstances that may indicate possible sabotage." In addition to these general guidelines, he received a memo dated April 27, with more detailed instructions:

When you are given a definite assignment, you are to send in a detailed written account covering your activities for each day, setting forth what you did, what you saw, and what you read.

It is essential that when you refer to any person in your report that you specify his name or time card number, if possible. If you are not able to obtain the name without arousing suspicion, describe the person in question in detail, in order that he may be later identified.

From time to time you will receive written instructions relative to your assignment. You are to read the instructions carefully and make sure that you understand what is called for; then mail the instructions, together with the envelope in which it was sent to you, back to this office.

One day, my mother wrote, while walking along Atlantic Avenue wearing his "uniform" of beat-up clothes, "he came face to face with a man he knew from the shipping commissioner's office, and Al said the consternation on the man's face when he saw him was so amusing. The man tried to get away from him and mumbled a greeting before sidestepping him. Al thought it was very funny, but I didn't. I thought it wouldn't be long before he was reputed to be a waterfront bum in the shipping circles who knew him, but nothing could be done about it."[3]

One week after he took on his false identity, he took on a true one, as a father. My brother Peter was born Good Friday, April 3. He had blue eyes, black hair, and cried all the time at first. But he ate well and grew. There is no record of how Al felt, or what he said, about the birth of his son, and, strangely, my mother didn't report his reactions. He was at home, so there were no letters about it. There is no question that to have a family of his own was a dream come true. This part, at least, of his life plan was coming to pass.

Two months later, he received a certificate that must have been the furthest thing from his mind, probably applied for while he was working at the Navy Yard: a state master plumber's license, No. 5230. He would not need it anytime soon, but later it would play an important part in his life.

• • •

As the guidelines above make clear, the navy was concerned not only with loose lips and disloyalty, but also with the presence of Axis agents on the waterfront, especially their landing from German submarines, and with any signaling along the coastline. There had been such landings and apparent signals. One set of Al's pencil notes in December recorded an interview with the mate of a fishing trawler:

> William Hanlon—Mate Dorchester. 0045 Monday 14th. Hauling back trawls—too rough. NW 40 miles wind on deck. High seas—to windward NW. Skipper in pilot. I hollered to him See that? I went up. He said, That's a sub. About abeam and then appeared under

our bow and then went to leeward & lay (couldn't hear motors). Light looked like a firebrand—not like elec.—as though cheesecloth over flashlight.

We doused and started steaming to NW toward shoal (location) Left there about 0115 and at 0300 we could still see him.

Skipper tried a couple of times at about daylight, several times. Orig. location SW part of Georges Bank approx. 66 55, 40 55 [i.e., 66° 55' West, 40° 55' North], 42 to 45 fathom. Ran NW about 40 miles.

Light was real low and looked to be showing up and flashed 3 times and then 2 when crossing our bow. Passed about 40 feet. Know what a sub looks like and I'm sure it was. We couldn't see the hull— but the conning tower. Night overcast but enuf light to see outline of tower when he lying to leeward.

We were doing about 8—he kept same distance about ¼ mile. Could see only the light once in awhile but not his outline—flash not like a signal flash—long minute & then second.

Stood by after calling in [i.e., to Boston by radio] but no one called back. Came over N edge of Geo. [i.e., Georges Bank] and started fish Monday afternoon. Didn't see any planes after our call.

The implication of the fisherman's report is that the submarine was signaling, perhaps trying to complete a prearranged rendezvous, but with the wrong boat.

Al kept notes as well of interviews with officers who had just come in on convoys, and some are as chilling as they are dry and factual. For example, an interview with Captain James Dunbar of "S.S. *Governor John Linch*" and navy lieutenant Rex K. Nelson, part of a convoy that had left Reykjavík, Iceland, November 8, for Boston via Halifax:

Between 9 & 10 p.m. Nov 15, 10 depth charges by escort. Nov. 17 54° N 36° W, 8:30 torpedo heard. 8:35 2 torpedoes heard. 3:30 a.m. 3 heard and observed.

Circling Comm. ship [commodore's ship] (which had been torpedoed). Our steering gear jammed and nearly rammed sinking

Comm. ship. Area called "torpedo junction." 4:30 another ship torpedoed. Eastbound [we had] 8 or more escorts for 55 ships. All action from starboard side. Don't think 5 enuf escort.

Nov. 19 11 p.m. escort 12 [depth] charges astern of convoy. Nov. 19 4:30 a.m. 2 charges, one flare and 20 mm [machine gun] burst from for'd on port.

Nov. 20 5:35 a.m. 20 mm burst port column, flares and several charges. One of my gun crew claims he saw periscope shortly after 9 p.m. Nov. 19 for'd of central part of convoy.

This was westbound Convoy ON 144, with forty-four ships from Oban, Scotland, via Iceland, to Halifax. Dunbar was captain of the S.S. *Governor John Lind*, not *Linch*, an American Liberty ship. Four ships in the convoy were sunk by U-624, including the commodore ship, British steamer *President Sergent*, torpedoed November 18 at 54° 18'N 38° 28'W, northeast of Newfoundland. The commodore, master, and thirty-seven crewmen were rescued. U-624's triumph was brief. The submarine was sunk three months later, February 4, 1943, in a depth-charge attack by a British bomber on patrol west of England.

• • •

Besides the waterfront work, Al was given offshore missions, and one of them led to the closest thing to a shipwreck in his seagoing career. In June 1942, he was ordered to try to get a position, incognito, as AB seaman on a coastal vessel. He found a job on a small tanker, S.S. *Lucy*, running from Boston to Portland, Maine. His exact instructions are not known, but my mother wrote that it had to do with watching for signaling or the landing of German agents. On July 3, a small item appeared in the *Boston Globe*:

> CAPE ELIZABETH, Me., July 2—Groping her way through dense fog, a small Boston tanker ran aground on Watt Ledge off this town this evening and was abandoned when a port tank split open and released hundreds of barrels of gasoline.

> Her crew of eight was standing by in the Cape
> Elizabeth Coast Guard station to help pull her off the
> ledge Friday morning.
>   Norman Olsen, a fisherman who went to the tanker in
> answer to her frantic signals, said she was not too hard
> aground. Her forepeaks and engine room still were dry,
> he said.

Describing this incident to us years later, my father said that the captain ordered them to get into the boats and row as far away and as fast as they could, for fear that the leaking gasoline, which they could smell, would ignite and explode. The ship was refloated, and once the danger of fire or explosion was past, the crew went back aboard. But then he got a letter from the coast guard in Boston, dated July 7:

1. Please be advised that in an investigation held with respect to the stranding of the Motor Tank Vessel LUCY, it was found that you had been wheelsman for 6 hours prior to the grounding.
2. You are hereby notified to appear before this board at your earliest convenience for a hearing.

The ironic implication of this inquiry is that he might have been a German agent deliberately steering the ship aground. He appeared as ordered and was not found to be responsible for the mishap. Neither the coast guard nor the captain or crew of the *Lucy* at the time of the stranding knew that he was navy undercover, although my mother thought the D.N.I. might have tipped off the coast guard before the hearing.

The grounding of the *Lucy* had a profound effect on her. She wrote in her autobiography and in a typewritten note clipped to the *Globe* story, which she saved:

> That was the night I woke with a terrible sense of foreboding, a
> feeling that something had gone terribly wrong with Al, that he was
> in some kind of danger. It was wholly irrational because he never

told me the specifics of his assignments. I was staying in Pemberton with my parents and Peter. I feel strongly it was a genuine psychic experience. I checked the time the ship went aground with Al later, and it was the *exact* time I woke up.

In addition to counterintelligence activity, Al actively sought information that the D.N.I might use. In early February 1943, he wrote to his old classmate Phil Mallard (it's unclear how the letter got back in his files, unless he later asked Phil to return it), asking for any recollections about "a certain island" on which Mallard had once been shipwrecked. Presumably it was a Pacific or Mediterranean island, since there were no uncharted German-occupied islands in the Atlantic. "If you have any recollections of the terrain, beaches, harbors, shore installations, contacts of any kind, this office may be able to use them. Pictures, drawings, sketches, letters of any kind may have value." He notes, "I'm connected with the above office." Under the letterhead "Headquarters First Naval District 150 Causeway Street Boston," he wrote "Zone 4 D.I.O." That is, District Intelligence Office.

A year after the *Lucy* mission, he was ordered to accompany a convoy to Halifax, Nova Scotia, where the convoy was to pick up Canadian escorts for the Atlantic crossing. My mother knew about this assignment, or figured it out later, because she wrote, "The ships were all painted gray, and [the convoy] formed off Pemberton. I could see it from the beach in the very early morning."[4] He told her later that it was a disturbing experience to be in a fleet of ships in total darkness. The purpose of the mission is not recorded, but it was probably to watch for lights breaking the blackout (whether deliberate or careless) or to note before the ocean crossing whether any ships did not, or could not, stay in position. Captain Walter Kingsmill, commander of H.M.C.S. *Blairmore*, a Canadian minesweeper, certified that he came aboard July 10 and disembarked at Halifax on July 12. His orders, after he arrived at Halifax, were to "report to the U.S. Naval Observer." Two days later, he left Halifax by train, crossing into Maine at Vanceboro, and returned to Boston on July 15.

• • •

Soon after the *Lucy* hearing, Al's superiors began to worry that he was becoming known on the waterfront and that his effectiveness as a civilian operative could be compromised. They suggested he enlist in the navy but remain in intelligence, carrying out different duties (such as the later Halifax convoy). Once again he applied for a commission, hoping at least for a lieutenant J.G., and given that his application was at his superiors' suggestion, he had every reason to think the appointment would come through this time. He was given a sample personal-history form to aid him in filling out his own and was amused that in the space for fraternal organizations, the examples given were "The Harvard Club, The Myopia Hunt Club." (The latter was an inbred tribe of the martini-and-manure set on Boston's North Shore.) Proudly he wrote on his copy, "Propeller Club; Quarterdeck Club [both merchant marine organizations]; two years Massachusetts Nautical School; Master, Mates, Pilots and International Seaman's Union, South Boston Yacht Club." In his view, these were better qualifications for a commission than having chased frightened foxes around Essex County.

However, as much as the navy wanted him, and notwithstanding his knowledge and record, he was still a night school graduate, and they could not see giving him a commission, not even as a junior lieutenant. He was offered the highest noncommissioned navy rank: warrant boatswain. His physical defects were briskly waived. He accepted and took the oath on September 22, 1942. Just before he was sworn in, the First Naval District informed Local Board 32 that he was about to enter active duty—essentially, to cross him off the list. From then on, he was Warrant Boatswain Alfred C. J. Mehegan, USNR, No. 201499.

His navy file, sent to him in 1954 when he was officially separated from the Reserve list, contains a remarkable correspondence that must have been a shock to him when he read it. It shows that his boss, Commander E. M. Major, had pleaded his case for a commission. Major was the D.I.O.—district intelligence officer. Right after Al received his warrant appointment on August 8, Major got a letter from Commander A. D. Chandler, in the office of the Chief of Naval Operations in Washington:

From: the Director of Naval Intelligence
To: District Intelligence Officer, First Naval District
SUBJECT: Mr. Alfred Charles Joseph Mehegan

1. In view of Mr. Alfred Charles Joseph Mehegan's shipping knowledge, his services could be utilized to great advantage by the Vice Chief of Naval Operations.
2. Therefore, information is requested as to whether or not the District Intelligence Officer would object to his assignment to the quota of the Vice Chief of Naval Operations.

A. D. Chandler

Somehow, navy headquarters had heard about Al Mehegan and wanted to get him on its staff in Washington. Such a post would normally have included a commission. Next is a handwritten note with an indistinct signature, dated August 18, to Major:

Memo to D.I.O

Mr. Mehegan is presently on duty as agent in Zone IV. All papers have been prepared and forwarded. No action from Washington. Shall I propose reply saying this office interposes no objection to Mr. Mehegan's being assigned to the quota of the V.C.N.O?

Then, another handwritten note with an indistinct initial-signature, undated, to Lieutenant Emerson Hunt, on the Boston D.I.O staff. In his security investigation as part of the warrant-application process, Hunt had written: "Subject is described by associates, employers, and references as being loyal, discreet, patriotic, level-headed, diplomatic and of officer-like material." The note to Hunt said:

1. DIO took a letter to Washington with him, copy in file, on Mr. Mehegan.

2. I believe this letter [that is, the copy] should be destroyed.

Finally, most remarkable of all, a transcript of a telephone call from Major to Chandler, on August 26. Excerpts:

Chandler: Oh, how are you, Commander?

Major: Pretty good. Sorry to have to call you here on Mehegan.... You asked for his services in Chief of Naval Operations. Now, there is a little complication about it. We recommended his papers and they went forward as a warrant. He was a graduate of nautical school ship, not a college graduate [inexplicably, Major seems not to know about Northeastern]. Now if he takes a warrant and goes to Washington the boy is suffering a $1,000 loss and it's going to make it pretty tough for him, so I wrote you a memorandum recommending, suggesting that you change his application from warrant to commission, which you can very easily do.

Chandler: Yes, we can do that.

Major: It seems to me he's a fine chap. He's got a good knowledge of everything concerning the shipping industry....We tried him out and we found he was an excellent man....He's a good man and if you're going to use him down there give him a commission.

It was for naught, despite Major's efforts. The "excellent man" received neither commission nor posting to Washington.

After he took the oath as warrant, he was sent to Novakoff Brothers, a naval outfitter in Charlestown, to buy his uniforms—the same store he had gone to a decade before to buy his Nautical School uniforms. When he tried on his dress blues, he and Mary puzzled over a slit at the waist of the coat and were amused to learn that it was for a sword. On the navy guidelines for uniforms, which he was given, it said, "The Sword [is] still part of the uniform, but is not required, due to difficulty of supply."

The warrant boatswain's uniform included a cap with a crossed-anchors medallion (rather than a commissioned officer's eagle) above the visor. The gold stripes on the shoulder boards and cuffs were so-called broken stripes, that is, interrupted by segments of blue, whereas a commissioned officer's would be uninterrupted gold. My mother wrote, "Wearing his uniform one day as he walked along Causeway Street, he met one of his old instructors from the *Nantucket*. When he noticed his rank, he said, 'You, of all people, with a broken stripe. There's no justice.' But to Al, it was a small thing and, as you can imagine, I was much madder about it than he was."[5]

Here was that pattern, reflected in his 1936 journal entry, of not nurturing resentment over personal slights, though my mother fumed about them on his behalf. He was inclined to try to see the big picture. She wrote that he believed strongly that the country and its way of life were worth fighting and, if necessary, dying for, and he was ready to do his part without letting personal ambitions get in the way. Still, it is hard to imagine that it did not gall him to see the gulf between what those who knew him—such as Commander Major and the old Nautical School teacher—thought of him and what those who did not know him and saw him strictly inside or outside standard categories thought. Is it possible that the young man who ten years earlier had written, "Instead of being a junior at Tech as planned, I'm a lowly Boot on the U.S.S. Nantucket," who had heard that he was in line for the top prize at the Nautical School for navigation and seamanship but then had it yanked away when the prize was cancelled that year, whose first merchant marine captain had told him, "You can't steer, you won't earn your pay, I never wanted you," is it possible that he was not upset now to see his reasonable ambitions thwarted by ignorance and prejudice?

He continued to hope for a commission (he applied one more time, in January 1943), and others tried on his behalf, but the door was barred every time. Knowing him, I find it likely that he tended to internalize these hurts, to believe that perhaps he had not deserved the recognition after all, to think that he simply must work harder to prove himself. If this is true, it might account at least partly for what he suffered after the war.

While staying at Pemberton with her parents the summer of 1943, Mary had a surprise visit from a person about whom she had long been curious but had never seen: Esther Carson, her mother-in-law. In 2002 she wrote:

> I first met Esther in 1942 [sic] when she and her sister May visited me.[6] Al must have driven them to see me because they were just visiting relatives in South Boston. I was amazed at how young they were, but of course Esther was only eighteen years older than Al and May was about five years younger [than Esther]. Esther had curly rather golden hair and May was dark. They were very well spoken, which I must say surprised me; Esther I knew had worked in carnivals, which was hardly a cultured environment. But they were charming and adored Peter, who was only a little over a year old.[7]

Esther was in her late forties. It appears from this brief anecdote that Esther did not mention to my mother that her son Andy, Al's oldest half brother, was a prisoner of war. If she had, my mother would have reported it. At the time, Esther did not know whether Andy was alive or dead. He had joined the army in March 1941, he wrote in his memoir, mainly because he could not find a job: "The Army offered good food, all of my clothing, a place to sleep, an opportunity to travel, and thirty dollars a month."[8] He was soon shipped to the Philippines, to a fortress, later to become famous, called Corregidor. On May 6, 1942, the fort surrendered to the Japanese. After enduring the infamous Bataan Death March, he was interned at the notorious Cabanatuan prisoner-of-war camp on the island of Luzon, a kind of Japanese-run Andersonville where thousands died from a brutal regimen of starvation, beatings, and hard labor.

The career of Agent M-26 came to an end that October. "On or about October 13," Al was told in written orders, "you will regard yourself as detached from duty in the First Naval District...will proceed to

Princeton, N.J., and report to the Commanding Officer, Naval Training School (Indoctrination), Princeton University." It was about a month before Mary was due to have her second child.

"Al got his orders to report to Princeton for indoctrination," my mother wrote, "not as an intelligence officer, but as a regular ship's officer. I knew for a long time that he really wanted to go and I understood it. Florence was due that November, but it was like Chief Justice Holmes wrote about the Civil War, when he enlisted: 'A man must partake of the passion of his times.'[9] It was terribly sad for us when he left, because we had no idea when we would see each other again."[10]

8.

~~~~~

For the Duration

B<small>Y LATE 1943, THE NAVAL TRAINING CENTER</small> at Princeton University
was one of four such centers in the country, taking thousands of green
officers and stuffing them with naval knowledge as fast as possible. That
fall, enrollment was increased to about seven hundred navy students,
in addition to three hundred or more marines. They were housed in
student dormitories and fed in the university dining halls and clubs.
Food service was provided by the Howard Johnson's restaurant chain. It
was an eight-week course for newly minted officers, both commissioned
and warrant, from October 15 to December 10. Academic departments
included Executive, Seamanship, Fundamentals, Supply and
Disbursing, Navigation, Ordnance, Visual Aids, Physical Training, and
Medical.

Al was assigned to Company VI, which had eighty-four men.
Seventy-seven were already commissioned officers, either ensigns or
lieutenants J.G. Only seven were warrants. All the commissioned men
were college graduates, with a variety of professional backgrounds, as
listed in the directory that Al saved: engineers, lawyers, teachers, social
workers, police officers, and a surprising number of athletic directors
and coaches.

Some would not seem to be obvious candidates for the naval officer
corps. Lieutenant Melvin Browning of Bowling Green, Kentucky, for
example, Wabash College '32, was a "Bowling Operator." Lieutenant
Kermit Overby of Falls Church, Virginia, Concordia '32, listed his

profession as "Public Relations." Lieutenant James M. Rogers of Asheville, North Carolina, University of North Carolina '35, was a newspaper reporter. There was a number from elite colleges: Purdue, Columbia, Cornell. Lieutenant Philip G. Willcox of Winchester, Massachusetts, Harvard '33, was an investment analyst.

None of them had professional maritime experience, except one: "Bos'n Alfred C. Mehegan, Milton, Mass., Northeastern U. '40, Propeller Club, U.S. Merchant Marine." This is not surprising, given the all-out national mobilization—probably few fighter pilot or aerial navigator trainees had ever flown before. But it did create another situation that galled Mary but evidently did not much bother Al. He was assigned to the navigation course. "As the classes proceeded," she wrote, "he found out that he knew more than the instructor, though he never let on. He tutored several of his friends for the exam."[1] They, of course, had already received commissions. His classmates, who called him Moe, were grateful for his help, and when he fell ill near the end of the course, thirty-two of them (including P.R. man Kermit Overby and stockbroker Phil Willcox) signed a letter saying good-bye, thanking him, and wishing him well.

With Mary pregnant and due any time, he called her as often as possible. On November 23, my sister Florence was born. Mary would stay in the hospital for at least a week, which was typical for that era. It was possible for a serviceman still in the country to get brief leave for such an occasion, especially if the Red Cross pleaded his cause. Julia Mehegan, a celebrated "Mrs. Malaprop," called the Red Cross, then reported to Mary, "I said to the girl, 'There is that feller down there in Princeton Anniversary and his wife just had a baby.'" The feller did get home long enough to meet his new daughter.

The class ended in December, but Al was taken horribly sick and missed the final exam (though he made it up later, and aced it). He was sent to the naval hospital in St. Albans, New York. Mary was worried and desperate for him to come home before his next duty orders came in. She wrote that he had ptomaine poisoning and "would never go into a Howard Johnson's again." But there's an indication that there might have been something more to this illness. Ordinary food poisoning doesn't normally require hospitalization. Paula added a few more details from my mother's memory: "They were all terribly ill for a week, and when Dad got home, he had lost a lot of weight, and he was very yellow, Mum said. He said they just got a little food poisoning, but I think he might have had hepatitis. He probably was a person who should never have had another drink."

In early January he was assigned to Dam Neck, Virginia, near Norfolk, the Anti-Aircraft Training and Testing Center, for a several-week class in naval gunnery. It was here, apparently, that he was also qualified for handling a pistol, because sometime later he received a bronze medal hanging on a blue ribbon. On the front it says "Expert Pistol Shot" and "United States Navy," and on the reverse, "A. C. Mehegan." I have often wondered why a boatswain aboard ship would have a sidearm, but perhaps in his later duty it was deemed necessary for potential situations in the management of large numbers of men.

After Dam Neck, he was ordered to the Twelfth Naval District, San Francisco, there to report to the port director at Treasure Island, which was navy headquarters for the district, for further orders. He had four days' leave before returning to Norfolk to depart for California. "It was a terribly happy/sad four days," my mother wrote. "The day he left, after we said goodbye, he said he wouldn't look back as he went out the driveway, and I said I wouldn't go to the window to wave, as I always did. But both of us did."[2]

He left Norfolk on January 24 and arrived in San Francisco on the twenty-ninth. His travel order says, "Issued transportation from Norfolk, Va., to San Francisco, Calif., via C&O CINCINNATI NYC CHICAGO C&NW OMAHA UP OGDEN SP BEYOND. First class travel all the way. Fare $97.47." On February 14, he appeared before notary public Marion M. Bender and signed a form appointing Mary "my true and lawful attorney and agent . . . and on my behalf to execute all instruments and to do all acts and things as fully and effectually in all respect as I myself would do if personally present." The same day, he signed a navy power-of-attorney form authorizing Mary "to receive, endorse, and collect checks drawn on the Treasurer of the United States." My mother wrote on this form: "Al said he had this done in case he didn't come back."

He had more than a month in San Francisco before he was ordered to report to a ship. He left no record of what he did during those weeks, but I have learned that he did one thing twice: He visited his mother in Los Angeles. Esther was living in a small house with two of her sons. Her marriage to Andy Carson, her third husband, had been over, officially or unofficially, for several years. The eldest of her three Carson sons, Andy Jr., was a prisoner of war (more on him below) in Japan. Jack, seventeen, and David, fifteen, were at home. Jack Carson, who died in 2016, always said that he never met my father. But David, who lives in Montana, remembered otherwise.

"He came to see us twice during the war," David said in a telephone conversation. "Once for overnight and once for an afternoon. He was a chief petty officer. As far as I know, he called Mom. He stayed for dinner and left about ten the next day. A few weeks later, he was there for four or five hours. When adults were talking, I was supposed to stay out of the way, so I personally didn't get much visiting with him, just a little. I thought he was a really nice guy, and I was kind of pleased that he was my brother." It is possible that there was one more visit, at war's end. One might assume that these would have been happy times, and perhaps they were. But they did not leave Al feeling closer to Esther and her family; quite the reverse.

My mother wrote in 2002, weeks before her death:

> Al told me that when he was in the Merchant Marine . . . he worked for the American Hawaiian Line out of Seattle and when his ship came in to Los Angeles occasionally he would always make a point of visiting his mother, his aunt May [Esther's younger sister, married to Mike Kirby] and also another aunt, a sister-in-law of Esther's, Mae Donahue, who was married to Esther's brother Bill Donahue and they also lived in Los Angeles.

But then Al told me the next time, or one time after his first visit, he visited May Kirby. To his amazement she was divorced and had a different husband. Then later when he saw her she had remarried Mike again! Al told me he was so disillusioned with the marital changes that he stopped visiting them when his ship came in, even his mother.[3]

Her memory of my father's account of these visits errs on the timing. Al had left his only American Hawaiian ship, S.S. *Pennsylvanian*, in October 1933. He had quit his last merchant marine ship, S.S. *Katrina Luckenbach*, in San Francisco in March 1936. But Esther was not in California until 1938.

In about 1935, she decided that the carnival was no place for kids, or at least that whatever schooling her three boys were getting was not adequate. She enrolled them in the Morris School for Boys near Searcy, Arkansas, a Catholic boarding school operated by the Brothers of the Poor of St. Francis. They were there for about two years. But then everything changed. "I guess the terrible Depression finally caught up to all of us," said Jack Carson. "Dad and Dave Lackman lost it all."

After the Lackman & Carson show failed in 1937, Andy and Esther Carson left Tampa, Florida, and lit out for California in Andy's old Packard. Esther had long dreamed of California, and neither of them was about to go to Missouri or Massachusetts, where their families were. They drove to Searcy. "Dad and Mom picked us up at school," said Jack, "and we headed for California. We stopped by Texas and met our half sister Betty—she was about eighteen or twenty—and then moved on to Phoenix, where we lived for six months or a year." Betty by then was married, briefly and unhappily, to an oil entrepreneur whose family, according to David Carson, didn't think much of Betty's carny mother. In this opinion they were not the first or last.

By the time they reached Texas, they would have been accompanied on the road by thousands of desperate ruined families fleeing the Dust Bowl, the migration immortalized by John Steinbeck's *Grapes of Wrath*, the sort of rural folk who, in better times, had flocked to see shows like Lackman & Carson. Esther was probably the only Southie-bred girl on those dusty, bitter roads.

"Once I remember seeing a wheel go by," said David. "A rear wheel had come off, and we had to stop the car and find the wheel."

They pushed on from Arizona as soon as they cobbled together enough money. "About 1938," Jack said, "we moved to L.A. In California we were on Relief and issued blue jean pants and shirts, got food stamps. Mom worked as a housekeeper for some priests, and Dad was a crossing guard at a school."

What Al knew of these details is uncertain, other than that his mother and her family had decamped to California. By 1939, he knew her telephone number when calling her on Mother's Day, and he noted her address, 6336 South Hoover Street, on his personnel questionnaire when he applied to the Naval Intelligence Service.

As for May's shenanigans, described in my mother's memoir, David confirms that she left her husband, Mike Kirby, and ran off with another man and sometime later came back to her husband. Though it seems odd that his aunt's behavior would so bother Al as to prompt him to stop visiting his mother, clearly that is the story he told Mary, and it is consistent with what we know about him: that he was alienated by the impulsive betrayals and estrangement he had witnessed on both sides of his family and was determined that his own married life would be different.

• • •

On March 7, 1944, Al was ordered to "report to the Commanding Officer, Naval Armed Guards and Troops, on board the S.S. *Young America*, docked at Pier 54 North, which is just north of today's AT&T Park. Seven years before, he had quit S.S. *Katrina Luckenbach* in this same port and, as he wrote at that time, "wended my weary way home from San Francisco, on the beach again." It is doubtful that he would have believed then that seven years later he would be a married father of two, heading back across the country to San Francisco, to report for duty aboard another cargo ship—this time to go to war. But this was no ordinary cargo ship.

The *Young America* was a freshly built, 459-foot, 14,000-ton C2 cargo ship, converted to a troop transport. It was "S.S.," not "U.S.S," because it was not a commissioned navy ship but an official government vessel owned by the New Orleans–based Delta Steamship Lines, leased by the War Shipping Administration. Its mission, according to a set of papers given to officers, was "to embark, transport, and successfully land combat teams with complete materiel and equipment on hostile shores. The boats of an amphibious transport are her principal weapons—the connecting link between the ship and shore, and by careful navigation and expert handling, the troops reach their objective in the desired tactical formation on time."

When he joined the ship, Al was one of several warrant boatswains, whose job was to supervise general management of the "passenger" operations. The passengers were the troops headed for such bloodily contested islands as Tarawa, Iwo Jima, and Okinawa, or Saipan and Tinian. The ship had bunks for 1,436 enlisted troops and 69 officers. Their gear and weapons were stowed in the hold. Tied down on deck were the thirty-six-foot plywood Higgins boats, the familiar rectangular landing craft used for beach assaults.

As a troop ship, the *Young America* had a bifurcated command structure. It had a civilian crew of about sixty-three and a master (that is, a captain) in charge of the ship and its crew. The captain was Roy Wilder, later succeeded by J. W. Clark. In addition, the ship had a naval commander, "in command of all passengers, military and civilian, as well as all Naval and Marine Corps personnel permanently assigned to the vessel. He is the master's military advisor and is charged with the vessel's armed defense." The naval commander was Lieutenant Commander Theodore H. (Ted) Little. Like most assault ships, the *Young America* had antiship and antiaircraft arms: four three-inch guns on the bow, a five-inch gun on the stern, and ten 20 mm machine-gun emplacements along both sides of the superstructure.

The civilian captain and crew had the same duty as they would had the ship carried ordinary cargo. Ted Little and his officers were in charge of soldiers, marines, and sailors, gunnery, and communication of military sailing orders—where and when the ship was to go and what it was to do when it got there.

Master and naval commander were supposed to work harmoniously, but it did not always happen. Reading the official explanation of the command structure, one can easily imagine potential tension:

> Orders and instructions for the crew will be issued by the Master. Orders and instructions for the conduct of military personnel and passengers subject to these regulations will be issued by or though the Naval Commanding Officer. It therefore follows that all communications between the master and members of his crew addressed to those subject to the regulations will be made through the Naval Commanding Officer. Likewise, any instructions or suggestions coming from those subject to these regulations and intended for the Master will be communicated to the Master through and at the discretion of the naval Commanding Officer.

What this meant for Al was that despite being a highly qualified ocean mariner, with a "heavy license," he had nothing to do with navigation or management of the ship, which must have been strange to him. His responsibility was to handle men and supplies, as well as landing craft and everything loaded on them. It was almost like being a camp director or running a hotel. He was also responsible for the stowing of gear and equipment, including weapons and vehicles.

While there is no record of friction between Little and Captain Wilder, the same was not true of Wilder's relations with his navy superiors. In September, he was stripped of his command after a navy hearing on a charge of insubordination by his task force commander, Admiral Alvin O. Lustie. In his 2000 memoir, *SSS*, J. W. Clark writes that Wilder, incredibly, "countered by charging that Lustie had interfered with the navigation of the vessel, which was the sole responsibility of the Master."[4] My mother wrote that Al told her later, "There were some terribly difficult times especially because the merchant captain was an 's.o.b.' who hated the Navy."[5] This must have been Wilder, who was captain for Al's first six months aboard, since Clark makes no criticism of the navy and writes of a friendly postwar reunion with Little.

The *Young America*'s officers noticed Al Mehegan and were attracted by his personality, character, and capacity. He had been aboard only four months when Ted Little recommended him for promotion to chief boatswain. The chief boatswain was the naval commander's "first lieutenant," essentially his overall chief operating officer. There were mates for gunnery and various other functions, but the chief would have his hand in everything. In navy culture it was sometimes said that the chief boatswain runs the ship. Ted Little was a warm and affable man who came to admire Al greatly, a regard that would result in a surprising incident after the war.

Among Al's many duties was that of chief mail censor. "I think I've censored 1000 letters since we arrived here [an unnamed Pacific port]," he wrote to Mary, "—maybe it was 1,000,000! After a while I hate the sight of mail! (I'm only joking, of course)." His letters were censored by someone else. He had to ensure that no letters contained information of value to the enemy. According to the mail rules, described in the policy handbook given to the ship's officers, "No information of a military or naval nature may be divulged in any correspondence. Accordingly, no mention may be made of the voyage, the name or the ship or ships, the composition of the escort, the route traveled, name of port of debarkation, etc. Only matters of a strictly personal nature may be written." Radios, flashlights, and cameras were forbidden aboard ship, and a total blackout was observed at night. Nothing could be thrown overboard: no trash, cigarette butts, tin cans, nothing "capable of floating."[6]

As it always does, wartime threw together people of diverse backgrounds, bringing Al into contact with men from worlds very different from that he had known. Two of his close friends on the *Young America* were Lieutenant Edward Dullea, gunnery officer and a lawyer in civilian life, whose father was the San Francisco chief of police, and Lieutenant William Sevier Trinkle, known as Billy, the supply officer, the son of Elbert Lee Trinkle, former governor of Virginia. Ted Little was also a lawyer, an assistant attorney general of Washington state when he entered the navy. A photograph of the officers, taken aboard the ship, shows them in a row in brown work uniforms, smiling and looking much alike. They seem to be friends. Little is at center, clearly not lording it over the others. Al is on the left, thin as an elf. His physical report for the July promotion listed him as 142 pounds.

• • •

He wrote to Mary almost constantly, and she wrote to him every day. "I have decided to try plain V-mail for a change," he wrote in March 31, 1944, "so note the date and tell me how long it takes the letter to reach you."

V-mail was a technical innovation invented by the British, designed to cut down on the tons of mail that had to be shipped from overseas. With V-mail, 150,000 one-page letters that would otherwise fill thirty-seven mail bags would fit into one. The writer used a standard-issue form, about 8½ x 11 inches, a combination letter sheet and envelope with spaces for addresses. The letters were photographed and reduced to a quarter inch on microfilm rolls (this presumably is what filled the single bag), shipped home, developed at centers near the recipient, printed at about one-quarter original size (5-⅝ x 4¼ inches), and delivered. Delivery was amazingly fast: one V-mail letter from Mary, dated April 24, arrived at a Pacific island port on April 31.

Mary kept many of these letters (except, she said, certain intimate ones), though hers to him have not survived. There was not much space on a sheet; the instructions cautioned, presumably out of consideration for the censor, "Very small writing is not suitable." Al would sometimes send two or three a day, as he did March 31. Excerpts from the three:

> I miss you very much, my love, think of you so very often. Our
> few years together seem so long ago and are part of another life,
> it seems. I have occasional flashes of the sense of unreality you
> mention in your letter—as though awakening would find me back

in our kitchen enjoying one of our Sunday morning breakfasts. I long for our peaceful happy way of life. I am as happy as separation permits. A good ship and a fine friendly group of officers and men. One couldn't ask for more. . . .

I long so for your serenity and soothing qualities. I wish I could write tender missives, the kind you could tie up with blue ribbons, but it's hard to write a love letter with a censor (however sympathetic) almost leaning over your shoulder!...

From now on, I'm not to tell you whether I'm in the States or not. My room-mate is a cheery likable young fellow. Last night we went ashore together and stumbled through mud and puddles and were soaked by a rain squall. We enjoyed two or three "cokes" and a hot dog—stop! . . .

I hope you enjoyed your birthday. You are officially older than I at this point. Give Peter two kisses from me for his birthday [April 3] and hold Florence close to your heart for a moment from me.

This is the first reference to drinking in his letters. Officially, no alcohol was permitted aboard ship, but officers could evade the rule. A month later, April 27, the ship was at sea: "Tomorrow, we expect to arrive at a Pacific Port (not U.S.A.)." He adds, "By the way, I've shaved my mustache—hope you had as much fun with the picture as I had having it taken." This photograph was taken April 4 with a friend he made at Treasure Island, Bob Hatch, at the Backstage Nightclub in San Francisco, showing both with drinks in their hands and Al with a Clark Gable mustache. The club occupied the ground floor of the Herbert Hotel, 151 Powell Street. They probably took the cable car and got off at O'Farrell Street. In May, writing from "a Pacific Island," he reports that "Hatchie's ship came in, so I hope to meet him today and have a couple of beers at the 'club.'" Next day: "Last night Hatch's ship came in and tied up right astern, so we 'tied one on.' He had some bourbon and rum & champagne and beer and oh-h-h-h-h-h...what a head today."

Reading this now and recalling Mary's uneasiness over his drinking at the yacht club that summer night of 1939, I wonder how she took it. Did she worry? Though she was virtually a teetotaler herself, she was not a temperance fanatic. She understood that he was lonely, a man at war, getting a bit of a break with a friend. Here he treats getting drunk and being hungover as normal and amusing, not as anything to hide or be embarrassed about. It's a reminder of the kind of social milieu he grew up in, so radically different from hers. Decades later, he would never speak of drinking directly, at least not to his children, certainly never speak lightly of being hungover. But by then he knew he had a problem.

In another letter, he has a fantasy:

> I've just been having the funniest thought. It persists, so I'd better tell you about it. I thought I'd like to try a winter very close to the ocean when we are together again. I wonder what it would be like to hear a wintry ocean raging at night—and be comfortable and warm withal. Do you think I'm going soft? A place like Hull or Hingham, or Cohasset, etc., where your house could be within hearing of the sea? Oh well, that's another one to be laid aside with our turnip farm and fishing boat. This is all the small boy in me, I guess.

In fact, they would live many years within sight and sound of the ocean.

In addition to writing to Mary, he told her, "I've made it a rule that whenever I write to you I must follow up with a letter to my 'fambly.' This won't interfere with yours, and will prevent any hurt feelings at '1115.'" Despite having a family of his own, he had not abandoned or forgotten about those he once refers to as "the inmates of 1115"—that is, 1115 Adams Street, Dorchester. Several of those letters were saved by Mary Rose, his sister: one to her, one each to his stepmother and his aunts, Mary and Catherine, and two to his father. Letters to my mother are signed "Al"; those to his family are signed "Alfred." He addresses Charlie as "Dad," and in this August 20 letter, there is no suggestion of awkwardness or distance, though not much feeling, either:

Dear Dad,

Still out "here" running 'em back and forth. I'll have a little to talk about when I get home again. It's too soon to guess, but there is a *chance* that I'll make a trip home before snow flies, but don't say anything because Mary might raise false hopes. As soon as they are home from the beach [they were staying with her parents in Pemberton] they'll probably visit you often. Hope this affair ends soon, because Mary must need a hand guiding the young ones along. I was amazed at the change in Peter in a recent picture. As for Florence, she is a heart-breaker already!...

Well, no news from out here, but I'm always glad to hear from you. Hope you had a good summer with some relaxation.

Love,
Alfred

The war reinforced his sense of the mutability of things. On June 1, 1944, he wrote to Mary:

Dearest,

Just a quick note before I hit the sack. I've just censored many, many letters.

I'm thinking of you constantly. You know I don't save letters any more—but just one you wrote me the day after Florence was born. You said, 'Our cup runneth over.' It still does, Sweetheart. I'm so grateful for you and all we have. Truly our treasured things can be neither measured nor weighed against any earthly standard. Only one thing to keep ever before us—nothing is ours; we possess merely to develop and then relinquish. We have a life to live apart from our children.

Your loving husband,
Al

The last sentence is a bit of a puzzle, given the preceding. It suggests an awareness of the unknowable future, that one must not cling to good things, only treasure them while they last. Children will grow up and go their own way. But then he and she will still have each other.

• • •

An account by an army passenger says the *Young America* left San Francisco on April 22 and arrived at Pearl Harbor, Hawaii, on the twenty-eighth. Jay Clark, who took command at Pearl Harbor on September 7, writes that the ship had taken part in the Marshall Islands campaign, which included Truk, Eniwetok Atoll, and Kwajalein, but these had been seized by landings in January and February, before Al joined the ship.[7] Eniwetok Atoll is a coral cluster of forty small islands, Eniwetok the largest, surrounding a large lagoon harbor. After it was seized from the Japanese, it became a major Allied base. At one point in 1944 there were as many as 488 ships anchored there at once. It appears that between late April and June, the *Young America* was, as Al wrote to his father, "running them back and forth," that is, ferrying troops and supplies between Eniwetok and other locations, but not close to any active fighting. On June "7–8," however, Al wrote to Mary:

> Last night…we had movies aboard, a news reel showing allied troops approaching Naples and a Notre Dame football game. Then followed…*Princess O'Rourke* with Olivia [de Havilland][8]—then the end with a flashing of white and distorted shapes—then over the P.A. system came the commander's voice—"Men —Rome has fallen. And — — —we have landed in France!" Shock—then an earsplitting roar from (censored) voices, mine included. Way out here in the Pacific we were thrilled to the spirit to hear the news. I hope *soon* we can make a major move toward victory in the Pacific.

He knew that something big was afoot. The "major move" the ship was headed for was the Mariana Islands campaign, code-named Forager. Its targets were Saipan, Tinian, and Guam. Forager was a gigantic operation, with eight hundred ships, including twelve aircraft carriers, eight battleships, and transports carrying 80,000 marines and

50,000 soldiers. Saipan was assaulted on June 15 and not secured until July 9, at a cost of 3,100 American lives and 30,000 Japanese. Saipan became most famous for the mass suicides of Japanese civilians, who leaped off the cliffs at the northern end of the island. Tinian was taken August 1 and nearby Guam August 10. An air base for B-29 bombers was soon constructed on Tinian, and from it a year later bombers took off to drop atomic bombs on Hiroshima and Nagasaki.

On July 14, Al wrote, "Henry Fonda (Lt. j.g.) entertained us here yesterday. Yesterday I went 20–30 miles by small boat to try to replenish my dwindling supplies, no luck." So it appears that the *Young America* was not part of the initial assault but landed troops possibly a week later, since it is clear that by mid-July he was back in port, probably Eniwetok. It is likely that the ship made multiple runs to the Marianas, ferrying more men and equipment.

Although he did not experience a direct attack on his ship until November, he saw the results of the island landings firsthand. Many times in that year, the *Young America* took wounded men aboard for evacuation. When he came home on leave the following March, he told Mary, she wrote, "of taking a rollicking regiment of paratroopers, kids really, who were so excited about going to war, but ashore they were decimated and they had to take some of them back to San Francisco, many seriously wounded. Some he said he would never forget were so mentally deranged from their experiences that they had to put them in cages."[9] Though he did not speak of such horrors to us, he did speak of Saipan and Tinian and the Battle of the Philippine Sea, soon after, at which so many Japanese planes were shot down that it was called "the Marianas Turkey Shoot."

There were long stretches at sea, and in a few V-mail letters he speaks of boredom or reading cheap novels, bridge games among the officers and of rigging up a cot on deck because it was impossibly hot to sleep in his cabin. Many American servicemen brought back Japanese war souvenirs from the Pacific, including rifles, swords, flags, and insignia. Some even brought back human skulls. Al's keepsakes were less martial. He saved a matchbook from the Pearl Harbor Navy Officer' Club, and a fifty-centavo Filipino note issued by "The Japanese Government." He walked the beach at Eniwetok and filled his pockets with delicate conchs, limpets, wentletraps, augurs, and one huge cowrie (I identify it as Cypraea *tigris*), which he kept for years in a glass jar. You might say, in a sense, that he didn't bring home the Pacific war, but the Pacific Ocean.

• • •

That summer of 1944, Al did not know that his half brother Andy was also on a ship in the same ocean. The Japanese occupation authorities of the Philippines in July selected about 1,500 prisoners from the Cabanatuan prison camp to work as slave coal miners in Japan. Andy Carson was one of them. They were loaded onto a convoy of ships, crammed into a totally dark hold day and night, with minimal food and water, and occasional slop buckets, lowered down to them. Andy's ship was *Nissyo Maru*. Conditions on these vessels, known as "hell ships," resembled those of the Atlantic slave trade. Prowling American submarines and planes did not know they were full of American and other Allied prisoners, and began to pick them off one by one. In a desperate bid to reveal the cargo to the enemy, the captain of *Nissyo Maru* brought the nearly naked prisoners up on deck and began to hose them off with warm seawater. At least six ships were sunk, including *Arisan Maru*, from which only a handful out of 1,759 prisoners survived. Somehow, *Nissyo Maru* made it through.[10] Andy spent the rest of the war in coal mines, but even this was better than Cabanatuan.

• • •

John W. Clark, age twenty-three, took command of the *Young America* on September 7, 1944, and soon learned his orders. The ship would be part of Task Force 31.5.2, which would head for Manus Island, a naval base in New Guinea seized from the Japanese earlier that year, to prepare for the invasion of the Philippines on the island of Leyte. The total force, composed of several fleets, was part of a massive operation, including seventeen carriers, six battleships, seventeen cruisers, sixty-four destroyers, submarines, and hundreds of transports and supply ships. The landings were to take place south of Tacloban. After a stop in Hollandia, the landing force, including the *Young America*, reached Leyte Gulf on November 4. The *Young America* and other transports anchored off Dulang, south of Tacloban. They moved as close to shore as possible, and the troops and equipment were landed the next day. Things went smoothly, but they were about to become acquainted with a new Japanese word: *kamikaze*.

The Japanese had first used kamikaze attackers, heavily bomb-loaded planes with just enough fuel to reach and try to crash into Allied ships, at Saipan and Tinian, but that assault was so well in hand by the time the *Young America* reached the scene that the ship did not experience the terror of that weapon. However, its turn would come in Leyte Gulf. Over the following days, as the initial invasion force was nearly bogged down inland, the attacks on ships in the gulf intensified. Three carriers, a cruiser, and several cargo ships, including one troop transport, were hit. Clark notes that most of the damage was to ships farther north, since the attackers would come low over the island of Samar, on the north side of the gulf, then go after the first ships they encountered.[11]

In mid-November, the *Young America* was ordered farther north, closer to Tacloban. Clark had noticed that the kamikaze attacks tended to take place in the early morning, so each evening he moved the *Young America* as close as possible to shore. The outcome of this maneuver, as Clark tells it, was that the ship escaped the attention of the attackers, who concentrated on vessels in the anchorages farther out. He does not indicate that he shared this clever trick with other captains.

Finally, however, the *Young America*'s turn came. Two surviving accounts do not agree exactly on the details. Without giving a date, Clark writes:

> Running low on fresh water, Clark [he always refers to himself in the third person] signaled the . . . command ship and requested water. He was allowed only 73 tons from a navy water tanker and required to shift alongside to receive the water. During the

maneuver there was another *kamikaze* attack with the guns of both ships blazing away at three enemy planes coming in low. P-38s from Tacloban airfield shot them down before they could hit the ships, and one plummeted down in the sea near the *Young America*. Early one morning at daybreak a bomber flew directly over the ship at about 1,500 feet after a bombing run at Tacloban, and the ship's gun crew let go with intense anti-aircraft fire, but missed....Despite close range targets the gunners never hit a single plane. Shrapnel from the fire of other ships rained down on deck, forcing the officers and crew to take cover.[12]

Navy radioman Howard Landon, whose memoir was written in 2000, the same year as Clark's, cites a date and gives a slightly different account:

> The planes, which took off from landing strips in the interior of Leyte Island, dropped bombs and strafed allied ships anchored in the harbor. During the air attacks members of the crew not on watch at their primary assignments assisted the navy gunners. During "general quarters" I was assigned to one of the 20-mm antiaircraft machine guns on the superstructure. It was my job to feed ammunition to the gunners. This was very exciting and took on the atmosphere of a football game. When a Japanese plane was hit and fell into the sea, everyone on the ship cheered.
>
> On the morning of 13 November the SS *Young America* was strafed by two low-flying Japanese zero fighter planes. We suffered no personnel casualties, but parts of the ship's superstructure were damaged.[13]

Aside from the difference in the number of attackers, two as opposed to three, one might assume that the captain would have a more accurate account, but it is strange that Landon recalls the ship being damaged, and Clark says it was not hit, and that Landon reports the antiaircraft gunners hitting their targets. Possibly Landon mistook the falling shrapnel for Japanese bullets. Both witnesses, of course, were looking back half a century. Landon credits the ship's gunnery for downing one plane, while Clark credits American fighters and says the *Young America*'s gunners "never hit a single plane," of which he could not have been certain.

My father, needless to say, never forgot this incident, and had one particularly vivid detail: As he told it, during the attack, he and the other exposed men had dropped down and "tried to dig foxholes in the deck." He could write to no one about it at the time, however. Two days later, the *Young America* was joined to a convoy of merchant ships and a flotilla of large landing craft and ordered to proceed to Hollandia, New Guinea. In a letter to Mary dated November 16, three days after the attack, he wrote:

> We are so many days at sea after an interesting stay in port, and I'm glad. We have a few days' vacation now, practically nothing to do but sun-bathe, eat and sleep. The food is not too good now, and water is rationed to one bucket per day, but what is that to an old salt? Yesterday I bathed, washed two suits of underwear, then four pair of socks in the same water—me first, of course. Then a pair of gray trousers and a gray shirt went to soak in [the] same bucket. Today, with my new bucket, I'll bathe, then rinse out the grays. See how simple it is?

The letter includes pencil sketches of the ship and of a crude deck chair that he built for himself.

The *Young America* steamed to Hollandia, then to Manus Island, and on December 6 reached the port of Nouméa on the French Island of New Caledonia. The ship's engine needed an extensive overhaul, which took weeks. On the twenty-first, a battalion of marines came aboard, and next day the ship headed for the island of Espiritu Santo, in what is now the nation of Vanuatu, then known as the New Hebrides, another Allied supply base and believed to be the model for Rodgers and Hammerstein's World War II musical, *South Pacific*. The ship arrived on Christmas Eve, took on more troops, then left the next morning en route back to Manus Island. Clark writes:

Once clear of the island and in deep water, Clark made a brief Christmas Day statement over the public address system: "On behalf of the ship's merchant marine and naval officers and crew, I wish all aboard as merry a Christmas as possible under the circumstances. Our good stewards and cooks have prepared a great meal for all hands and we trust you will enjoy it. We are presently bound for Oro Bay, New Guinea, ETA New Year's Eve. We're glad to have you aboard and we'll be even happier to transport you home." The Christmas dinner *was* great, with turkey, dressing, cranberry sauce and mashed potatoes, topped off with mincemeat pie....It was a meal to be remembered, and everybody on board shared the same fare.

Indeed it must have been memorable, because, amazingly, Al saved the menu. It's a mimeographed folio with a cartoon of Santa Claus on the front, ringing a doorbell. Over the door is a sign: "S.S. *Young America.*" The menu is astounding, under the circumstances. Not only turkey and cranberry sauce, but "ripe olives," "hearts of celery," "baked ham with raisin sauce," "T-bone steak, maître d'hotel," "whole kernel corn, buttered carrots and peas," and, in addition to mince pie, there is pumpkin pie and fruit cake. On the back of the menu is a message:

Have you noticed your shipmates' "Merry Xmas" has some indescribable zeal to it? You've extended this old familiar greeting to your friends in other years in a perfunctory way, but "Merry Xmas— 1944" among the bunch of fighting men aboard the S.S. *Young America* cracks with the resolve, "Let's get this whole thing over with and back to the only kind of a Merry Xmas—"Home Sweet Home." May God speed the coming of that great day!—T.H. Little, Naval C.O.

The ultimate destination, again, was Leyte Gulf. More troops came aboard at various stops, and the *Young America* arrived at Leyte—now completely under control, as opposed to two months earlier—on January 26, where it landed 1,500 men, with weapons and equipment, on beaches around Dulag.

One of the remarkable souvenirs in my father's *Young America* papers is a pile of issues of *Neptune News*, a four-to-eight-page stapled newspaper edited by army lieutenant Roy McIntyre, nephew of O. O. McIntyre, a celebrated New York columnist of the twenties and thirties. McIntyre's unit came aboard in Nouméa, and he produced the paper every day until he and his men were set ashore at Leyte. Besides war news, jokes, and assorted bits of gentle gossip and silliness about various men aboard ("Bo'sun Mehegan" is needled about his homemade deck chair), the paper is filled with cartoons by Sergeant George Ghyssels. Ghyssels later won a bronze star at the battle of Okinawa, and after the war he had a long career as a commercial artist. His cartoon in the last issue of *Neptune News*, January 25, 1945, shows a crowd of soldiers jumping off the *Young America* (using parachutes!) onto a beach, along with trucks, tanks, and artillery. Up on deck, waving good-bye, are figures labeled "Captain Clark" and "Cmdr. Little."

●　●　●

This was the end of operations for the *Young America* on the long voyage that began when it left San Francisco the previous April. It was and would be the longest that Al ever served on a single ship. With its bottom badly fouled and its overworked engines breaking down continually, it limped back to San Francisco, via Manus and Guadalcanal. After another engine breakdown near the Farallon Islands, with the ship rolling and drifting, it got under way again, entered the Golden Gate, and docked on March 11, 1945. Clark writes that after meeting with port officials, he went to his cabin, slumped over his desk, and thought, "Thank God this trip is over."[14]

Boatswain Mehegan was glad it was over too. He was stateside safely, for a while at least, with a special reason to celebrate. It was his fourth wedding anniversary.

9.

"My Private War"

"ON MARCH 11, 1945, OUR ANNIVERSARY," my mother wrote in 1989, "Al called me from the West Coast and said he was coming home on leave. I couldn't believe it was happening."[1]

There must have been a telephone booth on the pier, or not far away, and undoubtedly a long line of men waiting to use it. The telephone bill was a keepsake, probably preserved by Mary: The March 11 collect call cost $4.50. He called again on the fourteenth ($9.25) and the seventeenth ($6.00). My mother wrote:

> He had been gone fifteen months. He had a wonderful group of friends on that ship. One of them was Ed Dullea [Lieutenant Edward Dullea, the gunnery officer], whose father [Charles F.] was the chief of police in San Francisco. When the ship came in, he sent an official limousine to the dock to take them all to a dinner given by the city and all their officials from the mayor down, in honor of St. Patrick. They had a rollicking time and Al sat at the head table, where they were displayed as "heroes." Chief Dullea introduced Al as "a stalwart Irishman from South Boston," to frantic applause. Even in San Francisco, they knew the Irishness of South Boston, which amazed and amused Al.[2]

It was a thirty-day leave, and to get as much time as possible at home, Al decided to fly for the first time in his life. He only flew as far as Buffalo, New York; a freak late-winter snowstorm grounded planes, so he took a train to Boston. Mary waited for him, with Peter and Florence, Mary Rose, and his aunts Mary and Catherine, at South Station. Peter was just short of his third birthday, and Florence was fifteen months. The train pulled in at 9:30 a.m. The date is not recorded, but he called from Buffalo on the twenty-first, so it might have been the next day.

My mother wrote:

> Servicemen were pouring off the train. I can remember the incredible anticipation we had, until we saw Al come running towards us out of the crowd. Peter had had a little blue snowsuit when Al left, but when he met us that day Florence had it on, her first hand-me-down. Al picked her up in his arms and said, "Peter?" He couldn't believe it was her, she had grown so. But to my horror, she was very cool to him. Every time he touched her, she pulled away. She had no idea who this strange man was who wanted to kiss her. But Al was wonderful. He left her completely alone.
>
> Al and Peter were a joy to see. Peter remembered him at once and it was as if he had never left. Al was overjoyed with him. Then one day when Al was stooping down for something, Florence went over to him and put her arms around him. It was wonderful. Al had done just the right thing, although he said, "She's the coldest girl I ever courted!"
>
> I don't remember what we did that whole idyllic time. Talked, mostly, I think. Al had so much to tell me.[3]

One thing, it is clear, they did not do. When I was about fifteen, my father told me that on that leave, he and my mother did not "have relations." I cannot imagine now why he would have volunteered that information to me—I surely didn't ask about it—but he said that because he was going back into a war zone for no one knew how long, and with two children, he did not want to take a chance of leaving my mother with three children if he should be killed. When she wrote her memoir, she mentioned this as well. A few days before Al had come home, she wrote, a married friend had said to her, "'I'm so worried. As a Catholic, what are you going to do? Suppose you get pregnant again?' But Al had written to me and, without putting it into words, had said, 'You don't have to worry about anything happening while we are together. After waiting all this time, I can wait as long as you want me to.'"[4]

One little photograph from this leave survives, of Al in uniform crouching and holding Peter and Florence, and Mary slightly obscured by Florence's hat. He is smiling brightly. Julia is on a porch in the background.

"Al's leave was up on April 18th. The leave was 27 days, not 30, because the 30 included his transportation time. When he left, though, I felt so sad but cheerful, too, because *he* was, and though there was much more fighting to do, it did sound as if the war might soon be ended."[5]

• • •

He returned to San Francisco by air. "Consumed knockout drop on plane," he wrote in a telegram to let her know he had arrived. On May 5, German forces in northwest Europe surrendered, and V.E. Day was proclaimed, with huge celebrations in big cities, on May 8. But it was not over in the Pacific, and no one knew when it would be. On June 15, Al was ordered to report to the S.S. *Sea Runner*, which he did that same day, a Friday. The naval commander was Frederick Prince, a friend of Ted Little's.

The *Sea Runner* was a new C3 cargo/troop ship, built in San Francisco, owned by Grace Lines and chartered by the navy. It was bigger and faster than the *Young America*, at 492 feet, beam 70 feet, and a maximum speed of 20 knots. Its armament was similar to the *Young America's*. Besides the merchant crew (sixty-four) and naval guard (eighty-three), it had bunks for 2,154 troops, officers, and enlisted men, for a maximum company of 2,301. Al saved a photograph of it, tied up at a pier. It looks big, heavy, and dirty, like a ship that has been through a war. Indeed, before Al came aboard, the *Sea Runner* had served in the invasion of the southern Palau islands, September 6 to October 14, 1944; Iwo Jima, March 2 to 18, 1945; and two trips to Okinawa, March 10 to 16, where it had come under kamikaze attack.

If there are extended memoirs of the *Sea Runner* comparable to those of Howard Landon and Jay Clark, they have not turned up. Furthermore, there are no surviving letters from my father from that ship, though he must have sent them. At that late phase of the war, the *Sea Runner* would have been, in Al's earlier words to his father, "running them back and forth," moving men in the vast cycling of supplies and of fresh and tired troops over the huge Pacific theater. His job was the same as on the *Young America.* There is a photograph of him with a large group of officers at Hollandia, seemingly at some kind of nighttime cookout. Their khaki uniforms appear to be half soaked with perspiration, and he and most of the others are holding cans of beer.

• • •

As my mother wrote, there was hope that the war might end soon. Resistance on Okinawa ended June 22, and in the Philippines on June 28. But the hope seemed more like a dream to the American combatants, none of whom knew about the atomic bomb. The Japanese had fiercely contested every scrap of ground, every island, virtually to the last man, sending every rickety, ill-armed ship and plane, and every available soldier, on futile, suicidal missions. Having done so consistently thus far, they would, it was assumed, do so even more fiercely in the home islands. Indeed, the military faction in the Japanese government was talking of total resistance, to the last citizen. What the Americans now expected—those who did not know about the bomb—was a drawn-out, bitter land war, something like the war in Europe, after gigantic amphibious landings. The ships in such operations would surely be subjected to the same kamikaze attacks as at Saipan and Okinawa, only more intense. The Japanese would send everything that would fly against them. Projected U.S. casualty figures in the home islands invasion varied greatly, but extrapolating from previous losses, General Douglas MacArthur's staff had estimated the cost of a campaign on the island of Kyushu at about 100,000. General George Marshall had told President Truman at the Potsdam Conference that American casualties in fighting on the two main islands, Kyushu and Honshu, might range from 250,000 to 1 million. These numbers seem fantastic today, given that nowhere near such losses were suffered in Europe. However, the planners knew that most of the prelanding estimates of casualties in various island campaigns, including those in the Philippines, had proved to be too low. Furthermore, it was learned after the war that the Japanese command had correctly guessed the locations and timing of the invasions, and had planned a warm reception.

I do not remember my father expressing either strong moral approval or disapproval of the use of the atomic bomb. He did not regard it as criminal, given the savagery of Japanese warfare in China and the Pacific. But he was consistent in his opinion that an invasion would have been crazy because unnecessary. I can remember him saying, "By the end of the war, the Japs had nothing. *Nothing.*" My mother wrote:

> Al felt that though there was talk of invading Japan…it would never be necessary. He said they hoped the brass wouldn't decide to do that; that he felt all they need do was blockade Japan and force them to surrender. He was so confident that it would be the best course and it was the opinion of everyone he talked to. Why chance the incredible loss of American lives in an invasion when they could be starved into submission?[6]

That argument was made in the highest planning levels, but the counterargument was that it might take years, and in the meantime it would be impossible to maintain such a massive ground and naval force in a state of readiness, in case invasion might later be necessary. There was also concern, not necessarily entirely from humane considerations, that a prolonged campaign of bombing (raids of as many as a thousand planes at a time were already laying waste to developed areas in Japan) and blockade would leave the country in such a state of devastation and starvation that the cost and length of postwar reconstruction would be astronomical. Truman and Marshall did not want to be responsible for 90 million paupers.

My father remembered that in August 1945, the *Sea Runner* was fully loaded, part of a large fleet on its way to Japan in the massive invasion that had been code-named Downfall—an ominous name for all involved. Suddenly, the fleet turned around and headed back to base. The atomic bombs had been dropped on August 6 and 9. To the shock and amazement and delirious happiness of the men aboard, on August 15 Japan surrendered.

• • •

The day of the attack at Pearl Harbor, my mother had looked out the window on Adams Street in Milton and thought, "Nothing will ever be the same." Now, she wrote, "the war, the terrible, terrible war, was over at last. To be able to put our lights on again was one of the small joys. Boston exploded with parties and parades, as did the whole nation. To anyone who has not experienced a formal end to a war, as we did, it is hard to imagine the hysteria that we all felt. All I could think of was, 'When is Al coming home?'"[7] The normal life that they had dreamed about, and started four and a half years before, could finally resume. She wrote in her diary, "My private war is over."

It sounds like an easy catchphrase: "my private war." But to the millions who lived through that catastrophe in the middle of the last century, it was not a cliché, it was just so. They knew they had shared a piece of history and wanted to remember the details of their part in it. My mother saved a pile of home-front keepsakes, including the page of the *Boston Globe* (February 22, 1943) with the official rationing chart, showing how many points were assigned to "processed food": applesauce was 6 points for 10 ounces, canned carrots and corn were 8 points, tomatoes were 10 points. She saved several books of unused ration tickets, including those for fuel oil.

It is not clear exactly when the *Sea Runner* returned to San Francisco; probably not as early as August, possibly sometime in September. In any case, Al was not discharged until October. Presumably he remained aboard ship until he was officially detached from service. It was not full separation from the navy; he would remain on the reserve list for another decade, in case of need of recall. It never happened. When he walked down the gangway of the S.S. *Sea Runner* for the last time, his seagoing days were truly over.

On October 15, he sent a telegram to Mary from San Francisco: "Will leave here 0900 Wednesday morning should arrive Boston about 1000 Sunday morning will wire from Chicago. Alfred Mehegan CB." He boarded Southern Pacific train No. 22, on Wednesday, October 17, 1945, bound for Chicago. The serviceman's Pullman fare to Chicago was $9.25. He left Chicago on the New York Central train No. 28, at 1:30 p.m. Saturday the twentieth, and arrived, as promised, Sunday morning. The weather was clear, about 70 degrees—a beautiful fall day in New England.

He did not record in writing his feelings on the journey. But that he saved virtually every scrap of paper—the train reservations, even the Railway Express luggage tags—shows his awareness that this was a historic odyssey, which countless others were taking all around him, all over the western world. His private war was over too, and it was different from my mother's. We do not know all the details of what happened to him out there on that vast ocean as he helped ferry thousands of young men into battle, many of whom never saw home again.

Despite the details in her account of his arrival on leave the previous March, my mother wrote little about the last homecoming, except that Jack, her brother, "took us to the Back Bay Station to meet him." However, my brother, Peter, who was four and a half, has a distinct memory.

"It was the first time I ever saw my mother run," he said. "I didn't know she could run." Boston's Back Bay Station, which has been replaced since then but is in the same location, is a block south of Copley Square, on the edge of the South End. My mother was there, waiting with Peter, Florence, Jack, and Florence Humphreys, our grandmother.

"I remember the train came in," said Peter. "It was a huge train, a steam train, and it looked fifty feet tall. We were waiting, and all of a sudden Mum let go of my hand and started to run down the platform." She had spotted my father coming toward her. To make sure that he would see her, she had bought a smart pink coat. My guess is that she must have nearly bowled him over. He took photographs of her with Peter and Florence shortly after he came home. "He was amazed and delighted with us all," one caption by my mother reads. Another says, "I am in the bright pink coat I bought to wear when we all greeted Al at Back Bay Station." Alas, the photograph is black and white.

• • •

If he was aware of the fate of his half brother Andy Carson, he never mentioned it. Of the 36,000 Americans taken prisoner in the Philippines with Andy in 1942, only 15,000 survived the war. After a year of labor in Japanese coal mines—under conditions actually better than those in the Cabanatuan camp—Andy was liberated and returned home November 1, 1945, aboard the S.S. *Marine Shark*. It was a C4 troop transport, like the *Sea Runner*, and like his half brother's ship a few weeks earlier, it returned to San Francisco. In his memoir, he wrote nothing about a family welcome in Los Angeles. He was twenty-four. He married soon thereafter and eventually moved to San Francisco, where he stayed. Sometime after this move, he cut off most contact with his family. His younger brother Jack last saw him in 1956, at their father's funeral. The reason is not entirely clear, but the horrors of the war were part of it. Writing his personal story, Andy explained in that 1997 book, was part of trying to heal the trauma he had endured: "I still tremble as I write. . . . I built a wall that I could hide behind. The wall is still there. I have never been able to completely tear it down."[8]

There is more to that story, however. Andy married Elaine Maloy, a young woman whom he had known since high school. Jack remembered that the marriage was rocky at first, and that Andy's wife left more than once. Jack recalled, "Andy went after her, to get her to come back," and the second time, "Mom called him a sucker for doing it." In Jack's memory, this was the cause of the breach.

As we have seen, Esther could be quick to slam the door on people. But Andy and Lainie—despite more strife at times—were married for fifty years and had seven children. His memoir is dedicated "to Lainie Maloy, the only angel I ever met in the City of Angels." He eventually finished college and went to law school, but strangely like his half brother, Al, he never practiced law and was a workingman—a union dock worker—all his life. He died in 1998.

· · ·

Although he kept his blue uniform coat and cap, my father cut off and saved the brass buttons on his uniform whites and threw the clothes away. And there was one more thing he needed to do to put an end to his military life. In his papers there is a scrawled receipt: "Nov. 2, 1945. Received from Chief Bts. A. C. Mehegan. 1 Colt 45 cal. pistol #1332868. Anderson C. Gill. Fargo Building, Boston." The Fargo Building, which still stands at 451 D Street, South Boston, was the headquarters of the First Naval District. Given what happened about eight years later, it's probably a good thing that he didn't keep the pistol.

"I just can't remember what we did right after Al came home," my mother wrote in her memoir. "Perhaps we went away for a few days. We should have. But I know he did go to see his father and to accept his offer."[9]

10.

Peace

WHY DID HE GIVE UP THE LAW?

For many years, I could not understand why my father abandoned his dream of a legal career and went back to working for his father. It made no sense to me. He loved the law. He had worked at a killing pace to get his college degree, the first in his family. If there was anything he did *not* want, it was to be a plumber for the rest of his life.

That summer of 1945, my mother wrote:

> Mary Dillon [my father's sister, Mary Rose]told me that Al's father
> hoped that Al would go into the business with him after the war. In
> fact, I think I wrote that to Al. He had always nurtured a dream of
> getting back to school and eventually passing the bar, but of course
> we were married now with two children. I don't know why Al's father
> didn't write to him directly, but it was rather typical. He had told
> Mary that he would make Al a partner in the business. That would
> be his role, not just as another employee. It was a good business and
> promised to be an even better one, though I knew Al did not want to
> make it his lifetime career.[1]

He had worked for his father on and off since adolescence, but not with enthusiasm. He had long wanted to slough off Powers & Mehegan and Southie: go to MIT, be a master navigator, a merchant marine captain, a commissioned naval officer, a lawyer. After all he had done, the places he had been, from Athens and Istanbul on the training ship, to New York, New Orleans, and the West Coast in the merchant marine, to law school, and all across the South Pacific with the navy, and the accomplished people he had known (his law professors, great captains such as John Sorensen and Charles Bamforth, shipmates such as Ted Little and Ed Dullea), how could he go back to installing sinks and toilets in Boston, taking orders from Charlie? Why was that not unthinkable?

Reflecting on it now, I see it is not so hard to understand. For one thing, when the war ended, he and Mary were broke. They had no savings. The base pay in 1945 for a chief petty officer was $138 a month, $1,656 per year, which converts to about $22,698 per year in 2017 dollars. With that, Mary had to pay rent, utility bills, and keep herself and two children in food and clothing. She noted that when Al had been promoted to chief boatswain in the summer of 1944, the promotion had included a much-needed raise. Even so, it appears that she did not have access to all of his pay when he was overseas. On June 4, 1944, he wrote to her:

> In re your faint plea for money. I've written to my father and asked him to advance any amount you need (up to $75) as I have saved that much. The reason I asked him is that my money is tied up in my pay account in San Francisco and I haven't even a dollar in cash out here. Borrow what you need and I'll pay it back when I hit the states again.
>
> *Much love, my dearest of all,*
> Al.
>
> p.s. I can well understand your need. Let me know how much you borrowed.

Now his measly navy pay was ending. He had four dependents, counting himself, and with two children my mother could not work, though she had excellent secretarial skills. To start a legal career, he would need to refresh his basic knowledge, take a bar review course, pass the bar exam, then (or before) take special courses in admiralty law. Only a few firms specialized in that branch of law, most of them were based in New York, and for him to land a job in one of them, with his "night school" degree, might have been hopeless. It would have been years, at best, before he could make a living at the law. No, it was out of the question. As with my grandfather John Humphreys, who had also given up his dream of making a living with the law, Al needed to make money right away to support his young family.

At least, this is one sensible way to understand it. Still, I'm not quite sure. He was capable of persistence in personal goals. He was determined to hold out for a navy commission just before the war came, even turning down the chance to become a merchant marine captain, where there was good money and an avenue to a good career. Perhaps it would have been possible for him to have persisted in the law after the war, if that was where his heart was. My mother would have done all she could to support him in his dreams.

My assumption, knowing his rigorous sense of personal responsibility, is that he could not allow his dreams and ambitions to take precedence over his duty to support his family. He would sublimate his own desires in a way that neither of his parents would ever think of doing. And there was Charlie's offer. How could he justify turning it down?

I sometimes wonder at Charlie's motivation. He knew about my father's law ambitions and might have said, as many fathers would, "Go on, pursue your dreams. Do what you want to do." But no, his idea clearly was to get the son under his thumb again. Later on, my mother would hear a disturbing hypothesis as to his real reason. As her comment "It was rather typical of him" makes clear, that Charlie had not communicated directly with my father made her uneasy. It's as if she could not believe that he had Al's best interest at heart. Her tone foreshadows an intensifying triangular struggle that went on for another fifteen years. She would become indignant at what she saw as Charlie's mistreatment of his only son. But she had to constrain her expression, because she knew that Al loved and respected his father. As the years went by, she grew increasingly concerned at Al's deepening depression, which in her mind was clearly connected to Charlie's treatment of him. But she did not dare to break with her father-in-law, nor counsel my father to see him as she saw him.

Even before the war ended, my father had a physical symptom that sounds, given its weird denouement, as though it must have had a psychological origin. He developed a kind of neuropathy in his back and right leg. In a few V-mail letters, he refers to his foot bothering him.

"It was very much like sciatica," my mother wrote, "because it radiated from the right side of his back to his right leg and down to the toes. It was devilish because it wasn't really a pain. It was just an intense sensitivity, but he couldn't even stand the sheet on his leg at night. The Navy doctor he went to (I think it was ashore in San Francisco) said it was definitely not sciatica because it was not painful enough. At the end of his examination the doctor stood up and said darkly, 'In all my time in the Navy I have never accused anyone of malingering'"—faking an injury, that is, to get out of the war. "Al was devastated that he should be accused of such a thing," my mother wrote.[2]

The problem continued when he came home, and he consulted a Boston doctor, who was also unable to explain it. He suggested a diathermy machine, which uses high-frequency electric current to stimulate heat deep in tissues, a therapy sometimes prescribed for relief of arthritic pain. They rented the machine. It helped a little but not much. "He finally concluded he would have to live with it," my mother wrote. "He was not a complainer anyway. He never wanted to talk about any ailment, nor did he want you to ask about it."[3]

In October 1946, my sister Paula was born. My mother describes the birth as "an easy, fast delivery," and Paula as "an absolutely adorable blond baby." Now they were five in this small apartment in Milton. It was clear that they could not stay there as the children grew older. My mother, having grown up in the dense and crowded West End of Boston, loved the quiet suburban feel of the neighborhood, the flowering crab apples, the lawn, the birds. She bought a bird book, which I still have: Richard H. Pough's *Audubon Bird Guide: Eastern Land Birds*, a 1946 first edition. But then one day my father came home with a plan. They were to move to an apartment in a three-decker house at 133 Fuller Street in Codman Hill, Dorchester, a fairly tough neighborhood. To him, it was a great deal because Charlie owned the house. But my mother was appalled at the idea of moving back to the city. She called it "a regression," by which she probably meant not just toward the inner city but toward the world of Charlie and Southie. Al drove her to look at the place (they had an old green Nash, which he had acquired before the war and put up on blocks for the duration).

"I was aghast at the unloveliness of the street and the surroundings," she wrote. "There was not one tree." Nor was there any place for children to play, except for a vacant lot up the street full of junk cars and broken glass. While the thought of leaving relatively bucolic Milton upset her greatly, my father had no interest in suburbia or in nature. For him, nature was the ocean. He did not care about birds or animals or woods or meadows. He thought her objections unreasonable. The Fuller Street place was a roomy apartment with parquet floors and fine woodwork, in a well-built house. Here was his stubbornness again. It was not always a negative trait; it was just that he kept his own counsel. So she gave in. "Like my generation of women, wives and mothers," she wrote, "we deferred to the husband of the family."[4] They moved in November 1947.

She soon discovered that the whole thing was Charlie's idea. He had an angle. The house was fully occupied, and two elderly brothers lived on the middle floor. Right after the war, there were still controls on the right to evict without cause, since rental housing was so tight. However, there was an exception: You could evict to make room for a veteran. And that was Charlie's plan; he would evict the two old men to make room for Al and Mary. But there was still a catch. You could evict for a veteran *if* the veteran owned the building. So Charlie legally transferred the property to Al's name—it was a fiction; no money changed hands—and then told the tenants upstairs and down that Al owned the building and that they were to pay rent to him. Of course, my parents paid some amount of rent to my grandfather, presumably less than the other tenants.

My father was apparently content with this deal, since the apartment was large and Charlie paid for redecoration. But my mother was sickened over the fate of the two old men. "They took months to leave, with a daughter trying to find a place for them," she wrote. "Where they went I don't know. I was seething, inwardly as I always did. Anything to keep the peace and to maintain my goal of a stress-free family life for Al, always remembering that he had never had one before."[5] For his part, Charlie got a reliable live-in landlord for one of his properties. Al was expected to function as superintendent, which he did. "I remember Dad taking care of the house," my sister Florence said. "I remember his being in the basement with the coal bins, three bins because there were three units. And when the coal truck came, a big chute would come out the back and go through each individual window, and the coal would come down the chute with a great crash, black dust on everything."

•   •   •

If it is true, and no record survives, that Charlie made Al a legal partner in Powers & Mehegan, it did not mean that he, Charlie, was any less in charge. At the beginning, my father was not an office worker; he was doing on-the-job installations and repairs, a working plumber once again. I remember him, in the 1950s, coming home at night in khaki work clothes, tired and grimy. However, in addition to his labor, he had extra value because his master plumber's license enabled the firm to secure business for which it would not otherwise be a credible bidder. Charlie was not a licensed plumber. "That was the license that kept the shop going," Florence said. "Dad was the license for that shop."

An old business card, found in his papers, indicates that at least putatively he was more than just one of the plumbers:

Tel. SOuth Boston 8-4630

POWERS & MEHEGAN Co.
INCORPORATED
Plumbing, Heating and Gas Fitting
Oil and Specialty Piping

Alfred C. Mehegan   500 Broadway
                                                    South Boston, Mass.

It was never a big business. They had only a handful of full-timers
besides my father; the rest they would hire at the union hall for specific
jobs. Still, there was one steady source of business in the postwar period:
the vast expansion of the Catholic Archdiocese of Boston. As Florence
put it, "There were a lot of church jobs they got because of Dickie. He
was a friend of Dickie."

"He" was Charlie. "Dickie" was Richard Cardinal Cushing
(1895–1970), archbishop of Boston. Bostonians over a certain age will
remember the legendary lantern-jawed cardinal with the gravel voice.
Non-Bostonians may remember him as the old prelate who celebrated
the requiem Mass for President John F. Kennedy, in the Cathedral of St.
Matthew, Washington, November 25, 1963. He was a longtime friend of
the Kennedy family. At the end of the Mass, he called out, in his Jimmy
Durante voice, "May the angels, dear Jack, lead you into paradise."

Cushing's nickname in the old neighborhood really was Dickie. He
was almost exactly Charlie's age. They had been kids together at Gate
of Heaven Parish in South Boston, where Charlie and Esther had been
married, and their fathers both worked for the Boston Elevated Railway,
the predecessor of today's MBTA. John Mehegan was a motorman and
Patrick Cushing was a blacksmith who worked on the very streetcars
that John drove. Dickie Cushing had gone to the Oliver Hazard Perry
School, where my father went later, and dropped out of South Boston
High School on account of truancy. How friendly he and Charlie

Mehegan had been as youths is uncertain—I never heard that they had been pals. But parishes were close-knit social settings; everybody knew everybody else. Dickie, after he dropped out of high school, worked as a janitor at the parish hall, and managed its bowling alley. He probably knew the notorious story of Charlie and Esther but did not hold it against Powers & Mehegan later. He went to Boston College High School, a Jesuit school, then to Boston College, with the encouragement and financial support of a cousin, a priest. He graduated with honors, went on to seminary and ordination, and his career eventually took off. He was made archbishop of Boston in 1943, and the cardinal of Boston in 1958.

With the postwar baby boom, the general economic expansion, and the massive move of people from the cities to the suburbs, the number of Greater Boston parishes (each with a church, a rectory, and possibly a school or other ancillary buildings, or a cemetery) grew from 325 in 1944 to 411 in the mid-1960s. At the same time, there was a similar expansion of properties owned and run by orders of nuns, monks, or friars. These included many high schools and hospitals.

For Powers & Mehegan, church business (along with government work—Charlie had political friends as well) was always a big part of the whole, both installation and repair. Florence recalled accompanying my father on a job at a convent. She said, "It might have been in Jamaica Plain," a neighborhood of Boston. "He had to go into every one of the nuns' cells, tiny little rooms, to bleed the radiators, with a radiator key—remember the radiator key that you could borrow and use for a skate key? He had it on his key chain. We must have gone into forty little rooms and bled the radiators, and the nuns thought he was so sweet and fussed over me, and wanted me to come down and have cookies and milk."

Powers & Mehegan did not get all the church business, of course—no one firm could—but there was plenty of work, very close by, and it was not hard to get. For one thing, under laws passed with pressure from the Catholic bishops in the 1880s, the archbishop was (and still is) the "corporation sole." That is, he is the personal owner of every square inch of diocesan property, and every brick and pane of glass, in every church building. The main reason for this system was to prevent schism. When many Catholics were enraged at the archdiocesan "reconfiguration" (i.e., parish closings) in Boston of a few years ago, they could furiously occupy the closed churches—as some did—but they could not split off, start their own Catholic diocese, and take the churches with them. The archbishop owns the real estate. The power of the corporation sole also means that the archbishop can hire anyone he wants to do a job: He need not hire the lowest bidder, indeed he need not solicit bids. Under this system, personal contacts were important. Charlie was a friend of Dickie's, as well as of many pastors, monsignors, and mothers superior, and the business flowed.

• • •

Al and Mary settled in on Fuller Street. Then Charlie pulled another one. He informed my parents that he intended to evict the family, named Graves, who lived on the first floor—they were Irish Quakers—and that Mary Rose and husband Jimmy Dillon and their children would be moving in. The law had changed: You could evict to make room for a veteran even if he was not an owner, and Jimmy was the veteran. My father was nominally the owner, so Charlie told him he would have to deliver the bad news to the Graveses. My mother was horrified. It was worse than the case of the two elderly brothers because she had become friendly with the Graves family; furthermore, they were model tenants. When my father gave them the news, they were so angry that they refused to speak to my parents for the time they remained in the house.

Although my father did not want to live in the same house with his original family, as he had done until he was married, he loved Mary Rose and was reconciled with the idea. But it was all a ruse to get around the law. My father had been tricked into telling the Graveses a lie. After they moved, it was not Mary Rose and Jimmy who moved in. It was Julia, my father's stepmother. She had sunk into alcoholism, and Charlie wanted to get her out of 1115 Adams Street. As the final act of this long marriage of bitterness and silence, he moved her into 133 Fuller Street, along with her unmarried sister Mamie. The justification for this plan, attributed to Charlie, was that "Alfred knows how to handle Julia." It was true that my father loved his stepmother and would not be unkind to her. Henceforth she was to become his, and my mother's, problem.

"Julia moved in," my mother wrote, "and my lifestyle took a radical change. No longer did I have any privacy. Everything I did was subject to comment and analysis. When I went to the store, she would come up and take everything out of the bags. Then she would call Mary Rose (she decided she would use our phone instead of getting one of her own) and tell Mary everything I had bought."[6] The lock on the door was weak and Julia was able to push the door open. My father put a strong dead bolt on it to give my mother some peace. Then one day Julia was drunk and banging on the door, trying to push it open. But my mother had locked it and pretended not to be home. Later, Julia said to her darkly, "If I thought you put that lock on the door to keep me out, I'd break it down."[7]

• • •

My mother was pregnant that spring of 1948, and I was born in October. Meanwhile, the neighborhood situation, in her eyes, went from bad to worse. There was no place to play except the street. Six-year-old Peter was getting into fights. One day the school (the Robert Swan School, which he and Florence both attended) called to say he had hit a girl in the head with a rock. Another time he came home with his head bleeding from a rock. The local postman had seen the fight, bandaged his head, and brought him home. Mrs. Stravinsky, the crazy lady next door, would throw pans of water on children if they passed within range of her porch, and even hammered spikes into a board and pushed it through the hedge in hopes one of us would be injured. My mother yanked the board out and went to the police in a rage, but they told her they could do nothing so long as no one was hurt.

The tenants upstairs moved out and were replaced by George

McManus, my father's cousin, and his wife and children. They were kind people whom my mother liked. Still, now my father had cousins above and his alcoholic stepmother below. I have only my mother's account of all this, but the effect on my father, to have his family life invaded and compressed in this way, was evidently disturbing. Nor was this all. There was trouble at work.

"He was unhappy working for his father," my mother wrote, "because he had discovered that far from being a prospective partner, he was not even being treated like the other employees. Arthur Penney, for example, got a paid two-week vacation every year and Al actually got none at all."[8] Arthur Penney, mentioned above, was a childhood friend of my father's, and they remained close all their lives.

My father worked six days a week. Once he managed to get the family away for a weekend on Cape Cod. "We went down to Sandwich," Florence recalled. "We were going to sleep overnight, and we stayed in one of those cabins. You [that is, me] were in a playpen. Little cabins. It was on Route 6A—Route 6 was not finished then. And he got a call to come back, and we packed up and came back, and Mum was *so mad* at Grandpa."

It began to take a toll. "Al's leg was still bothering him," my mother wrote, "and he began to see a doctor again about it. I think it was that summer [of 1949] that he began to see Dr. Arnot for depression."[9]

• • •

Robert E. Arnot, M.D. (1917–2002), was a Wellesley psychiatrist. I do not know how my father heard about him; perhaps he was referred by the doctor he had consulted about his leg, or possibly by a priest. Arnot practiced in Wellesley and at St. Elizabeth's Hospital in Brighton. Born in Montana, a 1940 graduate of Harvard Medical School, he was a Catholic convert. He was an early proponent and practitioner of electric shock therapy and in some cases of partial lobotomy. That a person with my father's working-class background, who hated to get medical attention of any kind and tried to tough out any illness, would go to a psychiatrist indicates how troubled he had become. I do not know how long he went to Arnot, nor what sort of therapy was provided at the start. If it was talk therapy, it was no cure, because a few months later came the Christmas "heart attack."

We lived in St. Matthew's parish. The Spanish-mission-style brick church on Stanton Street had a school, but my mother did not enroll her children in it. She was wary of parish schools, having had the childhood experience in St. Joseph's School in the West End of bigotry toward Protestants and Jews. Some of the Catholic neighbors needled her about it, but she knew what she was doing, telling one of them, "I want my children to be with a mix of children so that they will learn tolerance for others."[10]

"That Christmas Day" of 1949, she wrote, "I went to early Mass and Al went to the 11:30 alone, when I got a telephone call from a doctor's office saying that Al had had a spell in church, which they thought at first was a heart attack." He had been carried out of church and taken to a local doctor's office (it is not clear how it would have been open on Christmas Day—perhaps the doctor was at the Mass). She raced to the office, which was near the church. "I was terribly upset, wondering what I would find, but the doctor said he felt it was just a nervous spell. He had checked out fine and it had not been a heart attack."[11]

She does not mention in her account—perhaps she had forgotten—that he was not alone. Peter was with him. "I do remember the episode at St. Matthew's," Peter said. "I remember being scared, and being out on the sidewalk, and someone attending to him. It happened a second time, at Fenway Park. He could not stand to be in crowds. I remember him back under the stands and someone helping him." There was another tense moment many years later, which I remember. It happened at Peter's college commencement at Boston University, in the spring of 1964, which was held at Nickerson Field, the old Boston Braves stadium. The commencement speaker was Walter Lippmann, the syndicated columnist. We had to sit back in the stadium, which was packed, at the end of a row near an exit because my father was anxious. He kept looking back at the exit as if he might have to make a run for it.

The term for fear of crowds is *enochlophobia*. If he had this disorder, where did it come from? My mother never mentioned it, in writing or otherwise, so it must not have manifested itself before the war. He went to church every Sunday in my lifetime, and I never remember him being anxious or reluctant about it, even on high holidays. Churches then were usually crowded. Moreover, he had served on two troop ships packed with men for more than a year.

I am inclined to think the anxiety was not constant but periodic, related to other, immediate pressures in his life—not so much crowds, perhaps, as a feeling of being hemmed in with no room to move, not physically so much as emotionally. The specific anxieties some enochlophobes have include feelings of being small and insignificant or being unable to block out the personalities and emotions of people crowding in on them.

Whatever was the cause, the Christmas Day incident had a strange result. "There was the most astonishing aftermath," My mother recalled. "His leg, which had been bothering him since he was in the Navy four years previously, never bothered him again."[12]

• • •

The situation with Julia worsened. My mother wrote, "Julia used to come into our apartment early in the morning (the children would of course let her in), and one morning when I opened my eyes there she was, sitting at the bottom of our bed and us in it." One day, my mother went downtown to shop. Standing on the subway platform at Washington station, later renamed Downtown Crossing, she watched a train rumbling in and thought, "'If I step in front of that train I'll never see her again,' and then I knew I had to do something." She went to her doctor, and when he tried to take her blood pressure, her heart was racing so fast that he couldn't take it. "What is troubling you?" he asked, and when the story spilled out, he said, "I am going to tell you what to do. Move out of that house at once."[13]

My father's family's craziness, which he had escaped for years by going to sea, was now threatening to push his own family in front of a train. He knew what a strain it all was on my mother and had put the stronger lock on the door to keep Julia out. But now he saw that he needed to do more. The old memory, which he had mentioned in the V-mail letter, of having a place on the South Shore of Boston, where they could hear the sound of the ocean, came back to him, and he asked my mother how she would feel about making such a move.

She was thrilled at the idea, even though at first he only meant a place for the summer. He went to Scituate, about twenty miles south of Boston and ten miles south of Pemberton, apparently alone. With his $600 navy separation bonus, he bought a 5,000-square-foot wooded lot in the Sand Hills neighborhood, no more than a quarter mile from the ocean. His old Northeastern classmate Tom Sheehan, who had been on the double date at the yacht club where the drunk had tumbled down the stairs, helped him clear trees from the site. In the end, he and my mother decided to build a small year-round house, not a summer place. Gene Blanchard, a local builder who became a good friend, began work in October 1950, and we moved to Scituate in February 1951. The little Cape Cod–style house, about eight hundred square feet, is the first home I can remember.

Fuller Street and the Charlie-Julia scene were left behind at last, and I am sure my father felt that the troubles were over: my mother would finally be happy with her situation; their family of six could thrive on a quiet street far from gritty Codman Hill, a short walk from the beach and within earshot of the calm or roiling ocean; and he would be happy too. Peter was nine, Florence seven, Paula four, and I two. In Scituate we grew up, and all but me have stayed. But it was not Shangri-La. For one thing, my father was still tied to Powers & Mehegan.

Helping a friend open a Hull summer cottage, spring 1938.

(Author's collection)

The engaged couple, summer of 1940.

(Peter Mehegan collection).

Northeastern University
Law School portrait, 1940.

(Author's collection)

In a 1939 publicity photo for the Red Feather fund drive, Mary places a
feather in a Boston policeman's cap. (Paula Weeks collection)

Boatswain Mehegan's Navy portrait, 1943.

(Author's collection)

U.S.S. *Sea Runner*, Al's second Navy ship, a C-3 cargo/troop transport similar to U.S.S. *Young America*, 1945.

(Author's collection)

With a friend at the Backstage Nightclub, San Francisco, April 1944. The Clark Cable moustache was temporary. (Author's collection)

Naval Guard Officers of S.S. *Young America*, 1944. Chief Boatswain Mehegan at far left, Commander Theodore H. Little, third from right. Gunnery Officer Ed Dullea second from right. (Author's collection)

Mary with Peter and Florence, October 1945. "I am in the bright pink coat I bought to wear when we all greeted Al at Back Bay Station when the war ended." (Author's collection)

(*Below*) "The terrible war was over." With Mary, Peter, and Florence by the Annisquam River, Gloucester, 1946. (Author's collection)

11.

The Townies

THAT'S WHAT SOME PERMANENT Scituate residents called themselves—
Townies—as distinct from the summer folk who had cottages on or
near the ocean. Before they built the house at 65 Seaview Avenue, my
parents drove there at night in the winter to get a sense of the number of
year-round residents. It turned out that there was no year-round house
on their street nearer the ocean. All those to the east were summer
cottages. That was fine with them. The houses were close together,
though not as close as on Fuller Street.

Sand Hills was and still is a densely built neighborhood of smaller
houses, many of them winterized summer cottages. The neighborhood—
lightly wooded but not forested—is barely above sea level, and at the
eastern end of aptly named Seaview Avenue there is wetland separated
from the ocean only by a barrier beach with a street, Turner Road,
that runs along it, lined with cottages on both sides. These houses
are frequently pummeled and demolished (and rebuilt thereafter) by
hurricanes and winter storms, annually observed nowadays by TV news
video crews. The sea is rising inexorably, by as much as eight inches
since 1900 and probably by a foot by 2100, and most of these houses
will disappear. Seaview Avenue, however, will remain, since it is sharply
uphill to the west. Number 65 was well above storm level and still is.

Sand Hills and adjacent neighborhoods never had seaside mansions
on the lavish scale of Martha's Vineyard or parts of Cape Cod. Older
houses have been replaced and sometimes expanded, but you don't see

teardowns replaced by monstrosities—perhaps because the lots are so small. Scituate is an old colonial-era town, settled in 1630, but by the late 1800s it had not been a Yankee bastion for a long time. The Yankees were and are still there, to be sure, but by the twentieth century they were thin on the ground nearest the ocean, greatly outnumbered by the Irish. In the late nineteenth and early twentieth centuries, beachfront areas south of Boston saw an influx of middle-class Irish Americans, especially in the summer. Though there were Italians, French, and a few Jews, Scituate was jokingly called "the Irish Riviera." When our family moved in, the names of our closest neighbors included Donnelly, Dooley, Kelly, McDonough, Rourke, Burke, Dwyer, Linehan, Flanagan, McGrath, and Connolly.

• • •

My mother immediately made friends and kept them all of her and their lives: Frances Kelly, Dorothy Cole, Sally McGrath, Bette Morwick, many others. My father made friends too, though not so many, and not so close. There were the husbands of my mother's friends, and others of his own, such as Gene Blanchard, who built the house, and Gene's laconic brother, Alvin. However, my father did not seem to have, at least not locally, well-educated friends—no lawyers or other professionals. My parents went to church at St. Mary's of the Nativity in Scituate Harbor. My mother joined the Ladies Sodality, and my father was at least nominally part of the Holy Name Society, the Catholic men's group. He was a charter member of the Knights of Columbus, the Catholic fraternal organization, and also joined the local post (Number 3169) of the Veterans of Foreign Wars. They went to different Sunday Masses, as they always had: my mother to the earliest, my father to the latest.

They had social lives, but my mother had more than my father did. Despite his membership in the Knights and VFW, he was not a clubbable person; he did not serve on boards, work on fund-raising or other community projects, or go to a lot of meetings. He did not coach Little League or teach Sunday school or volunteer for the PTA. He did not hunt or fish or play sports. He read some. He took care of the house and yard when we were too little to help. This was purely practical care; he had no interest in landscaping or gardening. Mostly, he worked. My sense was that he had little time for anything else, or did not make time.

Usually he would drive to work, twenty-five miles, mostly on Route 3, the coastal highway, now Route 3A, at least an hour's drive each way, longer in bad traffic. This was before the burst of postwar highway building: There was no Route 3 from Boston to Cape Cod, which today grazes Scituate, nor were there Interstates 95, 93, and 90, the Massachusetts Turnpike. There was a train between Boston and Scituate, the New Haven Railroad, and sometimes he went to work that way, getting off at South Station and taking the subway to 500 Broadway, unless he walked. But he spent a lot of time in the car, and we never had more than one, so my mother was usually carless during the week. That was not an insurmountable problem; she could and often did walk a mile or so (with us in tow) to Scituate Harbor, the retail area, where there was a post office and grocery and other stores.

In 1953, my parents got a surprising invitation: to the wedding of Ted Little, my father's naval commander on the S.S. *Young America*. Though Ted lived in Clarkston, Washington, in the eastern part of the state, he had met and was to marry Eve Grace Rockwell of West Dennis, Massachusetts. They were forty-six and forty-four, respectively. She was a graphic artist and a distant relative of the painter Norman Rockwell. The wedding was held February 14, 1953, at St. Paul's Episcopal Church in Brookline.

Ted Little was the most senior of my father's navy shipmates that my mother was to meet, and the occasion was a revelation to her about the quality of their friendship. She wrote:

> When we arrived at the church and the usher asked us, "Bride or groom?", and Al said, "groom," he brought us down the aisle to the very first pew. Al and I both thought it was a mistake when we saw the church filling up behind us, so Al spoke to one of the ushers and said, "We are not Commander Little's family and perhaps we should sit farther back." The usher said, "Of course" and Al and I

went practically to the back of the church. After a few minutes the usher came up to us and said, "Commander Little wants you to sit in the front pew," and though bewildered, we followed him back. It was really amazing but it turned out later at the reception that he had no family. We were his family. It was such a compliment to Al.[1]

Ted Little had a prominent postwar career in Washington state, among other things as tribal attorney for the Nez Percé Indian nation, and was instrumental in the creation of the Nez Perce National Historical Park. I have sometimes thought that had he been based in New England, he might have helped my father get his legal career back on track; at least he would have encouraged him and helped him in any he could. In Boston or Scituate, there were no others like him in my parents' social circle, that I can recall, which remains to me something of a puzzle. Perhaps there was just no way to meet such persons as Ted outside the accidents of wartime. And the plumbing business had its limits in social diversity.

• • •

It is difficult to keep the focus on my father at this point in the story because, while my mother wrote so much and in such detail, you might have noticed that his voice has disappeared. There are no letters, no journals, not a written scrap from after the war—only ours and my mother's memories of his acts and words. Those are considerable, not in contradiction to the character we have seen thus far, and they permit reasonable inferences. Still, a kind of scrim remains. What was he thinking and feeling? Exactly why did he do this or that? Informed guesses are all that I have.

• • •

In the summer at our seaside home, we could walk to the beach, which we did most days in good weather. There were good times at that beach. Paula was five that first summer and she remembers it as paradise compared to Dorchester. There is a grainy home movie of me "diving" off a rowboat pulled well up on the soft sand, pretending that I was diving into water, and the rest of us walking up the beach. Sometimes my father would go there with us on summer weekends. He was not the swimmer his mother was, but he did go in when it was not too cold, and as always, he was in the best of moods near, on, or in the ocean. "I remember Dad teaching me to swim in Sand Hills," Peter said. "He took me out in the deeper water, holding me up, and showed me how to swim. That was how I learned, not in swimming lessons."

He didn't have much free time. He was still working five and a half, or sometimes six, days a week. Much of it was still manual labor on construction jobs, but he also had moved into preparing bids. Contract estimating would become his specialty. In November 1951, for example, Powers & Mehegan was the low bidder on a job installing boilers in several buildings at the City of Boston Hospital Division. The bid was $3,940, a thousand dollars lower than the next lowest. P&M got the job.

The promised partnership in Powers & Mehegan, and the dream of succession, was a fiction. As my mother tells it, Charlie's treatment of his only son was a blend of exploitation and disparagement. He was grudging about time off, even for the move to Scituate, and loaded my father with extra duties: for example, making him each year deliver turkeys to valued customers on Christmas Eve, so that he would arrive home at eleven p.m. or later. Charlie needed my father's skills, license, and prodigious capacity for work. But it seemed to my mother, as she said above, that my grandfather did not think much of his son, and that others in the older man's circle had adopted that view.

She wrote, "One time Mr. Mehegan had told the pastor at St. Gregory's [the parish church near the Mehegan home in Dorchester] that Al would go there to repair something that had broken down, and Al forgot to go. The priest called him at home, and when Al got there, he was irate. He berated him for not coming as his father had promised and then he said, 'You'll never be the man your father is.' Al was heartbroken when he told me and I consoled him by saying, 'Thank

God you'll never be the man your father is,' though he didn't know what I was talking about."

Soon after our family moved to Scituate, a friend of Charlie's, a building inspector, built a house in the town, and Charlie, to return a favor (one can easily imagine an inspector's favor), volunteered my father to install the furnace, for free. He was not given time off to do this, and had to do it nights and weekends, which meant that the work went slowly. "One night their daughter came to our house," my mother wrote, "and rapped furiously on the door. 'Where is he?' she wanted to know. 'He promised to be at our house two hours ago and he isn't there yet,' and she added, 'He's nothing like his father.'

"Al heard one time at the union hall that someone had said, 'Charlie Mehegan is such a great guy but his son is an S.O.B.,' because if Mr. Mehegan let anyone go, he would leave a note for Al telling him to fire the person, while he went off with his yacht club cronies."[2]

One can infer the effect this would have on one who could not fathom, or refused to see, that he was being ill-used. As I wrote earlier, my father never blamed other people for his problems. He might hold them responsible for their own, but never for his. He was like Boxer, the draft horse in George Orwell's *Animal Farm:* "His answer to every problem, every setback, was 'I will work harder!'—which he had adopted as his personal motto."[3] Al loved his father, and craved love in return as much as any son could, and never stopped trying to measure up.

This fraught personal history reminds me of the memoir of the Irish writer John McGahern, whose father was a cold, arrogant, and brutal man.[4] John McGahern saw the truth about Frank McGahern clearly and broke free of him and his world, but his younger brother, Frankie (named after his father), was psychologically crushed and died of alcoholism in his fifties. In a telephone interview about his book, for a 2006 *Boston Globe* profile, John McGahern said to me of his father, "He never had any power over me. But poor Frankie was different. He admired my father." Charlie, it seems, had implicit emotional power over Alfred. What we should expect in a situation like this, where the ill-used person internalizes responsibility for mistreatment, perhaps even feels that he deserves it, would be deepening depression. And that is what happened.

The timing of my father's emotional illness is hard to plot, because aside from her single mention above of his going to see Robert Arnot for depression in 1949, my mother did not write down the details. She told us some things, and some we witnessed, but the exact arc is imprecise. My sense is that he would go to Dr. Arnot for a while, then stop, and then go again. One thing is clear: In these early years in Scituate, my father's internal stress and dissatisfaction over his work situation increased. In the meantime, there was another crisis, the last thing they would have expected in their peaceful nest by the sea.

We lived at 65 Seaview Avenue for only three and a half years. In September 1954, we moved to another new-built house, at 24 Blanchard Road, about two miles due south, almost exactly the same distance from the beach. We could see the ocean from our windows. One reason for this move was that the little Cape on Seaview Avenue was too small for a family of six. My parents had considered enlarging it but concluded that the lot, at five thousand square feet, was too small. But there was a bigger reason for moving.

The people in the next house to the west, at 61 Seaview, were a young couple with two small sons and a set of elderly parents. They had an Irish name, but here I'm going to call them the Neighbors. As their address suggests, their low white house, though it was close, was not the next lot, which would have been 63. However, sometime after my parents built their house and moved in, the Neighbors bought the narrow lot between. And one day, a truck arrived towing a mobile home, which it backed onto the site. It was apparently to be occupied by the senior generation.

Soon afterward, my father asked for a Veterans Administration assessment of the value of our property, which as a veteran he was entitled to at no cost. The VA inspector came, looked over the property, then pointed to the mobile home and asked, "Is that a permanent installation?" When my father said that it was, the inspector said, "Well, in that case I have to reduce the value of your house by 20 percent." It was not a shabby trailer, but its presence apparently had an implication of transience. Soon the other year-round residents were in an uproar, and a lawyer who lived across the street got up a petition to the town asking that the mobile home be removed because of its negative effect on property values. My parents signed it.

My mother wrote about this saga in exhaustive detail, more than once, and even saved newspaper clippings about it. The abbreviated narrative is that the town zoning board ordered the trailer removed, and the Neighbors sued the town and lost—the mobile home had to go. During this protracted squabble, the Neighbor wife and her mother conducted a campaign of screaming at my mother, whom they saw as the instigator, whenever they saw her outside. "Who do you think you are!" the woman yelled. "You think you're better than we are! You think we're trailer trash!" This was the first time my mother had heard this term. The woman repeatedly threatened to get even with my parents. In one of her diatribes, she screamed, "We will sell our house to a *nigger* and then you'll regret what you have done to us!"[5] This kind of talk— the content more than the tone—appalled my mother, who abhorred racial, ethnic, or religious prejudice. (I still have her well-worn copy of Gordon W. Allport's classic, *The Nature of Prejudice.*[6]) "Every time I went out in the yard to hang out my clothes," she wrote, "they would both start yelling at me. I suppose it enraged them that I never answered them back because they were itching for a fight."[7]

They nearly got their wish. One weekday afternoon, the husband, whom my mother described as "strange and sullen," was out in yard, apparently drunk, yelling that he had a gun and was going to kill my father. Paula remembers seeing the gun. My terrified mother called my father at work and told him not to come home. He told her, if she didn't think of it on her own, to call the police. He must have driven eighty miles an hour from South Boston, because not long afterward, my mother's friend Sally McGrath called in a panic to say that my father had showed up at her house and asked Paul, her husband, if he had a gun. The McGraths lived around the corner. He had said in desperation, "I have to protect my family from that madman."[8] Quick-thinking Paul said he did not have a gun, although he actually did. Sometime during this nightmarish episode, my mother called the police.

When my father got home, the police were there. Though I was only about five at the time, I vividly remember the cruiser backed into the Neighbors' driveway, a policeman standing holding the door open, and the man in an undershirt dropping heavily into the backseat.

It occurs to me now how fortunate it was that Paul McGrath had not lent his pistol, and that my father had turned in his own weapon in 1945 and had not been home when the threat occurred. He knew how to shoot straight; it could have been the Gunfight at the Seaview Corral. As for why he would have thought to get a gun and confront the Neighbor himself, rather than let the police handle it, it was like him to behave as though it was his responsibility, no one else's, to meet directly this threat to his family. He knew the Neighbor's type, after all. Peter said recently of the man with the gun, "He was just like the Irish punks Dad had grown up with in Southie."

The irony, of course, was that the contretemps was worse than anything on Fuller Street. Not even crazy Mrs. Stravinsky, with her pans of water and her plank with the spikes in it, had threatened to shoot us. Worn down by the vitriol and the tension, my mother concluded that they had to get out. My father, a gutsy, stand-your-ground kind of guy, was reluctant. "You know," he said to her, "you can't keep moving away from people."[9] But he heard that Gene Blanchard had available lots on a new dead-end street on the other side of town, and the two men soon agreed on a design and a price. The Seaview Avenue house was put on the market and eventually sold for $10,600 — "the exact amount that it had cost us," my mother wrote, "so we sold it at a loss after deducting the agent's fee."[10] We moved to the new house, also a Cape Cod style, in September 1954. From oldest to youngest, we were twelve, ten, eight, and six. My parents were forty-three.

12.

Sweet and Bitter

THE NEW HOUSE AT 24 Blanchard Road (Gene Blanchard had bought the land, laid out a street, and given it his own name), was twice the size of the old house, on a lot three times as large. My parents again thought, or hoped, that finally here they could be peaceful and happy. Besides nearby Peggotty Beach, about a twenty-minute walk, we were about the same distance from Scituate Harbor as we had been, and even closer to St. Mary's church. Jenkins Elementary School, which Paula and I would attend, was a fifteen-minute walk. Nearby were ponds for fishing and ice-skating, and at the Scituate Country Club, also within a short walk, we could coast on sleds in the winter. My parents got on pretty well with all the neighbors.

. . .

From our new house, the Scituate Coast Guard Station at the top of First Cliff was within sight, and from our windows we could see the marine storm-warning flags above the cupola. My father would look north on stormy days, spy a single red pennant, and say, "Small craft warnings are up." Or two pennants: "gale warning"; one red square flag with a black square centered: "storm / whole gale warning"; two flags: "hurricane."

He was stimulated and excited by dramatic weather, perhaps a memory of the great hurricane at sea. After storms, we would walk the beaches and see what had washed ashore. Usually it was driftwood, dead gulls or fish, skate egg cases, sea glass, bits of weathered rope, and wooden lobster traps and buoys. We kept our eyes down, hoping to come upon a blob of ambergris, a rare and valuable substance emitted by sperm whales and sometimes thrown up by the ocean, but we never did. In the late-winter blizzard of March 17, 1956, the flotsam was a ship. An Italian freighter named *Etrusco* (originally *Fort Poplar*, a Canadian-built World War II Liberty ship) was driven aground near the Scituate Lighthouse. Amid great excitement, my father took us all to see it. He enjoyed the event enormously (all the crewmen were rescued) and could share with us his expert's eye for what had happened and how. To us it looked like a gigantic rusty beached whale, awkward and ugly. Several months later, after it was stripped of all excess weight, it was hauled off the shore by tugboats at an astronomical spring tide.

Besides sometimes going to the beach with us in summer (never by himself), my father would also act as impresario of summer clambakes. In a new twenty-five-gallon galvanized steel barrel (what we then called an "ash can") he would lay stones and a few inches of water, a layer of rockweed, which we were detailed to harvest at the beach, and above that lobsters, clams, corn on the cob, potatoes, and possibly other foods, each course separated by a layer of seaweed. The water in the bottom would boil and cook the food with steam. The heat source would be a propane burner normally used to melt lead to caulk the joints in cast-iron plumbing pipe. He loved these times, which were family, not neighborhood, affairs, with the ocean in sight and the smell of steamed seaweed in our noses. He was happy, which brightened everyone's mood, especially my mother's.

Between our street and Peggotty Beach, the crown of which was covered with smooth granite oval stones, lay a tidal salt marsh. The estuary creek snaked and widened northward, a silvery river, and drained into the harbor, about three-quarters of a mile away, which meant that at high tide, you could row or motor a small boat right to the end of our street, perhaps fifty yards from our house. When I first saw Martin Johnson Heade's classic paintings of North Shore marshes, they reminded me of "our" marsh, minus the haystacks. The marsh itself was thick with eelgrass, spartina, and marsh heather, and in the water were horseshoe crabs, razor clams, and bait fish. At low tide, the air was heavy with a rich salty humus smell, and at unusually high tides, the marsh filled to the brim, like an inland lake, delivering flotsam and organic wrack, such as slipper shells, limpets, clams and all manner of driftwood, to the end of the street. Blanchard Road was built on filled marsh; today it would never be legal, but for us at the time there was a sense of drama to the tidewater so near. One spring the tide was so high that a friend of Peter's rowed a boat up to the back door to call for him. In winter, the marsh was filled with car-sized blocks of ice. Of course the cellar was often full of water, and we would hear the motor of the sump pump going on every thirty seconds or so, pumping the water through a hose into the backyard.

My parents had never had a boat in their marriage, though my father remained a life member of the South Boston Yacht Club. Sometime about 1955, he brought home, in the back of the Powers & Mehegan pickup truck, a wooden skiff that had been at Charlie's summer cottage in Wheeler Point, Gloucester. I do not know exactly how this happened. Was it a little-used extra boat? Did Grandpa buy a new one and not need the old? Did my father pay his father something for it? I know now, though I didn't then, that it was a sixteen-foot Lowell Amesbury skiff. Today I own a larger version of it, the Salisbury skiff.

For all of us, that little rowing skiff was a pinpoint of light in the midst of a darkening time. It was the first boat my father had had since *Mohawk*. He organized us in the backyard to sand and paint it, and caulk the bottom seams with oakum and caulking compound. He wore an old brown yachtsman's cap and called himself the captain. When it was ready the first summer we had it, we rolled it down the street on a wooden dolly and launched it at high tide. With the excitement, neighborhood kids following and dogs barking, you would have thought it was the *Queen Mary*.

It was not big enough to hold all six of us at once. I remember rowing down the creek on a flowing tide, my father seated in the stern sheets, my mother in the bow, and at least two of us at the oars. He taught us proper rowing technique, port from starboard, and such terms as "gunwales," "thwarts," and "catching a crab"—an oar slipping out of the oarlock—and to refer to the boat as "she." She never had a name. We rowed under the old bridge on Edward Foster Road into the harbor, crowded with moored boats of all sizes, including lobster boats, bottom draggers, and pleasure craft. Sometimes we anchored and swam (my parents did not), or pulled ashore and picnicked on the sand spit across from the town pier, watching the big cruisers and sailing yachts go by, not envying them a bit.

To be out on a boat with your family seemed to be completely delightful, simple as it was. We each have memories of that little vessel. Peter, for example: "We were pulling the boat up in the marsh [at the end of the street], and Dad was in the stern, and he told me to pull the boat, or maybe I did it without him telling me, and he went right over the transom into the water. It was high tide, maybe three or four feet deep. He came up sputtering and laughing hysterically." Anything to do with salt water made him happy, and if they had had any money at all, we might have done more. We might have joined the Scituate Yacht Club, or at least had a small sailboat, like *Mohawk,* and he would have taught us to sail. But there was no money for such things. I can't imagine how, or if, he paid the South Boston club dues in those years.

Then came an incident with the boat, a little dark cloud. Paula recalled, "One time he came out of his bedroom into the living room. He was in his bathrobe; he wasn't dressed. He looked out the window at the marsh, and he put his hand on the top of my head—he would always put his hand on the top of my head, pat me like I was a little puppy—and he said to me, 'Do we have a boat?' And I said, 'Yes we do.'"

He did not remember the boat. When I heard at the time that he did not remember the boat, I did not believe it; how was it possible? I thought he was playing some kind of prank. Several of us left the house with him and we walked to the marsh at the end of the street. There, pulled up in the mud amid the eelgrass, was the boat. He stood quietly with his excellent posture, hands in the pockets of the heavy navy-blue CPO shirt, untucked, that he often wore, and stared at it. I did not understand what was going on; I still thought it was a joke. But as Paula now says, "He was trying to piece his memory back together." He was suffering the side effects of shock treatments.

• • •

His depression had deepened. In the mid-1950s, even before we moved from Seaview Avenue, he fell into such a dark hole that for a while he could not work. The exact timing of this is unclear, but it seems that it was happening, or beginning, roughly in the same period as the mobile-home crisis, or perhaps just after. Other than the incident of the boat, I have no clear memory for details of this time, but my siblings remember it well. The worst of it must have been after the move; he could not have handled the building and financing of the new house, and the move itself, had he been in that condition.

"He kind of disappeared," Florence said, using a chilling word. "We were still little. I was maybe eleven." Florence turned eleven in November 1954, about two months after we moved to Blanchard Road. "He'd be in his room. He didn't work for a long time. He *couldn't* work. Mum told me later, I think, that Grandpa still paid Dad, even though he didn't work, which was really amazing." It *is* in surprising contrast with my mother's consistent view of her father-in-law. In her memoir she wrote, "One time [Al] had the flu and I called the shop to tell his father, and he actually said to me, 'It doesn't make any difference whether he is here or not. He makes no difference in the work we do.'"[1]

He must not have paid my father the whole time that he was disabled by depression, however, since there was a financial impact. Florence said, "I know Mum said she went to the South Scituate Savings Bank, which is where the mortgage was, and told them that he was sick and couldn't work, and they told her that as long as she paid the interest, which in many cases was the bigger part of the payment, she wouldn't have to pay anything on the principal until he went back to work."

It was probably after the move that the electroshock therapy began. My brother and sisters do not remember exactly when or where it occurred. I surmise, without certainty, that the recommendation, and probably the implementation, came from Robert Arnot, who not only was a proponent of shock therapy but also carried it out, and that it probably occurred at St. Elizabeth's Hospital, a Catholic hospital in Brighton, a neighborhood of Boston. That Arnot conducted such treatments himself is clear from a 1957 lawsuit against him by a woman who alleged that he had used shock therapy on her against her will. The woman had been showing severe psychotic symptoms, according to the testimony, during consultations with Arnot at Bournewood Hospital, a private psychiatric facility in Brookline, and her husband had signed the authorization for the treatment that Arnot had said was absolutely necessary. In 1962, the state supreme court rejected the complaint.[2]

Peter said, "I remember when Mum told me that he would have to have shock treatments, and said what it would entail: electrodes on his brain, etc. I thought, Would he be a zombie?"

"She would drive him in." Paula said. "Sometimes she would have to take me, for some reason, and he would come out looking like [here she made a face indicating a dazed expression]. They did it much differently then. They eradicated your memory."

• • •

Electroconvulsive therapy—usually called ECT—fell out of favor in the 1970s, though there was no question that it often had positive effects in cases of severe depression. It has been revived recently, with protocols as different from those of the 1950s as micro- or laser surgery is from Civil War surgery. Sixty years ago, the intensity and duration of the shocks were much greater, and electrodes were used on both sides of the brain, whereas today they are usually applied to one side, reducing the side effects. Also, there were many more treatments than is now typical for short-term treatment—as many as a hundred sessions. The effect on memory could be substantial.

I am uncertain how many treatments my father had, or how long the treatment went on, or how much it helped. My best guess is that it took place between 1954 and 1956. In that latter year, something else occurred, completely unexpected, an event that stunned all of us. Perhaps it did him good.

• • •

Over all these years, as well as before and after, he had another form of therapy, nowadays typically referred to as "self-medication." He was drinking. We children knew about it, and we took closer and more worried notice as we became teenagers and adults.

The best thing, and the worst thing, about my father's drinking was that he was famous for his ability to "hold his liquor"; that is, he could drink more than most people and not show visible effects. He could also stop at any point in a day or night; just not have any more, rather than swigging himself into inebriation. I've asked my sisters and brother about this, and none except me can remember him really drunk. We saw other kids' drunk fathers, or drunks in the street or in bars, or in movies or on television. They staggered, they could barely talk, they made fools of themselves or were violent. They went on extended benders; they were fired from their jobs. None of this describes our father.

If this was the best thing about his drinking, it was also the worst, because it meant that he never reached a crisis point where intervention was unavoidable. Drunks hit bottom, we expect, and when they do, they die or get help. Their wives leave them. They go to detox programs, or at least get into AA. But my father never hit bottom and so never sought help, and no one intervened. Neither he nor my mother knew, it seems, that the ability to "hold" liquor is a bad sign. With any kind of substance abuse, the addict gradually develops a tolerance and needs to ingest more to produce the desired effect. But my father always thought he had it under control, and my mother did not know enough to, or how to, disagree. She did not drink at all and had no experience of it in her immediate family. It was never easy for her to oppose him openly. He was stubborn. Furthermore, as with the move to Fuller Street, she accepted his primacy as head of the family. If he told her that he had it under control, she would not contradict him. There is no sign that either of them understood that you do not need to get drunk continually to wreck your health, even if you never miss a day of work.

In April of 1952, about a year after we moved to Scituate, Julia Mehegan died of cirrhosis of the liver. I cannot remember the actual cause of death ever being mentioned. She was a kindhearted soul and the closest thing to a real mother that my father had. My mother remembered his saying that it had been Julia, notwithstanding her rough edges, who had advised him, "Save yourself for that special girl." He had seen her decline and must have been uneasy at the cause, but he had his way of understanding it. "Dad said she didn't eat; she just drank," Florence recalled. "He was always very strict about food, which I always remember as such a sad thing, because he always felt that if he had a good diet, he could drink, which really wasn't true at all."

To me it is probable that fear of alcoholism was behind the preoccupation with his own and others' diets. "He was very careful about diet and he watched what I ate," Florence said, "and would tell me that I had too much bread, too much of this and that. I was very bothered by that when I was young, because he was watching what I was eating—'starch, too much starch!' he would say—and I was bothered by that because I was always a little heavy. I used to hide food from him." Paula, too, remembers hiding food, taking sandwiches to the bedroom.

He was caught in the addict's insidious cycle of denial: He cannot stop the behavior that is hurting him and others, so he tries to diminish the significance of the behavior by accentuating positive behaviors. "I don't have a drinking problem," he tells himself. "I eat well, I don't misbehave, and I never miss a day of work or fall down on the job. I'm a highly moral person and an upstanding citizen. See, I *couldn't* have a problem." As a result, he can be obsessive about these compensatory qualities.

Often I have thought over the years: If only he had become a Friend of Bill, the fellowship of Alcoholics Anonymous, he might have escaped the sinkhole he was in. With his character, intelligence, courage, religious faith, and sensitivity—not to mention stubbornness—AA surely would have worked for him, and he might even have helped many others. But for AA to work, the alcoholic has to admit not only how bad the problem is, but that he or she is powerless to fix it by him- or herself. Bill Wilson, the cofounder of AA, came to this insight on his own. But most people need to be told, forcefully, usually by a close friend or loved one, a person who understands that the message is necessary, no matter how much outrage or hostility might result. No one grabbed my father by his lapels and shouted in his face that he was a drunk and that his life and my mother's would be ruined if he didn't get help. My mother might have done it—though not in so many words—if she had been convinced that it was necessary. She would have done anything for him.

The attraction of AA for alcoholics who wanted help, its anonymity, was also its drawback, the more so in previous decades, when there was more of a stigma attached to alcoholism. It could be hard to know how to get into it, how to begin, whom to talk to. You never passed a public building with a sign saying, "AA meeting tonight! Need help? Join us!" I don't know if my father even knew any Friends of Bill personally, knew that about them, that is.

He did not drink much at home, in front of us, presumably out of discretion or worry about setting a bad example. He would have a beer with dinner, but never two or three, so far as I can remember. The lower shelf of the kitchen cabinet nearest the back door held his distilled liquor: never fifths, always pints. The brands I remember are Schenley and Seagram's Seven. There was no great variety, and he did not have martinis or highballs or mix any kind of cocktail. Rather, in my memory I can see him in the evening opening the cupboard, pouring a shot, and throwing it down. One time, when I was perhaps ten or so, I picked up one of the little flat brown bottles and asked him, "Dad, does this stuff taste good?" and was shocked and stung when he barked at me harshly: "Just put it down." He didn't want to talk about it, unlike many drinkers for whom adventures in boozing is a favorite subject of conversation. There was a cloud of reticence, of discretion, around this need in him, which signifies to me that by then he knew he had a problem and was worried about it.

I always knew he was drinking, but it never seemed to me, in retrospect, that the quantities were great. However, when Florence and I talked about it recently, she said bluntly, "He had a buzz on most of the time." She remembered one summer when she was in high school, she worked at Powers & Mehegan for a week while Mary O'Malley, the secretary, was on vacation. She rode in with my father. He took her every day to lunch at the Elite Lunch in nearby Perkins Square.

"When we went home," she said, "he would start. We would leave South Boston and he would stop at Billy Mitchell's Post Time and have a pop. It had a horse statue in front. And then in Neponset he would stop at the Circle Inn [at the Boston end of the Neponset Bridge] and say he was going to get peanuts." He might stop at another bar, she said, at the Quincy end of the Fore River Bridge. "And then he would stop at the VFW hall, on Route 3A in Scituate, and sometimes would go to the Satuit Grille [in Scituate Harbor] before he got home. So by the time he got home, he would have had at least three beers, and maybe a shot and a beer, or maybe four."

Most of his drinking was in favorite bars, and he had several. In addition to those along the way from work, there were two in Scituate Harbor: the Tap Room in the Satuit Grille restaurant, and the Grog Shop, part of the Harborview Restaurant. He frequented them both, but mainly the Satuit, and often one of us children would be with him, waiting in the car while he went in "to buy peanuts." Sometimes he actually brought us a bag. Another famous pretext was that he "had to borrow a wrench from Russ Hall," a local plumber. I remember many times waiting in the car outside the Circle Inn in Neponset, or the Satuit, for an hour or more. When he came out and got behind the wheel, he always seemed perfectly normal, never visibly impaired, and never seemed to think it amiss that I had been sitting there, waiting. I was used to it.

Often in the evening, he would be out for hours. There were times when my mother would be disturbed about it, and even call him at the Satuit and ask him to come home. She would ask him to stop drinking on a given day or night, just as she had at the South Boston Yacht Club dance, so many years before, and he would stop, as he had then. At least for a while. I never heard a quarrel between them about drinking. Perhaps my mother believed that he truly had it under control or at least that it was limited.

There is no way today to know just how much alcohol he consumed, or how big a bite it took out of the family budget. But there is no doubt that he drank steadily, daily, for decades, above the level that his body could tolerate. You could call it, I suppose, a form of lifetime shock treatment, with a mild stunning effect, that would help him forget what was troubling him. He did nothing else while he was drinking, didn't use it as some artists do to help them write, paint, or make music. Whatever immediate relief it gave him, it was also a depressant and a tremendous waste of time and money. That a price would be paid was inevitable.

Why was he depressed? There is no hint, in anything he wrote or in what anyone, including my mother, said about him before the war to suggest that he was afflicted then by serious depression. People do develop maladies of various kinds in middle age, of course, including depression, for strictly physiological reasons. It might have been that some chemical change took place, possibly as a result of the steady infusion of alcohol, to drag his mood to the floor. Or something might have happened in the war, although there does not appear to have been anything traumatic in his record to compare with those who experienced combat directly.

The best hypothesis as to nonphysiological causes, and certainly it was the one believed by my mother, was that he suffered from a crushing sadness about the lack of love in his early childhood, the abandonment by his mother, and, most of all, the lifelong implicit and explicit disparagement by his father, who was always near to hand. Sometimes, even if one has the same burdens in middle age as in youth, they weigh more heavily as one ages, because it becomes harder to be optimistic about the future.

We have seen hints of the differences between Alfred and Charlie, but I have no accounts of their actual interactions, no anecdotes of actual abusive words from Charlie. I never heard my father complain of mistreatment. But there was one thing his father sometimes did that he hated, enough to tell my mother about it. She recalled that Charlie would say to him, "You look just like old man Donahue"—John Donahue, that is, Esther's father. Apparently this taunt happened more than once: "When I see you coming," Charlie would say, "I could swear it was old man Donahue." My father once confessed to my mother, with real distress, "If he says that to me one more time, I don't know what I will do." Not that he would be capable of violence against his father. No, he would just try to sublimate his hurt, as he did everything else.

The truth, as noted above, is that he *did* favor the Donahues, which I realized when I met his half brother Jack Carson, though there was a hint of Charlie in my father's brilliant smile. Then, in October of 1956, in the midst of the shock therapy period, my parents found out that Esther was coming for an extended visit.

●　●　●

It would be impossible to exaggerate our amazement at this announcement. To that moment, Paula and I did not know that Esther existed, though Florence had learned about her by accident, shortly after Julia's death. We had always believed that Julia was our natural grandmother. Dad had another mother? How could that be? I cannot explain why that fact had been kept from us. Perhaps my parents felt that acknowledging Esther would have devalued Julia. Or perhaps they thought that since Esther had been gone from my father's life for decades, there was no need to reveal her and cause confusion in our minds. Possibly they decided it was all too complicated to explain.

My mother wrote that Esther's announcement was unexpected. "We were astonished to have her call us on the telephone from the Scituate train station to where we were living on Blanchard Road, telling us that she had arrived," she wrote. "Talk about being stunned, no one was more so than Al and me, but she said she had written us telling us she was coming, a letter we had never received."[3]

However, my sisters remember that we had had somewhat more notice. My mother and Florence, at least, went to the station to meet her. For some reason, I did not go, nor did my father—possibly because there would not be room in the car for all of us.

"She came by bus," Florence said. I remember the story of the bus ride from Los Angeles to Boston, and Esther saying that the trip had taken ninety hours. "She got on the train at South Station [in Boston] and we waited for her at the [Scituate] station, at First Parish Road, and we said, 'What are we going to do? We don't even know what she looks like.' We had no pictures. The train came in, and she got off with a bunch of bags and was looking at everybody. Her legs were all swollen."

They pulled into the driveway at 24 Blanchard Road and came into the kitchen, then into the living room, where my father was. I cannot remember what he said, only that his face lit up. He took her strongly in his arms and rocked her back and forth for a long time, the way I had seen him do only with my mother.

We sat in the living room that afternoon and evening, and we children listened to them talk and stared at her. It was all hard to believe. She was about sixty-two, every bit the little old lady grandmother in a plain coat, with gray short curly hair and a hat, and sensible shoes. That this respectable little person had once dived off a sixty-five-foot ladder into a tank was unimaginable. The only part of the conversation I remember is my father asking her to tell him something he had always wondered about: "Who named me Alfred?" In Irish families, it was traditional for the oldest son to be named after the grandfather; in his case, both were named John. Esther replied, "I did."

"Where did that come from?" he asked. He had always disliked his name.

She said, "I just liked it."

So much for tradition. Esther did all things her way.

She stayed for about two months, visiting cousins in the Boston area. One raw cold day we went to Minot Beach, in North Scituate, to walk and look at the ocean. At one point we came to a section of low seawall. Esther flung her purse onto the wall and hopped over. That a grandmother would do this was astonishing to me, given that our other grandmother was older than Esther and not vigorous. My mother wrote, "One day, she said she had brought her bathing suit and would like to go swimming, but I thought it was much too cold. But she disagreed and said, 'That wouldn't be a problem for me' and of course I realized it wouldn't be, professional swimmer as she was, but though she went to the beach I don't remember that she actually went swimming. Perhaps she found it really too cold to try." She did at least wade in at some point; I remember her saying that she wanted to feel the Atlantic again after so many years in California. Tidewater continued to draw her, as it did her firstborn in a different way.

She seemed to be a low-key, even-tempered person, though I learned years later from Aunt Betty Byars that she had a fiery temper when roused. "She was all Irish," said Betty. She whistled all the time when occupied with some activity—not melodies, but more of an unconscious twitter. She was agreeable but not, in my recollection, warm or affectionate. My mother wrote of a long conversation they had over the kitchen table:

"I thought she was really quite pretty but of course a little heavier than she had been when I met her thirteen years before in Pemberton. She was no more than five feet tall, and I noticed that she had lovely hands with slender fingers, a feature for some reason I always notice. In our family, Paula had these same hands and suddenly I thought, 'This is where Paula has inherited hers.' But Al had lovely hands, too, masculine, of course, but with the same long fingers. Of all our children, Paula resembled Al the most.

"Listening to Esther, I had a feeling that she was 'hard,' not tough or even tough-talking, as 'Southie' folk can be, but of course she had had a hard life." By this I'm guessing that my mother meant Esther had been hardened, toughened by life. This surely was true. "After they had lost the carnival [during the Depression], Andy [Carson] couldn't get a job and, desperate for money, she said, 'I told Carson (she always used the men's last names), "If you don't get a job soon, you're going." He didn't, so I threw him out.' It was tragic but so funny in a way, she was so casual about disposing of these husbands. And she said, 'I said to the boys' (whom I gathered were in their early teens), "You get jobs, too, or I'll throw you out like I did your father." They all did, too, because they knew I meant it.'"[4]

Jack Carson remembered this incident well, which seems to have happened about 1941. "Dad was crippled with arthritis and TB and could not work. Mom told all of us to 'get jobs and help or get out before I throw you out.' She kicked Dad out and he moved to a cheap hotel in downtown L.A. Andy got in the National Guard [actually the army]. David got a job after school stocking shelves and cleaning at a local store. I had an early-morning paper route and got a job after school working at a bakery." The boys were seventeen, fourteen, and twelve.

She might have said it to her husband and the two older boys (the ultimatum quite likely precipitated Andy Jr.'s joining the army in March 1941), but David, age twelve in 1941, has no memory of it. "It was not said to me," he said. "I had had jobs since I was nine and always gave half to the house, and sometimes all of it to the house." Whomever she said it to, Esther remembered it clearly enough to tell my mother twenty-five years later.

That Esther could have issued such an ultimatum to her own family, during hard times, persuades me that my father was fortunate that she was not a bigger presence in his life. Such a threat would have been unthinkable from his stepmother, from Aunts Mary or Catherine, or even his father. As for Andy Sr., the man once so quick with his fists, who would dive into any "Hey Rube," he was now too sick and weak to resist his wife. As in 1914, the year she dumped Charlie Mehegan, Esther had little patience with males who fell short of her requirements.

• • •

She apparently divorced her third husband. Jack said there was a divorce, though David is not sure, and it is possible that she did not bother. Andy Carson went to a sanatorium, David recalled, and recovered from tuberculosis, but he and Esther were finished. He was living in the hotel in Los Angeles at the time of his death, February 2, 1956. He was buried in the Pacific Coast Showmen's Association rest, a portion of Evergreen

Cemetery in the Boyle Heights neighborhood, set aside, according to the web site, for "indigent entertainers, including circus performers."

Esther was a survivor, with or without a man around. She told my mother that during World War II she had worked in a defense plant, and my mother commented "Esther was the living prototype of 'Rosie the Riveter.'" David remembered this small factory, at the corner of Slauson Avenue and Hoover Street in South Los Angeles. It made Bakelite knobs for aircraft cockpit controls. He worked there for a while himself, until it was discovered that he was underage.

One feature of Esther's character that startled me in 1956 was her open dislike of black people. She called them "jigs"—an epithet I had never heard before—and would make cutting remarks about them. I wondered if this was something she had learned in South Boston or picked up in the carnival. If so, it was ironic in that Jack remembered that a black man named Shorty took care of the boys while their parents were working in the Carson show. That my mother in her writings does not mention this prejudice suggests to me that she had not heard it. Endlessly interested as my mother was in human character, she noticed Esther's nature in detail, including traits that were absent. "There was one more personality trait Esther didn't seem to have," she wrote, "which was so strange: a sense of humor. I don't think I ever saw her laugh."⁵ In this she was nothing at all like my father.

She had cut loose three husbands, though apparently she did her best, by her lights, by her three Carson sons. For years, she lived with Jack and his family, later with David. But as Betty wrote, "She was never happy living with anyone" and lived alone in her last days, though brother Bill and his wife, Mae, were nearby.

It is clear to me that Esther Donahue and Charlie Mehegan, despite their stormy history, were cut from the same bolt—tough, watchful, willful, always ready to seize the main chance and the devil take the hindmost. My mother was right that my father did not resemble either of them. Given their history, one would expect contempt or even hatred between the two old antagonists, but, as with most couples, their chemistry was mysterious. Incredibly, even after all the decades and bitter early history, there was still some kind of current between them, although probably more on Esther's side. My mother wrote:

> One day, she showed me a pretty little blue hat and a dress she had brought with her and told me, "I am going to wear this when I have a date with Charlie" and to my amazement she called him on the phone right then, evidently got him and made an appointment to see him, telling him that "Alfred" would drive her to Boston. Then, evidently sensing my surprise, she said, "You know, Charlie can be very sweet," an adjective I could not imagine being used to describe that irascible man.[6]

The reunion happened; my father did in fact drive her to Boston. That my father should have been drafted to serve as quasi chauffer for this bizarre "date" between his estranged parents seems to me extraordinary, and I wonder how he felt about it. It is not beyond the realm of possibility that Esther, knowing that Charlie was widowed and had a good business, might have been harboring a nostalgic fantasy. She tried to see Charlie again during a later visit, but, my mother wrote, "He refused to see her, and she was obviously bitterly disappointed."[7]

Although my mother always described Esther's first visit as a complete surprise, Paula has a different understanding, which came to her during Esther's second visit, six years later, in 1962. Paula was sixteen at that time. Esther confided in her, especially about the early history of the divorce and the court fight. "She was sending money home when she was on the road," Paula recalled Esther telling her, "and Charlie was gambling it away. When she tried to get him [i.e., custody of Alfred], they said she had money but was not sending it."

The most startling revelation to Paula, which I had never heard before, was that Esther's first visit was not a surprise. "The first time she came," Paula said, "was when Dad was very sick and having shock treatments. That was why Mum had her come. They had a conversation about how sick Dad was and Grandma said she thought it might help if she came. So she came."

"Mum had her come" is Paula's distinct recollection of Esther's explanation for the visit. It would not be like my mother to be dishonest about this, and I can easily imagine that she might have telephoned Esther, desperate for answers that might explain what was happening to my father, and that Esther either offered to come or inferred that my mother wanted her to come and did so unbidden.

In any case, Esther found out about my father's illness and about his fraught relationship with Charlie. She had a shrewd theory about it that rang true to my mother, who wrote:

> Esther told me, when she heard about the strained relationship between them, "He's doing that to get even with me, striking at me through Alfred." I was bewildered and couldn't imagine anything so hideous, so perverted, especially [since,] despite his patent rejection, Al loved his father. I used to think, "What a play that would make, the father taking the son into the business with the intention of making him fail." Did he know that he was doing that? I don't know. I hate to think anyone could be so malevolent.[8]

My mother was straining to give Charlie some benefit of doubt; that is, that he might not have known what he was doing. That seems to me a stretch for this canny fellow. She was not deeply read in psychology and the power of the unconscious; did not, that is, read Freud and Jung and their generation. But she did believe in the permanent scarring effect of childhood trauma. A book that supported her thinking later was psychiatrist W. Hugh Missildine's *Your Inner Child of the Past*, which posited that the childhood self continues to live within and affect one's feelings and behavior at any age.[9] She had no doubt that my father's insecurities, anxieties, and depression were caused by Charlie and Esther, especially Charlie, since his mistreatment, as she saw it, was virtually lifelong. She did not know enough, as many intelligent people did not at that time, to consider the physiological, sometimes called chemical, drivers of depression, even in those without traumatic histories. Even if my father did have such drivers, however, to me it is unquestionable that the sadness and coldness of his "ill-started life" were intensifiers that a less sensitive person might have been able to shrug off.

My mother wanted desperately for my father to get away from Charlie. Once again she hoped that, in my father's words, "moving away from people" might be the solution. Most of all, she wanted to break Charlie's indirect malign effect, however unconscious on his part, on our family. She had begun to think that her resentment had hardened into hatred and was so disturbed at this possibility that she went to Confession—the common name then for the Catholic sacrament of Penance—about it. I know this because she described this encounter to me many years later.

There have been wise and humane priests in every generation, and my mother was lucky enough to know a few. The priest listened to her confession of anger, then said, "You're being too hard on yourself. I very much doubt that it's true hatred you're feeling. Let me give you a little test. If he had a heart attack in front of you, or were bleeding, would you not call for help? Would you just let him die?"

My mother said, "Of course I would help. Of course I wouldn't let him die."

"Well, then, I don't believe that you have hatred in your heart."

13.

On His Own

If the worst of my father's depression—the inability to work, the need for intensive therapy—abated in the late 1950s, his decision finally to leave his father might well have had something to do with it. There is no record of precisely when it happened, but my estimate from my siblings' recollections puts it about 1958 or '59.

"Leave his father." It is strange and suggestive to call it that. But that is the way my mother always phrased it. How the decision to quit Powers & Mehegan once and for all was made, at my father's initiative or my mother's prompting, is not known. I never heard anyone speak of Charlie's reaction. He could not have been pleased; after all, it was no compliment to him or expression of confidence in the future of the business. My father's skill as an estimator—and his master plumber's license—was undoubtedly a serious loss and not easily replaced. But given the coolness of the father-son relationship, and Charlie's comment to my mother that "he makes no difference in the work we do," he might well have expressed little or no reaction. After the separation, my father's relationship with his father, such as it was, apparently did not change for the worse. He remained in touch with him and saw him when he visited Mary Rose and Great Aunt Mary and Aunt Catherine.

I know of no indication that the break was traumatic for my father; on the contrary, it seems to have been a relief. When I was about fifteen, in 1964, I asked him if he thought he had done the right thing to "leave his father." His response was an unequivocal yes: "I didn't want to be walking up and down Broadway in South Boston, plunging toilets in my fifties and sixties." This minimizing comment about the business, and his prospects in it, suggests that he had faced the truth that Powers & Mehegan was a dead end.

At first, he had some idea that he might hang out his own shingle. He even had business cards made: "A. C. Mehegan, Plumbing and Heating, Residential—Commercial." He must have concluded that this was not practical, however. His situation was not much different from that at the end of World War II, when he might have dreamed of resuming his quest for a law career but scrapped it for the need to make money right away. Fifteen or so years later, he had a family of six, and without capital, there was no way he could support us while trying to build a plumbing business. No, he had to find a job, which he did, as an estimator for a plumbing contractor in or near Providence, Rhode Island.

I have not discovered the name of the company. My siblings do not remember either, and the name is not mentioned in either of my parents' papers. That he went so far afield to find a job indicates that there were not many opportunities in the Boston area. That seems incredible today, but the economy then was sluggish, especially in backwater Boston. There were two recessions in four years—the "Eisenhower recession" of 1957–58, and the so-called rolling adjustment recession of 1960–61. The Catholic Church postwar building boom was ending, and not much industrial or commercial construction was going on.

He had this job for about three years. In that time, he would drive to Providence in the family car and stay over several nights a week at the Providence YMCA. It is not hard to imagine what he did in those lonely nights in Providence, away from his family. He drank. But a Boston reader of this story might puzzle over why the stay-overs would be necessary. Isn't Providence about an hour's drive from Boston? Today, yes. But in 1958 or '59, the interstate highways had not been finished. His most likely route from Scituate to Providence, via winding two-lane secondary roads such as Routes 123, 18, and 44, would have taken him as long as two hours.

He hated the lonely drive, and for a brief time he and my mother had decided to move closer to Providence. "We were going to move down there," Florence said, "to a place called—it was very funny—Hicksville. They said, 'We're moving to Hicksville.' We said 'Over our dead bodies.'" The idea was abandoned, perhaps because of the children's opposition. I cannot find any such place as Hicksville in Rhode Island, but there is a Hixville, Massachusetts, part of Dartmouth, not far from the Rhode Island state line. In addition to this job, he needed to make more money, so he began to install plumbing on weekends in houses built in Scituate by old friend Gene Blanchard.

He did this heavy work alone, on Saturdays, lugging lengths of cast-iron soil pipe and bathtubs, melting and pouring hot lead to seal and caulk pipe joints, installing copper water-supply lines, fitting toilets, tubs, and sinks. Gene, besides his genuine liking for my father, was impressed by the meticulous quality of his work, far above that of the typical small-town plumber.

Sometimes Peter and I helped him on these jobs, but I was not much help at age twelve or thirteen, except to carry tools and supplies. I did learn to pack oakum in soil pipe joints and, after my father poured the lead over the oakum with a steel ladle, to drive the hardened but still soft lead down with a cold chisel and a ball-peen hammer. I learned how to cut copper tubing, dress the ends and elbows with "pipe dope," and solder the sections together with a propane torch. On any new house, his objective was always to "get the [vent] stack through the roof the first day," and he always succeeded.

He was as proud of this work as of any he had ever done. There must have been satisfaction in having no boss, but the labor was hard—too hard, really. Once, working with Peter in a house, he slipped in a bathroom and crashed down on the side of a tub. He was OK, he said. It was the end of a day, and he and Peter carried his tools out to the car. But soon after, the pain was so bad that he had to go to the hospital. It turned out that he had broken three ribs. Besides keeping him out of his weekday job, the injury made sleeping, coughing, and especially laughing almost unbearable. We were careful not to say anything funny or to laugh in his presence. But for kids, this was almost impossible—like the famous exercise of trying not to think of a polar bear.

In the late 1950s, my mother decided that she too would have to work. It was her call; my father would never have asked her to work and might even have resented it as a reflection on his ability to provide. But it made sense. She no longer had small children. She had excellent secretarial skills, fast and accurate typing, and fluency in Gregg shorthand. She was also, of course, intelligent, efficient, extremely dependable, and a clear writer. With her gifts and experience, she might have become a well-paid executive secretary in a bank or a law firm. Instead, she took a job at *Plays* magazine, in the Back Bay of Boston. *Plays* was one of two magazines edited and published by Abraham and Sylvia Burack of Brookline. It featured scripts of school plays for children. The other magazine was *The Writer*, a guide for freelance writers on technique and self-marketing. Both magazines still exist. In the 1950s, the office was at 8 Arlington Street, in the same little brownstone building opposite the Boston Public Garden that housed the *Atlantic Monthly*.

My mother loved being in her old neighborhood again, just a short walk from her widowed mother, who still lived at 76 West Cedar Street, on Beacon Hill. Sometimes she would ride in and out with my father in the car, or take the bus to Boston, after commuter rail service to Scituate was discontinued in 1957. She liked the job and had a warm regard for Abe Burack, whom she referred to as "Mr. Burack," or sometimes "the man who owns the business." She thought the word "boss" was not respectful.

As hard as my parents were working, there still was not enough money. My mother made her own clothes and many of those of my sisters. We did not eat out in restaurants and never traveled. We had a basic diet, nourishing but plain, and I cannot remember "seconds." I remember a weekend trip to Cape Cod, which seemed to me like a trip to Paris. There was a promise, alas never kept, that when Peter finished junior high school, we would take a family trip to Washington, D.C. There was always one plain car, standard transmission—I remember a blue 1955 Chevy, and before that a black or dark-green Plymouth—

and when the car broke down, it was a serious matter. Sometimes they would get behind on the mortgage, and this would be a huge worry. My mother once gave me a five-dollar bill to go to the movies—a movie at the Satuit Playhouse (Satuit was the old Indian name for Scituate) would have been about seventy-five cents—with the expectation that I would return the change. She was exasperated when I unaccountably lost the change, though she did not stay angry; it was not in her nature. It was just that every dollar counted.

When I look back on it now, I wonder why they could not make ends meet. We lived very frugally. They both had professional skills. Yes, we were a family of six, but with three jobs between them, there should have been enough. Peter and Florence had part-time high school jobs. I can only speculate, sad as it is to think of, that he was drinking away a lot of the income. Surely the three or four dollars I lost after the movie were as nothing compared to what he was spending at the Satuit Grille, the Grog Shoppe, or Billy Mitchell's Post Time, and that must have been the real source of my mother's exasperation.

My father was, needless to say, exhausted much of the time. He was also, I am sure, discouraged and down on himself, like so many of his generation, that he could not do better, could not get ahead. In situation, though not in character, he resembled Willy Loman in Arthur Miller's *Death of a Salesman*. His work life was something of a treadmill. To some extent, at least, he could drink the edge off his worries and disappointments.

In about 1961, he got a new job, in Boston. The company was B. Snyder, a commercial plumbing contractor at 120 Braintree Street in Allston, about halfway between Union Square and the Massachusetts Turnpike. B. Snyder was the last employer my father had, and he was happier working there than he ever had been ashore. He scored some big jobs with his bids, of which he was very proud. One was 535 Boylston Street, Boston, a fourteen-story building at the corner of Clarendon Street, now called the McCarthy Building.

It was fitting that he landed happily at a firm like Snyder. It was a kind of Jewish Powers & Mehegan, with the difference being that the second generation really did inherit a valuable business. B. Snyder was Benjamin Snyder, the founder, and his sons were Milton, Ralph, and George. I cannot recall which of them was CEO, but my father most often spoke warmly of George. The feeling was mutual. Like so many others in my father's life, the Snyders held him in high esteem, not only for the quality of his work but for his work ethic.

He no longer had to make the long drive to Providence, but he still had to drive, or take the bus, to Boston. He wanted to be free of commuting for good. By 1962, Peter and Florence were away at college and never would live "at home" again. Paula and I were fifteen and thirteen. We hated the thought of leaving Scituate, but my mother too by now was tired of the provinciality and cultural poverty of the Irish Riviera. They decided to move back to Boston.

In the fall of 1961, they rented a three-bedroom apartment at number 60 the Fenway, at the corner of Westland Avenue, in Boston's Fenway neighborhood. The landlord's name was Pizzi—pronounced like "pizza" with an *i*. They put the house on the market, but for some reason they (or more likely my father) decided not to use a real estate broker, opting instead to advertise it and sell it privately. He had made both of his home purchases informally with a builder, so it must have seemed reasonable to him that the sale could be simple and informal. Their asking price was $16,800.

Number 60 the Fenway (not Fenway Street or Avenue, but "the Fenway") is still there, with the odd name Rusridge still carved over the door. From my parents' point of view, it was a fantastic location. The apartment was on the top floor, the fifth, with a view of the Fens— the park with the sinuous Muddy River that was part of Frederick Law Olmsted's famous Emerald Necklace. Beyond the Fens we could see the light towers of Fenway Park, and both the Museum of Fine Arts—free to the public in those days—and Symphony Hall, home of the Boston Symphony Orchestra, were no more than a five-minute walk. St. Ann's Parish church was at the end of nearby Gainsborough Street. From my bedroom, I could see the flashing rooftop sign on the Huntington Avenue YMCA, where my father had gone to law school.

My parents were delighted. We would be close to "cultural advantages," always important to my mother, and my father could get to work, three miles away, in a ten-minute drive or twenty minutes via the T. We had a car, a white 1961 Dodge Polara, and strange as it may seem to residents of that part of Boston today, my father could usually find a legal parking space on the street. There were no parking meters on that part of the Fenway.

We moved in September, and the most astonishing thing happened on moving day. The telephone rang that morning in Scituate. It was Esther. My grandmother was in Boston, just arrived for another visit. My mother was dumbfounded. Esther insisted she had written to say she was coming, but the letter, if there was one, never arrived. It was just like her not to wait for confirmation. As usual, she had made up her mind what she was going to do and plunged ahead. Wearily my mother gave her the address of the apartment and suggested she meet us there, which she did.

She was now sixty-eight. All that day, she helped with the move-in. She would pick something up that the movers had brought in from the curb and ask, "Where should I put this?" and my dazed mother would point randomly and say, "Put it there." I can see myself carrying a mattress down a hallway, me at the rear and Esther in the lead. She was still fit and sturdy, and I remember her saying, "It was all that swimming when I was young." My father was happy, as always, to see her and have her there. "He called her 'Mother,'" even though, my mother wrote, "he had seen her no more than six times in his life."[1] By now my mother had had her fill of this unpredictable, impulsive person. My grandmother slept in a small room off the kitchen, probably once a servant's room, which had a Murphy bed in the wall. She stayed for months and made no financial contribution, which nearly had my mother at her wits' end, the more so in that she had to hold her tongue, since my father would not tolerate any criticism of either of his parents.

An incident during this visit is a perfect character cameo of my grandmother, or at least part of her. She was going downtown to do some shopping on Washington Street, perhaps at Filene's or Jordan

Marsh, and I went with her. I was thirteen. We walked along Westland Avenue and down the stairs of Symphony Station, on what is now the MBTA Green Line, in front of Symphony Hall. (There was no color scheme for the subway lines then: What today is the "E" route on the Green Line was commonly called the Huntington Avenue car or just the Arborway car.) A trolley train had pulled into the station as we came down the stairs, with passengers climbing on and off. Esther was ahead of me and she rushed to drop her token in the turnstile. As I fumbled with my token, she dashed ahead and leaped up into the car; the door slammed shut, and the train took off, leaving me standing there.

There was no danger to me; I was familiar with the system, using it alone every day to get to school. I boarded the next train and got off at Park Street, and there she was, waiting for me. We probably all laughed about it later. But today it strikes me as a strange thing to do. If I had a grandchild with me in such a situation, even a thirteen-year-old, I would never leave him behind. I would let the train go and wait for the next one. She meant no harm. It was that she was not the hesitating kind when opportunity presented itself. There would be a similar episode at the end of this visit, not funny at all but terribly sad, involving my father.

While she was staying with us Esther spent much time visiting an elderly sick aunt in South Boston, who died in November. My father took a day off from work and went with her to the funeral. "He looked so nice in his gray topcoat, gray felt hat, white shirt and black tie," my mother wrote. She always thought he was a fine-looking man. "He had gained some weight, but he had wonderful posture." That was true. He was straight as a stick, never slouched. "She took him by the arm as they left the apartment, and I could see how delighted he was, as she was too. She had many relatives in South Boston, whom neither he nor I knew, who were all at the funeral, and here she was, so proud to be escorted by her son."[2]

Just before Christmas, Esther was to return home by air. My mother wrote that she wanted to see her cousin, daughter of the deceased aunt, one more time. So a couple of days before leaving, she went to South

Boston with her suitcase to stay with the cousin, whose name was May Bartick. My father talked to Esther by telephone the night before departure day, and she told him that May would drive her to the airport, where he would meet her and see her off. Next morning, he drove to Logan Airport with a package of Christmas presents for her that we had put together.

My mother wrote:

> About an hour later, Al called me from the airport in great distress because she had not made the plane. He tried to get her at the Barticks' house, but there was no answer. He waited at the phone booth at Logan while I phoned the Barticks several times, too, but still there was no answer. Then when I got him again, where he was waiting at the phone, and told him I had been unable to get anyone at the Barticks', he decided to come home, not knowing what else to do. When he got home, he immediately called the police, thinking that she and May, who was driving, might have had an accident. But none was reported. Then he started calling hospitals, one after another, but again there had been no accident reported.
>
> May was a teacher at Charlestown High School, but the school was closed for Christmas vacation, and there was no other way Al could think of reaching her. Why we didn't call her other relatives I don't know, but it might have been not to alarm them. It occurred to me that she might have taken an earlier flight, although it was outlandish to contemplate. I suggested it to Al, but he dismissed it as impossible.[3]

A few days later, they received a letter from Esther in Los Angeles. She *had* taken an earlier flight and apparently not thought to tell my father.

"Al was so hurt, really devastated," my mother wrote, "and could not believe she had done that. In all the years I had known him, he had never said an unkind word about his father, his mother, indeed about anyone in his family. But he did then, for the first time. He said, so sadly, 'Selfishness has always been my parents' main fault.' That was all he said."[4]

This was such a strange thing to do, even for Esther, that I wonder if she simply did not want an emotional scene at the airport. Presumably it was no simple matter to take an earlier flight; she had a ticket for the later one. More likely, though, my father was right—surely no one knew them better—that both of his parents had an instinct to put their personal interests first. Whatever Esther's exact motive, once again, and for the last time, the swimmer had left the boy standing alone on the beach. He never saw her again.

• • •

My mother got a job as a secretary in the admissions office at Northeastern University, on nearby Huntington Avenue. She would walk home for lunch each day. She and my father would have spent the rest of their lives in Boston, I guess, but for two problems. First, Paula and I were miserable in school. Neither of us was threatened. It was more that we suffered from the shock of the suburb-to-city change. Paula went to Girls High School on Green Street in Roxbury, near Egleston Square, which had been Practical Arts High School when my mother had gone there in the 1920s. It was in a poor neighborhood, and what with Boston's de facto racial segregation (the epic battle over which, memorably documented in J. Anthony Lukas's *Common Ground*, was already under way), Paula was one of very few white girls in the school. She suffered, like her black classmates, with the fact that the black-majority schools were severely underserved and neglected. Another point of stress on Paula and my mother at this time was that it was the height of the Boston Strangler terror. One of the first victims, Ida Irga, was murdered August 19, 1962, on Grove Street, Beacon Hill, one block east of West Cedar Street, where my grandmother lived. I went to all-boys Boston Technical High School, also in Roxbury, which was one of the city exam schools, like Boston Latin School and Boston English High School. It sounds like a trade school, but it had a college-preparation program, along with courses in such subjects as mechanical drawing and metalworking. Despite the segregation of most neighborhood high schools, the students at Boston Technical were mostly white, from all over the city, with a fair number of black and Asian students. I was unhappy there. I didn't care about mechanical drawing, and I was picked on relentlessly in a low-voltage way by the tough guys who always go after the quiet types with glasses. It was mostly insults and random punches.

Paula's and my unhappiness was a trial to my mother, who suffered whenever we did, but my father was not sympathetic. However, there was a second problem, which he could not brush off. The house in Scituate had not sold. Probably they should have listed it with a broker. For several months they were carrying the mortgage on top of the apartment rent, which could not continue. In order to cover the gap, my father borrowed a thousand dollars from Aunt Mary Mehegan. I imagine that to borrow from Charlie—ask him to bail them out at that time in their lives—would have been out of the question for either of my parents. Dear Aunt Mary, a person of wisdom and kindness (the one who had bought books for my father when he was a child) who understood everything about the history and dynamics between Alfred and Charlie, probably better than they did, was undoubtedly discreet. I doubt that the loan was repaid, not that Aunt Mary would have cared.

After six months, with me and Paula both failing in school, skipping as often as we could get away with, my mother told my father that we should give up and go back to Scituate. We could not afford to do what we were doing. He was furious. Years later, she told me that they had a quiet but intense quarrel over it, lying in bed one night. He said to her, "You want to go back, you go ahead. I'm not going. I'm staying here."

She was shocked at the idea of separation. "I can't believe you're saying this. How can you talk that way," she said to him, "after all we've been through together? *We went through the war together!*"

There it was—the unanswerable argument. They went through the war. The war had been the primary bonding experience for them and their generation. For her, that they could have endured that ordeal "the terrible, terrible war," but not survive this crisis was unthinkable.

Against that position, I don't believe he could have stood his ground. My mother was his whole world, along with us. So, this time, he relented. We packed up and moved back to 24 Blanchard Road, across the salt marsh from the sounding ocean. He would go back to commuting, more unhappily than ever. As for the house itself, they never had a single serious inquiry.

Looking out to sea in Scituate, 1951. "He was always happiest near the ocean." (Author's collection)

At Minot Beach during Esther's surprise visit, October-November 1956. From left: Florence, Esther, Paula, Al, and the author.

(Author's collection)

Esther with Peter, age 14, at Blanchard Road, Scituate.

(Author's collection)

At Florence's wedding reception, September 1965, age 54, just before he became ill. (Courtesy of Florence Ely)

Christmas 1965, Al's last, with Mary and grandchild Nancy Mehegan.

(Author's collection)

Life of the party: Charlie with friends, undated, probably mid-1950s. (Courtesy of Virginia Dillon)

Esther at home in Norco, Calif., 1980, age 87.
(Courtesy of Jack Carson)

14.

What He Was Like

IF HE WERE TO COME BACK and read this work, would my father think I got it right? Probably not. Probably he would say, "Nice try, but you don't really understand. There's a lot you know nothing about." That surely is true. To explain any person fully is more than difficult; it is impossible. As much as I squint and strain to see, I am stuck behind distorting lenses, displaced by the gulf of time, like a terrestrial stargazer peering through the murk of the earth's atmosphere. I and you will never comprehend more than a fraction of any life—ours included. Because my father held so much within himself, here I pause to try to fill in aspects of his character and personality that might otherwise only be implicit.

. . .

My mother was saddened and frustrated at my father's limited ability, and unwillingness to try, to be close to his children, and always excused it on grounds of his history. She wrote:

> Al had no role model as a good father, as I had. He was in addition quite clear in his idea of his role and mine. One time when in desperation I asked his opinion on some problem concerning one of the children, he said, "That's your business. My only responsibility is to support you." He would often dictate a punishment that was too strict and then call me the next day from work and say, "That was

too severe a punishment." He was so fair like that, so that next day
I called him at the shop and I asked him, "Last night you said your
only responsibility was to support us. You didn't mean that, did you?'
And he said, "Yes, I did."[1]

Perhaps not unusual for the time, his view of their respective roles
was rigid, which my mother overlooked, though not always easily. Years
after his death, she once referred to him, not harshly, as "the original
male chauvinist." I doubt that he ever changed a diaper, and I never
saw him touch a broom or wash a dish, or make a meal. However, he
would mildly criticize her if he thought she was not holding up her
end, which would bring her as close to a boil as she was capable of.
One frequent petty complaint, for example, was that the coffeepot was
not properly cleaned. Once, he picked up the aluminum percolator
that she had just washed, took a toothpick, and, without saying a word,
began methodically to poke it through the holes in the grounds basket,
holding up the oily toothpick for her observation. She walked over to
him, also without a word, snatched the pot from his hand, and slammed
it into the trash barrel. He backed off, and they laughed about it for
years. He loved it when she showed that kind of spirit.

With bigger issues, it was not funny. She wrote:

> It was really a source of deep grief to me that I couldn't talk over
> my problems with the children with him. Once, I said, "Al, there
> is something that has come up with Peter I would like to have your
> opinion on," and he said to him instantly, "Go to your room!" I said,
> "It's not that serious" and he said it again, "Go to your room!" which
> Peter did. I remember that night, lying in bed crying to myself and
> thinking, "It is not that he has a bad relationship with his children.
> He has *no* relationship with them." But maybe the children saw that
> all differently then, as well as now. I hope so.[2]

In talking to Peter, Florence, and Paula about this, I found that indeed
they have a more nuanced, generous view of that long-ago relationship
with their father than my mother's account would suggest.

When Peter was fourteen, he had what he now calls "one of my capers." After a winter gale had damaged some beach cottages, he and a couple of friends went into a house laid open by surf and took a few things, including a toboggan from the outside porch, which they used to coast on a nearby golf course hill. They were seen, unluckily for them, arrested, and brought to juvenile court. Peter recalls the headline in the town newspaper, the *South Shore Mirror*: "Police Crack Teenage Reign of Terror." Such was the spectrum of crime in that little town that a joyride on a toboggan was a grave act of juvenile delinquency.

My parents and Peter drove to Hingham District Court, about ten miles north, to appear in the juvenile session of the legendary Martha Ware, the first female judge in Plymouth County. Recalling this drive, my mother once told me, "All the way there, the only thing Dad talked about was the plumbing business"—an example of what she saw as his detachment from the fatherly role. However, Peter has a different memory.

"When we went to court," he said, "the police read the list of particulars, and I was accused of larceny of a toboggan, a box of golf tees, and an Ivy League cap. On the way back in the car, I remember how quiet Dad was. He didn't yell, he just talked to me about 'what this is doing to your mother.' He wanted me to be mindful of how hurtful and grieving this was to her."

Each of us had a different relationship with him. I was somewhat fearful of him in childhood, of his anger and his lack of patience. I was always a poor student, especially in math, at which he excelled. Once he sat me down to "help" me with my math homework, but he was so brusque and impatient, treating it as a disciplinary session, accusing me of pretending to be stupid, that all I wanted was to get away. I could not have added two plus two in that situation. For me, to avoid him as much as possible became a pattern. That I was a mama's boy did not help.

I wrote in an earlier chapter of his attention to eating habits, which Florence found dispiriting and even a bit demeaning. As well, he could be hypercritical about any perceived deficiency of neatness or personal cleanliness. That might have bothered the girls more than it did Peter and me. Boys don't mind as much being called slobs. He was also strangely obsessive about table manners—I can't imagine that he learned that from Charlie, but perhaps he did. The predictable effect, for children, was to make mealtimes an ordeal. I can still hear him growling at us to "get your wing off the table," that is, our elbow, and *never* to use the butter knife to spread butter on the toast (crumbs in the butter—the *horror*). If one of us were to reach too far for the salt, the fork in his hand might flick out like a snake's tongue and rap us on the knuckles. And though we all had foods that we abhorred (Florence's was sliced potatoes fried in bacon grease; mine were liver and beets), he was implacable about our eating what was put before us. Looking back, I have the impression that for some reason, with many of these obsessions he was hardest on Florence. That was unjust, because in truth Florence was a model child, as she has been in every stage of her life.

Paula's memories of her relationship with my father are the brightest. "For me, he was amazingly approachable," she said. "From the time I was born, he was home. He didn't die in the war, he had a place to live, he had a family. Everything he could possibly want he had, and then they had me, and he thought I was the greatest thing in the world. With Florence and Peter, he was away [in their earliest years], and they were closer to Jack [my mother's polio-disabled brother]. As I got older, he didn't put me off. Even when we argued, I had that basis in those early years. When I was ten, I would climb up in his lap when he was sitting at the table. I wouldn't ask him, I would just do it."

He was not violent. I remember no real spankings, nothing you could call a beating, though a moderate slap at moments of wrath was known to occur; it was just that his overwhelming first instinct toward us was to make a judgment, to instruct, to moralize. In his mind, it was not important to enjoy us, simply to have fun (the rowboat history described above was a notable exception). He did not take me fishing— perhaps once or twice when I was very small—or to a ball game (but I think now of his fear of crowds), never pitched batting practice or even played catch with me. He did sometimes play cards with us, always draw poker, and there were those occasional trips to the beach when we were very small. He did not participate in school or extracurricular activities such as Boy Scouts or Little League. I don't mean this to sound like whinging—it was just that undeniably there were empty spaces.

His social life was limited. He went to Mass every Sunday but never taught Sunday school, as other Catholic parents did, nor was he especially active in the Holy Name Society, the parish men's organization. He had no hobbies, activities that were personal and individual. He did not play golf, or cards with buddies, or go bowling. He did not hunt or fish. He did not read much, other than the newspaper, although he did read paperback detective novels before bed. He would take us to the library in the evening and pick us up an hour or so later, but would never go in and take out books for himself. He was not interested in the arts: no museums, movies, or music. Although he had understood mechanics since his youth, he had no interest in gadgets: no ham radio, cars, model railroads, tinkering of any kind. We had a suburban home, but he did not garden or do anything about improvements (unless something was broken) or the yard. Lawn-mowing was the kids' job. My mother, a lifelong New Dealer, had strong views about politics, and I have no sense that he disagreed with her on any of it. But he didn't say much about it. I remember no interest in town politics and do not recall that he went to town meeting.

It is hard to put into words, but from the late 1950s onward there was a kind of slackness about him, almost as if he had given up trying, except to make a living. He did not bestir himself in anything outside work. Yes, he worked hard and this was tiring, but that was not the whole of it. Undoubtedly, drink and its associated causes and effects were a large part. I do not know that we were conscious of this slackness, this disengagement—aware, to be sure, but not conscious; we could not imagine him any other way, although surely we noticed how different some other fathers were. But there is no question that we would have prized and welcomed his interest and involvement in our lives.

He did show *some* interest. "I was always playing baseball," Peter said. "Little League, Pony League, Babe Ruth, whatever. He would sometimes come to my games. Mum never came, for some reason.

Maybe she was busy with the other kids. Whenever he would come to my games, I would always strike out."

That last detail suggests how important it was to Peter to do well when my father was watching, not to disappoint him. We all looked up to him, we cared about what he thought of us, and in spite of his criticism and negativity, we knew that he loved us and our mother. She once wrote that the parental authority of her own father, John Humphreys, was rooted in the deep respect that she and her brothers had for him. "He never punished us physically," she wrote. "Just the thought of his even slapping me was so awful to contemplate that I always tried to please him. As a result he had complete control of us, yet none of us were ever afraid of him."[3] Something like this applies to our orientation toward my father—and again I note the oddness that in this respect he resembled his father-in-law more than his father. His authority was an outgrowth of his formidable integrity.

• • •

Here was another of his traits that my mother marveled at, given its contrast with his parents' tendencies. He and she both were rigorous about speaking and acting honestly, but she was trained to it by her parents, especially John Humphreys, whose oft-spoken rule was "Never compromise a principle for gain." My father had had a less inspiring model. "One time he got a speeding ticket," my mother wrote, "and he paid it. His father was irate. 'Are you crazy?' he exploded. 'Why didn't you ask John to fix it for you?'" Uncle John Mehegan, Charlie's younger brother, was a Boston police lieutenant. "And Al said, 'But it was a stupid thing I did and I'll never do it at that intersection again.' His father had no comprehension of what he was talking about."[4] That he would get his uncle to fix a ticket was unthinkable. In his view, that would have been to corrupt John as well as himself. An inborn instinct for honesty was part of this; another part was respect for law. When I learned in school the legends about Honest Abe Lincoln, walking miles to repay a five-cent debt, I recognized the resemblance to my father.

I called his integrity "formidable," and by that I mean that it was something he stressed and insisted upon with us, and that reaching his standard felt to us mere mortals like scaling Mount Everest. In this quality, I suspect that none of us felt (or yet feel) ourselves to be in his league. And when we *did* fall short in his sight, as kids will do, we took it hard.

I can think of two occasions when he marched me off to make restitution to someone I had offended. The first time, I had broken a window in the garage of the Gallaghers' summer house at the end of Blanchard Road. He took me to see Mr. Gallagher (I guess the family had not been in residence when the deed was done) and made me apologize and pay some amount of money to cover the cost of the window. Mr. Gallagher was raking leaves, stopped to listen, looked at me gravely, and accepted the apology. The second time, I and my friend Eddie stole a pumpkin from the patch of Alfred Gomes, a prominent member of the local Cape Verdean community. The field had been picked and a few stunted pumpkins left behind, so Eddie and I thought it wouldn't matter if we gleaned. But Mr. Gomes had seen us and called my father. Again the forced march—this time me and Eddie, whose parents must have been consulted—to apologize to Mr. Gomes and to pay him for the pumpkin. I think it was twenty-five cents. My father must have supplied the cash; I certainly had no money. To him, you might say, these payments were like the fine he had paid for speeding. It was not that the money mattered. It was about making things right.

I was fascinated by fire in those days. It's a wonder I did not burn the house down. Once I accidently set the woods ablaze behind our yard—not really woods, but a narrow line of chokecherry trees. The fire department came with their brush-fire truck and put out the smoky blaze. No one had seen me do it, but my father was immediately suspicious. That day or night he confronted me. "You did it, David, didn't you?" he said. "You started the fire."

I denied it. "Not me," I said, "I didn't do it."

He looked at me for a long time, and then said, quietly, "I don't believe you," and turned away.

I have never felt more ashamed of myself in my life than I did at that moment. I had lied to my father and he knew it, and I knew that he knew it. His tone of contempt was worse than a beating. Here was a lie that caused me real pain — not an unprofitable experience. But he had no proof that I had done it and so, with his fine legal mind, could not punish me.

One day in the summer of 1964, when I was fifteen, I was in Boston for the day, visiting my grandmother on Beacon Hill. Late in the afternoon, I took the old Brighton Avenue trolley out to Union Square, Allston, and walked over to 120 Braintree Street to meet my father at his office at B. Snyder, to ride home with him. He was not quite finished working, so I sat and waited. I noticed a slip of paper taped to the wall opposite his desk. On it was written in pencil, about an inch in height, "10¢." I said to him, "Dad, what's that?" He looked up briefly, said "Ten cents a minute," and turned back to his work.

"What does it mean?" I asked.

He explained that it was his pay rate. He had divided his salary by the number of minutes in the forty-hour work week and posted the quotient to remind himself that he owed his employer every minute of his time when he was on duty. To those in the habit of thinking of union workers as layabouts, I point out that this was the stance of a committed union man who believed that a contract was binding. There was to be no goldbricking, no hanging around the water cooler. He was not pulling down big money for his loyalty and his efforts, notwithstanding his skills and experience. Ten cents a minute adds up to a gross salary of $12,480, or about $98,000 in 2017 dollars. He always had more self-respect than money.

I would have to say, looking back, that admirable as his integrity was, he dialed it up unreasonably at times. Perhaps, as I wrote in the last chapter, this was in partial counterbalance to the nagging addiction of which he could not have been proud. Or perhaps he stood so strongly upright because deep inside he feared that he was actually not much good or that, as some had said to his face, he would never be the man his father was.

Aside from its application to us, which he took as a parental duty, his moral code was always pointed at himself. That is, he was not generally a finder of fault in others to his own advantage. He was not like the biblical hypocrite who says, "Thank God I'm not like that tax-collector over there." Nor did his code make him a tiresome, solemn old owl. If it had, no one would have wanted to be around him. Finally, there are three things to say about his integrity: He was not a hypocrite, not a cynic, and not naive. As to the latter, on land and sea he had known enough of the "crooked timber of humanity," in Isaiah Berlin's famous phrase, not to be naive about human failure or evil. He took what he saw as the moral high road and did not care if it was less traveled by.

• • •

Notwithstanding his seriousness in ethical matters, he could be extremely funny, and when funny things happened, he would laugh until tears ran. No matter what its problems, unless a family is beset by rancor, bitterness, or tragedy, there are going to be such times. One Thanksgiving, as a practical joke, he bought a Cornish hen—about the size of a pigeon—along with the turkey. Unknown to us, he and my mother roasted both together. When the time came to take out the turkey and bring it into the dining room for carving (he always carved the turkey at the table), we heard a great commotion in the kitchen, and shouts of "Oh, *no!*" The door burst open and in he came, holding a huge wide platter with a tiny bird at the center. "The turkey shrank," he said with a poker face. We children stared for a long moment. We had no idea what a Cornish hen was. Was Thanksgiving ruined? My mother stood in the doorway with her hand over her mouth; finally she could not help cracking with laughter. He enjoyed such moments, and the great holidays themselves, enormously. "Dad did not drink on holidays," Paula said. "He might have had a little glass of wine. He loved family stuff. He loved all of us around the table. Peter might be flicking peas at us, but we were all there."

There was the legendary incident of the nighttime mosquito. My mother was an early-to-bed, early-to-rise person. One summer night, she was sound asleep while my father was propped up in bed reading a magazine, with the light on. She stirred suddenly and sat up, not fully awake. At that moment, a mosquito landed on my father's face. She snatched the magazine out of his hands and whacked him across the face, knocking his glasses off. When she came fully awake and realized what she had done, they started to laugh uncontrollably, and they laughed all night. Indeed they laughed for decades. "She knocked my *glasses* off!" he would say, and the hilarity would begin again. There were many such moments, salted among the difficult times.

It was always apparent to us that he adored my mother, and that he saw her arrival in his life as a saving grace. One thing above all others that would make him lose his temper was our showing any disrespect to her. I once asked him what he thought his life would have been had he not married her. Without a moment's thought, he said, "I would have been a bum." While perhaps he would not truly have ended as a derelict or homeless person, I do not doubt that his devotion to her (and through her, to us) was like the sea anchor that saved the *Nantucket*, keeping him upright and headed into the wind. Admiring her as we did, to know that he was the admirer-in-chief was to make him an even bigger man in our eyes.

He was openly affectionate with her, and I remember often his sweeping her up in an embrace unexpectedly, in the kitchen or elsewhere. At such moments, he would often tell her that he loved her, in front of us. In my memory, he was always the initiator of these embraces, although she didn't resist, would never push him away, never say, "Oh, Al—*stop!*" Sometimes he would sing snatches of the old George M. Cohan song "Mary's a Grand Old Name," pronouncing the name with an exaggerated "*May*-ree": "For it was May-ree, May-ree…"

• • •

I have said that he tended not to find fault with other people, at least not loudly and openly, but there were exceptions, and one exception relates to sex. He made no effort to hide his loathing for a certain woman in the town whom we all knew. I didn't understand it. She seemed nice enough to me. I knew her husband and kids. I'll never forget my father saying to me, spacing the words out and stressing the object: "She . . . is . . . a . . . *pig.*" I had no idea what this meant when I was eleven or twelve—I took it to mean that she was a slob or somehow vulgar. Then my mother explained, with some sort of euphemism, that the woman had told someone that my father had made a pass at her. This got back to him. The imputation that he would take even a step toward cheating on my mother was so offensive to him that it put the accuser, in the Irish expression, beyond the beyond.

I have little to report about my father's sexuality, since I don't know much about it. My mother wrote more than once that "he surely was a normal male."[5] I'm not sure exactly what that means, probably that he had a healthy appetite. There is no doubt, from my mother's description of their wedding night, that he had had some sexual experience, which she had not, but she did not think less of him for that, didn't think he had ever been a roué. She wrote, "He had had such a rough life, carousing, as he told me, in all the seamy ports of the world. He went to brothels with his friends, his young friends even from the *Nantucket,* but for some reason he could not explain, he would wait for his friends in the parlor and never go in to the back rooms. He never felt critical of them, though."[6]

I suppose this story provokes a smirk in some readers, but its very oddness makes it believable to me. It would have been simple, after all, for him to have told my mother that he never went to whorehouses with his shipmates. But to have told her that he did go but sat in the parlor is consistent with his way of going in at the narrow gate, so to speak—doing exactly what he thought was right, not caring what anyone else thought, but at the same time not judging his shipmates for the difference.

I don't know how well their needs matched, yet I am not aware of, and find no reference in her writings to, any conflict over sex. As Catholics, they did not use artificial birth control; rather they used the "rhythm method," sometimes laughingly called Vatican roulette. Even though my mother wrote that she was extremely irregular, they never had more than four children, probably because most of the time she was too tired, or they both were. It's not all that surprising, I guess: She was thirty-one when her first child was born and had three more over the next six years, ending with me at age thirty-seven. Even so, she wrote, "No one got pregnant more easily than I did. Had Al been more demanding, I could have had fifteen children." There was one last, terribly sad comment about it late in her memoir: "I do think now that had I responded physically then, Al might not have drunk as much as he did."[7]

• • •

Between him and me, there was always a reserve; unlike Paula, there was no climbing onto his lap for me. I am sorry to say that I don't remember any physical affection, not a hug or an arm around the shoulders. A kiss would have been unthinkable. It was not, it would seem, what he knew fathers to do, and at the time I did not find the absence of affection strange. That was doubtless due as much to my nature as his. Yet the day would come, very late, when he would look back at his way of relating to us with regret.

I was always amazed to hear my mother talk about what he was like when he was young—lively, fun-loving, a snappy dresser and a "fabulous dancer"—and about how much he had enjoyed us as babies. It was hard to reconcile that figure with the often silent, brooding, overweight, pontificating, even boring fault-finder we knew, who so much of the time did little except work, watch a bit of television, read cheap detective novels, and stare out the window. It was not as if a young stud had lost a few steps in middle age. Rather it was as if two persons with the same name had occupied different parts of one lifetime.

You learned to approach him cautiously, since you never knew what sort of mood he might be in. This is a very common experience for the children of alcoholics. He was caught in the alcoholic trap, where you drink to relieve the pain, but in its effect on your body and psyche, the drink makes the pain worse in the long run, which prompts you to drink all the more. At a certain point, whatever its causes or tangled psychologies, the drinking becomes an independent vortex. Paula said, "It was in later years that he became much more difficult, and that was all because of the drinking, and his drinking was how he self-medicated.

A man with that much torture in his soul was not going to be able to live without something else."

"Torture in his soul." Something was gnawing at him from the inside. Possibly, as I have suggested, it was classic depression with a physiological basis, accelerated by feelings of failure and inadequacy, the sense of never measuring up to his own high standards for himself, that had dogged him since his poignant conversation with his guardian angel on the *Nantucket*. Or perhaps most strongly it was the fear of being abandoned, of being ejected from, or being found unworthy of, a circle of love.

Nevertheless, somehow we knew that underneath his often stern or grumpy facade he was a sensitive, emotional, and tenderhearted person. Paula and I both remember accidents that happened in his presence (in her case a car door closing on a finger, in mine a fall onto my back from a height) in which he leaped to grab us up in his arms, with fear in his eyes. I also remember an incident between him and me that I'm not sure my siblings have ever heard about. It had to do with a dog.

We had dogs and cats, birds and guinea pigs, like all families, and none of the pets, I would have to say, worked out well. I had two dogs several years apart, Daisy and Mac, both mongrels. Daisy bit the mailman and my father gave her to John Andrade, a Cape Verdean friend who had a landscaping business and needed a watchdog at home when he was out working. Happily, John told my father later, to his great amusement, "She best dog I ever have—she bite *everybody!*" But Mac was different: quiet and sweet, affectionate, with soulful eyes. He was mostly beagle, with a piebald face.

Though we had pets, we did not necessarily take proper care of them. Veterinary care cost money. Mac must not have had the usual immunizations, because one summer when I was about twelve, he fell ill, listless with running eyes, and then could not stand up. I don't know how, but I suspected that it was canine distemper.

It must have been on a Saturday that my father and I took the dog to the veterinarian, whose name was Dr. Carr, at Hingham Animal Hospital. Not knowing that distemper is almost always fatal, I was worried but expected there would be some sort of treatment. Dr. Carr examined the dog, and said, very gravely, "You're right, David. It *is* distemper." We were to leave the dog, and he said he would call us. No one said "The dog is going to die," but the realization had dawned on me that the call would be to give us the bad news.

Dr. Carr gathered Mac up gently—he was too sick to stand—and carried him behind a counter and through a doorway to a stairway to the basement. I can still see his frightened, sad black, brown, and white face looking at me over the doctor's shoulder as he receded down the stairs.

We got in the car and started to drive home, south through Hingham, Cohasset, and into Scituate. Neither of us said anything. As we came to the VFW hall, my father suddenly steered to the left, into the small parking lot, and pulled up behind a delivery van. It was a pale color, about the size of a UPS truck, with two semicircular windows in the rear doors, parked along the grassy strip parallel to the road. I do not remember if he turned off the engine—probably not. I suppose I thought he was going to visit the bar, as he often did. Instead, he crossed his arms over the steering wheel, put his face down, and began to weep. I don't mean whimpers, but hard body-wrenching sobs. Here was something I had never seen, a grown man crying uncontrollably. That it was my father was all the more shocking. I stared straight ahead through the windshield at the back of the van.

After about a minute, or possibly less, he grew quiet, sat up and sighed, wiped his face with his sleeve, turned to me, and said, "I'll bet you think I'm an old softy, don't you?"

I said, "No, I don't." It was true. I never thought there was anything soft or weak about him. I knew he was human. I was dry-eyed about the dog that day. It was all too stunning and strange. Besides, my father's response was enough for both of us. He never spoke of it again.

Years later, someone who heard this story said to me, "He wasn't crying over the dog; he was crying over you." That hypothesis was clever and plausible. Nevertheless, they were *his* tears, not mine. There is no doubt that he was capable of that kind of feeling about a pet. For those few moments it was as if we had traded roles, and he was the grieving boy while I was the adult who sat stonily and did not shed a tear, because men do not.

• • •

His captain-of-the-ship act, his emphasis on exemplary behavior, discipline, and moral standards, changed when we reached our later teen years and adult life was in the offing. We could have real conversations with him. We could even challenge him a bit, respectfully, and he would listen and reconsider his position.

Before that change, he and Peter, especially, had the worst of the conflicts, perhaps because Peter was the oldest, more high-spirited than I, and for the most part not much of a student. I remember one vivid quarrel when my father slapped Peter and tried to pin his arms behind him, after which Peter ran out of the house. It was an argument over what my father believed was Peter's unsafe handling of a shotgun. Peter was into duck hunting at the time, and my father was a fanatic about gun safety. My mother wrote of this incident, "It was awful because Peter was as big as he was and I thought for one paralyzing moment that Peter was going to hit him back, but he didn't."[8]

There was more to it than the shotgun, undoubtedly. Peter's lackadaisical attitude toward school surely reminded my father of himself at that age, as recalled in the conversation with the guardian angel, and he worried about the consequences for Peter's future.

He needn't have worried. Peter got serious about schoolwork in his senior year of high school, earned good grades, and was accepted at Northeastern University, my father's alma mater, in the fall of 1959. He was to live with our grandmother and Uncle Jack on Beacon Hill for his college years. That was a wise move for him—it was probably my mother's idea—because Jack and my grandmother thought he was the cat's meow. It turned out also to be the turning point in his and my father's relationship. Years later, my mother told the story of coming into the house sometime that fall and hearing two men's voices in animated, laughing conversation. Who could that be? she wondered, then realized that it was my father and Peter, who had come home on a weekend. She had never heard them actually *talk* before, without the tone of criticism or defensiveness.

Florence went off to college a couple of years later, living in a residence hall. With her, too, his relationship changed for the better. His two eldest, the war babies whose births had made him so happy and filled him with hope for the peaceful future, had grown up, were on the verge of making their way in the world, and he discovered that he was proud of them. It would happen with Paula and me too. But time was short.

15.

Sickness

Iт must have been apparent to some people how relatively unhealthy my father looked by 1965. I did not recognize it because I had no basis for comparison. The few pictures of him from that time show a florid-faced, somewhat portly man with graying hair. He was fifty-four that fall, but now I think he looked at least ten years older. Still, he did not show any obvious signs of illness.

The year 1964 began painfully, as Uncle Jack Humphreys, who had been a surrogate father to Peter and Florence in wartime, as well as a great friend to Peter during his college years, died of a heart attack in New York in February. He was forty-nine. My grandmother never got over the shock. He was the only one of her children to die before her and, as my mother later wrote, "Truly I don't think she ever did grasp it. . . . Jack with his polio had been a special child."[1] For months after his death, she would continue to speak of him in the present tense.

Brother Peter and Julianne Sliney were married at Our Lady of Mercy Church in Belmont, September 26, 1964. The reception was at the Sheraton Commander Hotel in Cambridge. Alas, Pooch (our pet name for our grandmother, pronounced like the German word *putsch*) collapsed at home a few days before the wedding and died, age eighty-one, while the couple was on their honeymoon. They cut their trip short.

As the only brother, I was to be Peter's best man. The week before the wedding, before my grandmother's collapse, I rode with him in his two-tone green 1958 Chevy Bel Air to Lechmere Sales, a Cambridge department store, to buy tie bars for me and the ushers and a can of green spray paint to cover the rust around the headlights. He did not want his car to look like a junk box as he drove away with his bride after the reception, with everyone looking on and waving.

On the way back to my grandmother's place on Beacon Hill, Peter mentioned my father's drinking. I had never heard him speak of it before. As we drove along Memorial Drive, just before crossing the Longfellow Bridge over the Charles River, he said he was worried. "It's not the beer I worry about," he said. "It's the hard stuff." He was only twenty-two and had not lived with my father for four years, but he knew enough to be concerned. What had he seen or heard? My mother might have said something. Or perhaps the long stretches away revealed to him visible changes in my father that I, still living at home, had not noticed.

The wedding was festive, although shadowed by my grandmother's condition. She had not regained consciousness, but we were hopeful and did not know that she would not recover. My mother might have suspected as much; she knew that her mother would never be able to live alone on West Cedar Street, with Jack and Peter both gone.

It was a happy occasion for both my parents—they had worried so much about Peter in earlier years, and contended with each other about him, and now he had graduated from college, started his broadcasting career, and was about to be married. I wasn't watching my father, but I do not believe that he drank more than a bit of champagne at the reception, perhaps a glass of wine or two. He was not even tipsy. As Paula said, he did not get hammered on holidays or happy occasions, as so many people do.

I did not know how much he was drinking in those years, notwithstanding Peter's words of worry, and still do not know. I knew he drank, but the amount was obscured by all the discretion. I was too young to be counting empty bottles and of course did not accompany him into bars. One thing is certain: I had never seen him drunk—staggering, misbehaving, slurring his words, or violent—as I understood drunken behavior from movies and television. Nevertheless, even with his legendary ability to "hold his liquor," there were signs that change was afoot.

Sometime in the winter of 1965, I was riding into Boston with him on the commuter bus. He was going to work and I was going to school at Shaw Preparatory, a small inexpensive private school in which my mother had enrolled me because I was failing at Scituate High School. That night, he told me that on the morning trip he had been sick on the bus and vomited inside his topcoat, all over his suit. I cannot imagine how I did not notice, sitting right next to him, that that was happening. He was not obviously ill in any other way; he did not have the flu.

Then one night in Scituate, he picked me up in the car somewhere, I can't remember where, perhaps the library or the movie theater. He had not driven far before I knew that he was inebriated. He nearly ran off the road at a curve. This I had never seen before, nor would see again: Dad was *smashed*. He was incoherent. The next day, he apologized to me. He said he had not had much to drink. "I don't know what happened," he said in a tone of bafflement. "All at once, the roof caved in." It seems likely that his liver was beginning to fail.

● ● ●

I turned sixteen in October of 1964 and got my driver's license the following spring. Peter and Julianne's first child, Nancy, was born the next summer. Both of my parents were thrilled to be grandparents, and there are a few pictures of my father with Nancy, the only grandchild he was to know. In one picture, he is leaning back on a sofa with the white-swaddled newborn lying asleep on his stomach. He looks utterly contented.

A second wedding was coming, that of my sister Florence and Wally Ely. It was held August 21 at St. Mary's in Scituate. As at Peter's wedding the year before, my father had a fine time, with the added pleasure of giving away the bride. He was in rare form, full of jokes and laughter. After the ceremony, we were all piling into cars outside the church, about to go to our house on Blanchard Road, where the reception was to be held in the backyard, when my father strode down the driveway to the car I was in, looked in the window, and said, "They tell me the bride's father is supposed to walk home." He could barely get the words out, so hard was he laughing. Somehow, all the cars were full, and he had been moving from one to another looking for a seat, until finally one was found. He had arranged to borrow a lot of brown wooden folding chairs for the reception from the local funeral director, Ernie Richardson, but did not realize that all of them would have the words "Ernest A. Richardson Funeral Home. Serving all faiths" stenciled in white on the back. They were arrayed on the lawn, just as they might have been for a funeral. It was the sort of accidental joke that he loved.

It was a beautiful late-summer day by the sea. The reception was informal and merry, as backyard summer receptions usually are. By this time, we had inherited a second Lowell skiff from the Gloucester cottage, bigger than the first, but it was hopelessly rotten and leaky, and my father had not had a chance to enjoy it. It was never launched in 1965 and was on blocks in the backyard. It had a perfect role at the reception, however. My father built a plywood platform on top and it served as a table for the punch bowl and food—a clever nautical touch. As he had the year before, he enjoyed himself immensely, and again I don't think he drank much—there would not have been hard liquor, anyway; certainly there was no catered bar. Evinced by one picture of him taken on the front lawn that afternoon, as Florence said recently, "He looked hale and hearty, and a month later he was in the hospital."

After I got my driver's license that year, sometimes during the day or evening I would be allowed to take the car—we still had the sixty-one Dodge—and drive a bit around town, for practice. One night in September, a couple of weeks after the wedding, I went for a ride. When I got home, my mother met me at the door, frantic with worry, and told me that my father had been hallucinating. He thought there was a dangerous animal in the backyard. He was wild-eyed, talking crazy. The physiological term for hallucinations related to the alcohol-damaged liver is alcoholic hallucinosis, or alcoholic psychosis. Usually the hallucinations come on suddenly, often involve some perceived threat, and can end as abruptly. We did not know that then. She got him to go to bed finally. Sometime later, she told me that her imagination had run wild that night. "I imagined him completely insane," she said. "He would be committed to McLean [McLean Hospital, the psychiatric hospital affiliated with Harvard Medical School], and I would go there every day to visit him." By the next morning, he was himself again. He even joked about the hallucinations.

Soon, however, it became clear that something was seriously wrong. He began to have severe abdominal pain. He went to Dr. Blanchard, the family GP, whose preliminary diagnosis was a stomach ulcer. He was treated for that, but the pain and sickness did not abate, and he was admitted first to South Shore Hospital in Weymouth, and later to Massachusetts General Hospital in Boston, at the foot of Beacon Hill, where my grandmother had died two years before. He came under the care of Dr. Robert Schapiro, a young internist specializing in gastroenterology. We learned that it was not an ulcer but liver disease. I do not recall that alcohol was mentioned to me as the cause, but perhaps that went without saying.

Soon after he was admitted to MGH, I met my mother somewhere downtown, perhaps after school, and walked with her toward South Station to get the bus to Scituate. She had just come from the hospital. When I asked her how long the doctor thought it would take for him to get better, she said something like, "He may not be getting better." I was stunned and questioned her further, but she did not say much more, and she never took that pessimistic tone again. From then on, his illness was always treated as serious but not necessarily fatal. I assumed that he would get better eventually. We were told about the remarkable regenerative powers of the liver. But I suspect now that Dr. Schapiro had given her a grim prognosis—or had told her that at best the outcome was in doubt.

My sister Paula and Tommy Stone were married in February 1966. My father was very sick by then, which made everything quieter. Again the reception was at our house, indoors because it was winter. There is a picture of him, looking thin and frail, holding up a glass of white wine for a toast in front of the fireplace. I don't know that he actually sipped it.

That spring, he was in MGH for extended periods, and my mother was anxious to get away from Scituate so that she could be closer to him. She said to me, "I just need a *perch*." About this time, she got a job as a secretary at the *Horn Book*, the children's book review magazine, which was then at 585 Boylston Street, Copley Square. It was an old small specialized Boston magazine, of the same sort as *Plays*, and she liked the quiet, bookish atmosphere set by the editors, Paul and Ethel Heins.

My parents agreed to sell the house on Blanchard Road to Peter and Julianne, an arms-length sale with no brokerage fees. My mother rented a tiny one-bedroom apartment at 88 Exeter Street in the Back Bay, behind the Boston Public Library at the corner of Blagden Street. I was still at the Shaw School at 739 Boylston Street. She would walk to work and I to school.

Eighty-eight Exeter Street is a yellow-brick building with a wrought iron door. We lived on the second floor, with windows overlooking Blagden Street and the south wall of the library. Since there was no door between the bedroom and the main room, we hung a curtain in the wide doorway. She had the bedroom. I slept in the main room, on a twin bed, which we made up into a kind of sofa during the day, with bolsters. An efficiency kitchen was built into the end opposite the two windows. The bathroom was ancient, with a wooden water closet mounted at the ceiling, and an Essex bathtub with ball-and-claw feet. There was no shower. Years later, 88 Exeter Street became a pricey boutique hotel, with several ugly stories stacked on top.

At some point that spring, my father came home to that apartment, which made it extremely tight. He was somewhat improved, but thereafter his condition moved steadily downhill. He was weak and frail and sometimes a bit delusional—not hallucinating but beset with uncharacteristic obsessions. For example, he began to think about having stylish new clothes and would pore over department store catalogs. One day, he tried to leave the apartment to go to the Anderson-Little men's store to buy a lot of clothes. He could barely walk, and my mother refused to let him leave. She literally blocked the door to the corridor and said, "No, Al, no, you can't. You're too weak." He argued with her angrily, but he *was* too weak to force his way, and he relented.

His hopes would rise and sink. One night at the hospital, he had a dream. Two crows were sitting on the footboard of his bed, having a discussion. One said to the other, "I don't want him. Do you?" The second crow replied, "No, I don't want him either." Although he was not superstitious, my father found this terribly funny, told everyone about it, and thought it was a good sign.

Of course he hoped to get well but could not be sure that he would, which made him sometimes think of the past with regret and promise to turn over a new leaf, especially toward us. My mother wrote, "When Peter, Florence, and Paula were married and David was 17, Al said to me, 'I have been so wrong about the way you brought up the children. I'm so proud of them and someday things will be different.'"[2] They already were different, of course, and I don't believe any of us felt that he had anything to make amends for. The gathering sorrow that something terrible was happening to him eroded any residual complaints we might have had about the past.

Sick as he was, he was still strong-willed and never complained of his plight, never whined or said, "Why me?" One day I came home from school, or my after-school job in the garment district, and my mother met me at the door. She told me that he was in terrible pain, in the bedroom, and was refusing to take medication. He wouldn't listen to her. She was desperate and asked me to try to reason with him. She said, "He loves Dr. Schapiro. Tell him that Dr. Schapiro wants him to take it." I parted the curtain and went in. He was sitting up on the bed, shirtless, with his back to the headboard. He was pathetically thin. His stick-like arms were arched straight back over his shoulders, gripping the top of the headboard. He was staring straight ahead, trembling, and paid no attention to me.

"Dad," I said, "please take some medicine."

"I'm not taking it," he said roughly, without looking at me.

"Dad, Dr. Schapiro wants you to take it."

He hissed at me, "I don't give a goddamn *who* wants me to take it. I'm *not taking it!*" This went back and forth. Suffering though he was, he was trying to be strong, to overcome this adversary by force of will and character. Then I resorted, in desperation, to begging.

"Please, Dad. Please. Please take it."

Finally, he gave in.

All of this, now that I look back on it, was hard for a teenager, especially one as awkward and socially inept as I was—I had no close friends, no one to confide in about what was happening. We were living in that shoe box of an apartment, me and my mother and horribly sick father. And so, early that summer, I asked them if they would let me rent a room somewhere. They agreed, and I rented a room on the second floor of 543 Commonwealth Avenue, on the corner of Gloucester Street, for seventeen dollars a week. It was on the third floor, facing Gloucester. Even seventeen dollars proved to be too much for me, with the small amount of money I was making at my part-time job packing and shipping neckties, so I had to take a smaller room, on the top floor facing the avenue, for eleven dollars. It was the size of a walk-in closet, with one door, one window, and no fire escape, and it was hot as an oven. It was just a place to sleep; I came home to Exeter Street in the afternoon and for meals.

If this was hard for me, at least I had a life ahead of me, but my mother and father must have known that theirs together was ending. Still, she was as tough and brave as he was. I don't remember her ever shedding a tear, at least not in front of me. She coped and managed and never complained or was distraught or hysterical. She once said, during this time, "I have a calm place in myself, and if I can just get to that place, I'm all right."

Sometime early in that summer, probably in June, we were to go to Scituate for the afternoon to visit Peter and Julianne, just to get my father out of the hot city. We rented a car. My mother drove, I was in the passenger seat, and my father slumped in the backseat. She had never driven a car with an automatic transmission, with no clutch, and she could not understand that you just took your foot off the gas pedal and put it on the brake. "Why doesn't it stall?" she asked. There were tense moments as the car jerked along Arlington Street, past the Public Garden and the Ritz Carlton, to Herald Street toward the Southeast Expressway, with my father growling at her from the backseat. Somehow she figured the car out and we got to Scituate. I'm not sure why I did not drive. Perhaps the rental contract forbade it.

It was a hot day. Peter and Julianne had hung over the fireplace mantel a framed painting, a print of Émile Renouf's *En Coup de Main (A Helping Hand)*. It depicts an old sailor in a dory, holding an oar with a little girl beside him. The sailor is wearing a yellow sou'wester, with a pipe clamped in his teeth, and is smiling down benignly at the child. She is wearing a dress and apron, and a red cap, and holds on to the oar with him. We had had lunch and were sitting in the living room. Peter pointed to the picture and said, "Dad, that will be you and Nancy in a few years." My father looked up at the picture and said, "If I live that long." Peter answered brightly, "Oh, *sure* you will!"

He was weak and needed to rest for a while before we started back to Boston. The nearest bedroom was on the second floor. Peter and I helped him climb the stairs, slowly, one of us on either side of him. My mother stood at the bottom and watched. Later, she said to me, "David, when I saw you and Peter with Dad, all I could think of was the proverb 'A mother's beauty is renewed in her daughters; a father's strength is renewed in his sons.'" I never until now looked for the origin of this saying, assuming that it was somewhere in the Bible, perhaps the Book of Proverbs. But I found to my surprise that it is not from Scripture, nor did it turn up in any dictionary of quotations. It might have been a Celtic proverb that she had learned from one of her parents or grandparents, from Ireland or Cape Breton.

Eventually he went back to the hospital. My mother went there every day, though she did not always stay a long time. There was one other daily visitor: my grandfather. Charlie, now seventy-two, would come every day and sit there for hours, saying almost nothing. He had always been a chatty, sociable man, but not now. My father said of this, with some surprise and amusement, "He's like a faithful dog."

He was dying, it was now clear, though no one said so. Then his beloved aunt Catherine died without warning. My mother, anxious not to add a broken heart to his other sufferings, decided to keep the news from him. But when she went to see him the next day, she discovered to her horror that Charlie had been there ahead of her and had briskly delivered the news, without thought of the possible impact. She found my father utterly crushed. For the first and only time in his sickness, he told her to go away. He was so depressed that he could not bear to see anyone, not even her. His life was all pain, sickness, death, misery, regret.

My mother was outraged, though she said nothing to Charlie. To her, it was his final act of stupidity, ignorance, and cruelty. It was unforgivable. By this time Charlie was showing signs of dementia, though I don't believe that my mother was aware of it. My father's old friend Arthur Penney, who was barely holding together what was left of Powers & Mehegan, told me that Charlie was regularly losing his car and doing other strange things that we now see as symptoms of Alzheimer's disease.

● ● ●

The last time I saw my father conscious was, I believe, Monday, July 11. I was in his room and he asked me to shave him. It is not easy to shave another person. You don't know how much pressure to use. I didn't want to cut him. When I finished, his face was still very stubbly, but he seemed satisfied. A day or two later, he fell into a coma, and he died on Friday, July 15, two weeks short of his fifty-fifth birthday. I cannot remember why I was not there. I do not think Paula was present either; perhaps Peter or Florence was, or Mary Rose. My mother must have asked me not to wait at the hospital, possibly out of concern for my feelings. That Friday I was in the apartment at 88 Exeter Street when the telephone rang. It was Dr. Schapiro. He spoke to me with extraordinary kindness and sympathy. All I can remember saying to him in response was "Thank you."

Dr. Schapiro was surprised that the patient had declined so rapidly and asked my mother to consent to an autopsy. She agreed, because she wanted to help the understanding of cirrhosis, because she was grateful for Dr. Schapiro's care and kindness, and, as she said to me, because my father had loved him. Later, he wrote to her about the results. She showed me the letter but must not have kept it, because I never saw it again and it is not among her papers. In my memory, he wrote that my father's liver was severely scarred and shrunken, and that "his disease was undoubtedly progressive." He had never had a chance.

Peter remembers looking at the autopsy report with my mother and her telling him that Dr. Schapiro had said that it was nonalcoholic cirrhosis. As Paula said, it is possible, considering his severe illness in Princeton in 1943, that his liver had been previously damaged by hepatitis, rendering it more susceptible to attack. Nevertheless, it is hard—for me impossible—to believe that decades of drinking were not the foremost cause. Laennec's cirrhosis, noted on the death certificate, is closely associated with alcohol abuse. Perhaps my mother was advocating for him as she always had, clinging to the possibility that he bore no share of fault for his fate.

As to the exact mechanism and driving forces of his death, Peter sensibly says, "Who knows?", to which I add, It doesn't matter. The apposite fact is that something terrible happened to him. One could only wish there had been mercy, wish that he could have had more time, given how hard he had tried, how much he had loved, throughout his life.

16.

The End of Time

Hᴇ ᴡᴀs ʙᴜʀɪᴇᴅ ꜰʀᴏᴍ sᴛ. ᴍᴀʀʏ's, in Union Cemetery in Scituate, in a double lot now shared with my mother. Wakes at that time, incredible as it seems today, typically went for three days before the funeral, and there was much sitting around at home before going to the funeral home—Ernie Richardson's, of course. Once when we were sitting in the living room at Blanchard Road, someone asked my grandfather, who had been mostly silent over these days, no longer the hail-fellow-well-met with cigar in his mouth and pockets full of cash, "Are you retired, Mr. Mehegan?" He hesitated, then mustered one word: "Semi."

I do not know if my mother ever saw her father-in-law again. Probably not, unless in his casket. He lived another three years in steady mental decline. My cousin Ginny Dillon remembered, "One day when my mother was not home he dressed himself, pants over his pajamas, and somehow made it to the yacht club via train. They found him wandering close by but confused about where he was or how he got there. He had little short-term memory, but detailed memories of Southie. His health declined and he needed round-the-clock medical care." He died in 1969, age seventy-five, and was buried with Julia. Presumably he had bought the lot before the mysterious quarrel and eventual breakup. For Mary Rose, at least her parents were in some manner together again, no more silent, perhaps, than they had been in life.

My parents had long assumed that Charlie had accumulated

substantial assets, given his sharpness in real estate and business, but they did not know the details. It turned out there was nothing. A few years after my father's death, Mary Rose learned that Charlie had been going around Wheeler Point in Gloucester, knocking on doors, offering to sell his little summer cottage on the Annisquam River. She moved quickly to get control of his affairs, including the cottage. By then it was obvious that his assets, whatever they had been, were mostly gone with the mind.

Whatever Charlie's true feelings about his firstborn, he had not forgotten or erased him. In his will, which he had made in 1956, before my father left Powers & Mehegan, my grandfather left:

1. To my daughter, Mary R. Dillon of said Boston, my real estate on Wheeler Street, Wheeler's Point, Gloucester.
2. To my children, the said Mary R. Dillon, and Alfred C. Mehegan, in equal shares, all the rest, residue and remainder of the property of which I shall die seized and possessed or to which I may be entitled at the time of my decease.

At the time of his decease, Mary Rose already had the house. There was nothing else to divide, other than a few personal possessions, even had there been anyone to divide it with.

I had always supposed that my grandfather had no real interest in religion, notwithstanding his friendship with various priests and bishops (including Dickie Cushing) and his longtime business connections with the Church. He didn't seem the type, somehow. But of course that assumption was colored by my mother's view of his character. Still I was curious, so recently I asked my cousin Jean Dillon, older sister of Ginny, who lived with him for much of her childhood, "Did Grandpa go to Mass?" She replied, "Every day."

I was startled. "Every *day?*"

"Yes, he would go out early and go to St. Monica's in South Boston." St. Monica's was on the way from Dorchester to Powers & Mehegan.

So Charlie, "that irascible man" in my mother's words, was a "daily communicant," the sort held up in Catholic tradition as a model of piety. I venture to say that she would have been surprised.

• • •

Immediately after my father died, my mother wrote to Esther, who lived in Mira Loma, a suburb of Los Angeles, and enclosed a picture of my father before he was sick, perhaps from one of the weddings. She received a reply, dated July 23:

> *Dear Mary,*
> Thank you for your very kind letter and picture of Al.
> I know that Al had all the care that he needed and all he really wanted he got from you. Mary, you have been such a loving and devoted wife. You have had such sorrow in the past two years. God grant you peace and happiness now.
> I wish I could have seen Al this year but the trip was more than I could make on the bus and finances wouldn't permit air travel.
> I have so much regret. I can truly say that I loved him, but am afraid I never convinced him of that. Mary, I am so grateful for you and what I know without anyone telling me that you have done for Al.
> *I love you all,*
Esther
>
> *Please keep in touch with me.*

Two details in this remarkable letter leap out at me. First, Esther knew all along that her oldest child had never felt loved by her. He could and would not have told her that, but she knew. Second, she knew that my mother had filled that empty space—"all he really wanted he got from you"—as well as any wife could do. She could not know how closely her words echoed my mother's own, in her love-struck 1940 letter to Rita Greene, announcing her engagement: "He is *everything* I've ever wanted."

They did keep in touch. Esther died in July of 1987, age ninety-four.

She was in a nursing home in Norco, another Los Angeles suburb, blind and unable to eat. There was no Mass, only a prayer and rosary service at the funeral home, conducted by a deacon from the local parish. She had planned the service to the last detail, including the reading of a poem by Scottish-American clergyman Robert Freeman, "In My Father's House."[1] An excerpt:

> *No, not cold beneath the grasses,*
> *Not close-walled within the tomb;*
> *Rather, in our Father's mansion,*
> *Living in another room.*
>
> *Living like the man who loves me,*
> *Like my child with cheeks abloom,*
> *Out of sight, at desk or school-book,*
> *Busy in another room.*
>
> *Nearer than my son whom fortune*
> *Beckons where the strange lands loom;*
> *Just behind the hanging curtain,*
> *Serving in another room.*

She was buried in the San Fernando Mission Cemetery in Mission Hills, under a small simple flat stone that I found in 1994: "Esther Carson, 1893–1987." I wrote her obituary in the *Boston Globe*, before management made a sensible rule prohibiting staff-written obituaries of relatives. It ran mostly intact on July 16, 1987, except for one line trimmed by the copy desk, which I had written to make it clear why this item about a West Coast carny girl would be in a Boston paper: "Her oldest son, Alfred Mehegan of Scituate, died in 1966."

Not long afterward, a small package addressed to me arrived in the mail from Mae Donahue, Esther's sister-in-law, who was in her late eighties. In the package was another, smaller lumpy envelope. Written on the outside, in a spidery hand, were the words, "Esther's rosary."

• • •

Aside from whatever equity might have remained from the sale of the Scituate house and settlement of the mortgage, my father left nothing but possessions and whatever cash was in the bank. Fortunately, besides her own pay, my mother had had his salary from B. Snyder Co., which continued to pay him throughout his illness. After his death, she wrote to the company to ask whether my father had been eligible for profit sharing. On August 19, she received this reply:

> *Dear Mrs. Mehegan,*
> With reference to your letter of August 12, 1966, Al was nine months short before he would have any equity in the Profit Sharing Plan.
> Al had a personal loan from my brothers and myself for $500.00. He repaid $200.00 on his debt and in order to help him we did not press him for the balance due. We do not want the balance due us, because considering Al's past performance with the Company we will consider the balance paid in full.
> With kindest personal regards from my brothers and myself, I remain
> > *Sincerely yours,*
> > *Ralph Snyder*

It was not so small a loan as it now seems. Five hundred 1966 dollars would be roughly equal to $3,800 in 2017, so forgiving it was a significant kindness, although, I suppose, they could have done it silently. She hadn't known about it; he might have been embarrassed to tell her. Later, the company secretary told her that the Snyders had admired him greatly and considered him to be "the best contract estimator in Boston."

As for insurance, there was a $10,000 Veterans Administration policy, for which she received $10,030.80, and a $250 VA benefit for death expenses. From Local 12 of the Journeymen Plumbers and Gasfitters, of which he had been a steadfast member from the time he first got his license, she received $1,500 on a group life policy. The state refunded his last plumber's license renewal fee: $30. Aside from these, all she had as a survivor's benefit was his Social Security.

She was never bitter and never complained. She continued to work at the *Horn Book* and eventually became the circulation manager, a position from which she retired when she turned sixty-five, in 1976. She survived my father for thirty-six years, reading and writing, keeping up an active correspondence with friends and relatives (and politicians), volunteering in schools, and maintaining her interest in public affairs. She made phone calls for Michael Dukakis during one of his gubernatorial campaigns, which, with her shyness, nearly killed her when phones were slammed down in her ear. She died in 2002, after only a few days of illness. At her funeral Mass at St. Mary's, I read aloud portions of a letter she had left for us. It was partly instructions for the service and partly reflections on her life. Looking back, she wrote in part, "There were sad times, too, none more than when Al died, so unexpectedly, at only fifty-four. But we had twenty-five wonderful years, which have sustained me ever since."

Once I asked her if she had ever thought of remarrying. She replied, "Oh, no. Once you've loved someone like that, you couldn't ever love another the same way." It seems to be true of both of them that what they wanted most from life was each other, and us.

● ● ●

I think of him often, virtually every day, and probably more than I would had I been five or twenty-five when he left. When I'm trying to hoist the bow of my boat on its trailer, to tip the rainwater aft to the drain hole under the stern sheets, I imagine him behind me, saying, "You're going to hurt yourself doing that. You need to get some mechanical advantage, like this." Or when I'm sailing awkwardly in Hingham Bay, I can hear his voice: "Steer closer to the wind before you come about. That's it—now: *hard-a-lee!*" And I can just imagine his harrumphing as I fumble on my knees with a leaky toilet or a plugged sink: "Those old pliers are useless. What you need is an eight-inch Westcott wrench. Don't you have a Vise-Grip?"

It's not the voice of a centenarian I hear, as he would be today, speaking to a man in his midsixties, which I am. It's the voice of a fifty-year-old speaking to a fourteen-year-old. A man who is gone, speaking to a boy who is also gone.

EPILOGUE

Bright Deep Water

MAY 29, 1931: "Rain. Still under sail. Canteen open today. Filled up with candy. Racing season opens back home. Would give a year of my life to be aboard *Mohawk* today instead of U.S.S. *Nantucket.*"

Until I read that entry in his 1931 *Nantucket* log, I never knew the name of the much-loved Indian-class sailboat my father spoke of fondly all his life. The Indian was a twenty-one-foot lapstrake sloop made by the Alden Yacht Co. of Boston. Alden, which closed in 2008, is best known for its large yachts, but the Indian was a hit for the middle class. Designed by Sam Crocker, about one hundred were built, mainly for the local racing members of the yacht clubs of Massachusetts Bay. They were individually named for Indian tribes: *Micmac, Huron, Chippewa, Cayuga, Mohawk.* The first was built in 1921.

In the autumn of 2014, friend and master painter Butch Ustach of Hull was painting our garage. An affable bear of a man with white hair, Butch is a sailor and longtime member of the Hull Yacht Club, an unpretentious club, more about boating than socializing. During a break, I was telling him about a maintenance problem—a spot of rot—with my wooden skiff, which was sitting on a trailer in my yard. "I once restored a twenty-one-foot wooden sailboat," he said. "I had to go to Newburyport to get the right width cedar planks."

"What kind of boat was it?" I asked.

"It was an Indian."

"You had an Indian?" I said. "My father had an Indian that he learned to sail on. It was called *Mohawk.*"

Butch gave me an amazed look. "*Mohawk.* That was *my* boat. It was *Mohawk.*"

In the mid-1970s, he had bought the old boat, which had been out of the water for years, from an elderly member of a Quincy Bay club, replaced the rotten wood, put it back in the water, and sailed it for several years. He later showed me a framed photograph of it, with the name *Mohawk* in bronze letters on the transom, himself at the helm. It had never occurred to me that it could still exist, although I know that wooden boats, like furniture, can last for centuries if properly cared for. "What happened to it?" I asked.

"My kids were born and I had to stop putting money into it. I sold it to somebody in Hull." His memory was fuzzy about what happened to it after that, but later he remembered that it had been acquired by someone else in town. He couldn't remember the name, only, "It was the guy who restores the wooden horses on the carousel. It was in his yard for years."

The 1927 carousel is the last relic of Paragon Park, the old amusement park that for most of the twentieth century had stood along Nantasket Beach in Hull, where young Esther Donahue had dived off a tower into a tank in the summer of 1910. A nonprofit foundation owns and operates the carousel, near the beach, and its sixty-six beautiful wooden horses are being carefully restored and lavishly repainted, one by one, as money is raised. The restoration shop is part of the Paragon Park Museum.

Not long after our first conversation, Butch stopped by my house to bring me the one relic of the old boat that he had kept. It was part of the original bronze gooseneck fitting, which connected the boom to the mast and allowed the sail to swivel freely in the wind. He had replaced it with a new one but kept the old.

• • •

I am not sentimental or given to magical thinking. By the laws of probability, strange coincidences are inevitable, and while they strike us as weird when they happen, they are not omens. They do not, in my view, carry messages or instructions. Even so, coincidences and weird dreams can put unexpected thoughts in our heads, raise poignant questions. I could not stop thinking about *Mohawk*. The thought in my mind was this: All the steel ships Al Mehegan had served on, from the U.S.S. *Nantucket* to the ocean liner S.S. *Manhattan*, to the S.S. *Young America* and the *Sea Runner*, are long gone. One was scuttled off Omaha Beach the summer of 1944, two were sunk by U-boats, one was lost in a storm, the rest were scrapped. Was it possible that the graceful, delicate little wooden bird that he had loved and sailed as a youth in Boston Harbor, before he had ever thought of the ships in his future, had survived them all and was still afloat somewhere? I decided that I could not leave that question unanswered.

The wood carver restoring the horses on the old Hull carousel is James Hardison. He has been working on the project for years, and as money is raised, eventually all the horses will be like new. Here was a second coincidence: My sister Florence is a board member of the carousel foundation and knows James Hardison well. She asked him if he had bought an Indian named *Mohawk* from a man in Hull. He told her that he had. Eventually, he told her, he had given the boat to the South Boston Yacht Club.

I went to see James Hardison on a hot summer day by the sea. He was in the shop adjacent to the museum, facing the ocean, and pulled the sliding door aside to let me in, then closed it to try to keep the cool air in. He has a ruddy complexion and thick white hair. The small shop was crammed with lumber, tools, cans of paint, and wooden horses in various states of restoration. A horse behind him had a base coat of white, with brown on the mane, without yet the extraordinary decorative enamels and glass jewels that would be applied last. The artist held a brush in his hand, with copper metallic paint on the bristles.

He told me that he had bought the boat from a local wooden-boat fancier, who had bought it from Butch Ustach. He had hoped to restore it (Butch's work had been incomplete), but he said, "I just couldn't get to it." Gesturing backward and sideways with the brush, he said, "I had all this work."

"Why did you give it to the yacht club?" I asked.

"Because I was told they wanted to rebuild the Indian fleet." He was leaving it in good hands, he thought.

I got in touch with my cousin Frank Manning, son of my father's cousin whose family he had stayed with during the battle between his parents in early childhood. Frank is the unofficial historian of the South Boston Yacht Club. We met for lunch, and when I told him the story of *Mohawk* being given to the yacht club for restoration, he nodded and said, "George Kulda." At my puzzled look, he explained.

"George Kulda is an old member of the club, who lives in Burlington"—that is, Massachusetts. "He has restored many wooden boats, rebuilt them from the waterline. My recollection is that boat was in the cellar of the yacht club for years. Then I think George and his sons David and Billy took it away, intending to restore it. But when they got it home and looked at it closely, they decided it was too far gone to save."

"What happened then?" I asked. Frank did not know. George Kulda, he said, was in his late eighties and not in vigorous health. He promised to try to contact the sons but never succeeded in reaching them by phone.

I decided to try on my own. With some Internet digging, I found an address for a George Kulda in Burlington. I wrote a letter explaining my mission: simply to find out what happened to *Mohawk*. It can be hard to reach people by phone or email, but the postal service is still reliable, and my experience is that anyone will read a letter. A week or so later, I got a telephone call. It was Billy Kulda.

"We got your letter," he said. "My father doesn't remember too much these days. That boat has been gone about three or four years. Carpenter ants took the boat apart. There might still be the rudder and tiller. You should talk to my brother David. He's the one who saved it from the dumpster." He gave me David's number.

David, too, proved to be difficult to reach. Eventually, though, he called me.

"It was in the cellar of the club for years," David said. "It was a pigsty down there. They would throw trash in it. There were cats living in it." Finally there was a move to clean out the cellar, including throwing the old hulk away, but David objected. "I said, 'You're not going to throw that in a dumpster.' One of the old-timers, Whitey Doyle, told me it was one of the first ten Indians built. It still had the hull shape, still had the ribs." The brothers put it on a truck and took it to Burlington. But when they inspected it closely, they concluded it was too late. "It was all full of dry rot," David said. "Nothing could be saved."

This should have been the end of the story, but David said he thought the mast and boom were still in the shed behind the house. I could have them if I wanted them. "You could make a nice flagpole out of the mast," he said, adding that he had thought of doing so himself, at his father's cottage on Cape Cod.

The image appealed to me. A flagpole from the original mast. Wouldn't that be a fitting memorial, of a sort?

Nothing happened for months. The winter of 2015 came, with mountains of snow everywhere. When the storms abated and the snow had melted enough to move around, I called David again and made a date to drive up on a Saturday in mid-March to see him and look at the mast and the boom.

That Saturday, it was raining. The address was on a short street with a cul-de-sac. The house was a 1960s split-level with a pickup truck in front and a black mailbox. There was no name or house number, but it had to be the place, because all around it were old boats covered by tattered tarps. It was clear that not much had been done to them recently. I knocked, and a burly man of about sixty came to the door. "David?" I said.

"No," he said. "Billy. Was David supposed to meet you?" When I said that he was, Billy made a hurried cell-phone call to his brother, who was in his car miles away and, it was clear, had forgotten the appointment or lost track of the time. "What were you going to show him?" Billy asked him. "OK," he said after a moment, "OK," and hung up. He lit a cigarette.

"Maybe I could explain what this is all about," I said.

"Pull up a chair," said Billy.

Billy Kulda was a machinist for the Massachusetts Port Authority, at Logan Airport in Boston. Younger brother David was a carpenter and all-around construction worker. The two brothers lived here with their ninety-year-old father, who was currently staying with their sister in Illinois.

I had not told him the whole story during his first brief call to me, months before. Now I explained about the book, about the boat and what it had meant to my father, about the strange coincidence with Butch. I just felt, I said, that I should follow this story to the end, find out what happened to *Mohawk*, and that David had told me there was a piece of the boat still here. At least I would like to see it.

Billy listened and said, "You're making me feel guilty. The boat was here for years, but it was completely eaten up by carpenter ants"—the oak, the mahogany, everything but the cedar. The knees were warped, the seams were opened up. It was a wreck.

"We were going to just get rid of it," Billy said, "but then my brother Scott knew of a guy in Maine who wanted to build a replica of an Indian and would buy the old hardware." They called the man, made a deal, and stripped off the old bronze hardware. He drove down from Maine, paid, and took the parts.

"Did he ever build the boat?" I asked. Billy didn't know.

We got up and went out the back door, wending our way around mountains of snow and old boats to a shed. It was not a building but a large wooden frame covered with plastic. Inside, there was an old powerboat, in need of repair, along with an assortment of junk, tools and leftovers from numerous projects. Billy led me to one wall, and there on a set of hooks was a long mast of very old wood, and a boom lashed to it. We made a rough measurement. The mast was about twenty-three feet and the boom about sixteen. I looked at them for a long time, and a practical inner voice said, "OK, you can't carry this mast on your Subaru, and if you did take it, or even just the boom, what are you going to do with it?"

I knew what I would not do. I would not stick it in the ground for a flagpole. I would put it in my garage, and it would hang there, untouched alongside my oars and the mast of my boat, just as it was hanging here. Sometime in the future I or someone else would have to get rid of it. It did not make any sense for me to take it. Maybe I *was* being sentimental. My father would say, "Forget it. It's a piece of wood. It's not me."

"I think," I said to Billy, "I won't take this today. It won't fit on my car anyway. I want to think about it some more." This was the truth. Then I asked him, "After you took the hardware off, what happened to the boat? Did you take it to the dump?"

He said, "I feel like it was a sin, but I knew that boat was never going in the water again. I had my chainsaw here, and I sawed it up in pieces."

"It wasn't a sin," I said impulsively. "It's like when you have an old dog who can't get up on his feet anymore. You do what you have to do."

He nodded.

"What happened to the wood?" I asked.

"It went in fireplaces."

"So it gave some warmth."

"That's right," he said, brightening a bit. "That boat was useful its whole life."

Before I left, for some reason I said to Billy, "Tell your father Charlie Mehegan's grandson was here."

He said that he would.

• • •

It was the end of the *Mohawk* trail. I hope the old bronze hardware was used by the man in Maine on his replica Indian, but I did not find out because Billy and David did not remember his name. It's better not to know. I like to think that the bronze blocks, shackles, and cleats, which link the working parts of a sailboat and make it go before the wind, all together form a kind of ghost of *Mohawk*, still giving pleasure to someone in Casco or Penobscot Bay, as they did once to a boy in Boston Harbor, with brisk airs, the boat heeling smartly, and nothing but bright deep water ahead.

Acknowledgments

I am greatly indebted to my sisters, Florence Ely and Paula Weeks, and my brother, Peter Mehegan, for their memories, photographs, and strong support for this project. With longer and more detailed memories than mine, they helped to make this story come alive.

Uncle Jack Carson (1927-2016), who did not live to see the printed version, was an invaluable source of details and photographs of Esther Carson's professional and private life after 1920, as was David Carson, his younger brother.

My research was greatly aided by Janis Duffy, archivist at the Massachusetts Maritime Academy; Valerie Uber, archivist at Boston Latin School; and Michelle Romero, assistant archivist for special collections in the Snell Library at Northeastern University. Many thanks also to my cousins, Jean and Ginny Dillon; to cousin Frank Manning, historian of the South Boston Yacht Club, carousel wood-carver James Hardin, David and Billy Kulda, and especially Frank (Butch) Ustach, all of whom helped in the search for *Mohawk*. For their support, thanks also to Katherine A. Powers and Sir Christopher Ricks, who understand problematic fathers. Thanks to my wife, Julianne, who is always patient, and to my son, Owen, who said, "Tell me about Al" and helped me track down *Young America* and *Sea Runner*.

Works Cited

Ackerley, J. R. *My Father and Myself*. New York: Coward-McCann, 1969.

Allport, Gordon W. *The Nature of Prejudice*. Boston: Addison-Wesley Publishing Co., 1954.

Bamforth, Charles A. and Richard A., eds. *Iron Jaw: A Skipper Tells His Story; Captain Charles N. Bamforth*. Pittsburgh: Dorrance Publishing, 2002.

Bier, Lisa. *Fighting the Current: The Rise of American Women's Swimming, 1870–1926*. Jefferson, N.C.: McFarland & Co., 2011.

Boswell, James. *The Life of Samuel Johnson*. Garden City, New York: Doubleday and Company, 1946.

Bowditch, Nathaniel. *The American Practical Navigator*. Washington: United States Hydrographic Office, 1918.

The Bulletin. Buzzards Bay, Mass.: Massachusetts Maritime Academy, vol. 25, no. 11, December 1974.

Carson, Andrew D. *My Time in Hell: Memoir of an American Soldier Imprisoned by the Japanese in World War II*. Jefferson, N.C.: McFarland & Co, 1997.

Catalogue of the Public Latin School in Boston. Boston: Jamaica Press, November 1925.

Clark, J. W. *SSS*. Kings Point, N.Y.: American Merchant Marine Museum, United States Merchant Marine Academy, 2000.

Freeman, Douglas Southall. *R. E. Lee: A Biography*. 4 vols. New York: Charles Scribner's Sons, 1936.

Freeman, Robert. *The Land I Live In and Other Verse*. Pasadena, Calif.: privately published, 1921.

Gibson, Emily with Barbara Firth. *The Original Million Dollar Mermaid: The Annette Kellerman Story*. Crow's Nest, NSW, Australia: Allen & Unwin, 2005.

Graves, Robert. *I, Claudius: From the Autobiography of Tiberius Claudius, Born B.C. 10, Murdered and Deified A.D. 54.* New York: Modern Library, 1961.

McGahern, John. *All Will Be Well: A Memoir.* New York: Alfred A. Knopf, 2007.

McKennon, Joe. *A Pictorial History of the American Carnival.* 2 vols. Sarasota, Fla.: Carnival Publishers, 1972.

Mehegan, Mary. *As I Remember It.* Unpublished, 1989.

——. *Memories of My Mother. Memories of My Father.* Unpublished, 1983.

——. "Some Notes about Al's Father—Charles Mehegan." Unpublished memorandum, 2000.

——. "The Story of 'Grandma Carson,' Al's Mother." Unpublished memorandum, 2002.

Missildine, W. Hugh. *Your Inner Child of the Past.* New York: Simon & Schuster, 1963.

Orwell, George. *Animal Farm.* New York: Harcourt Brace & Co., 1945.

Trillin, Calvin. *Messages from My Father: A Memoir.* New York: Farrar Straus & Giroux, 1996.

Walter, Ahto. *Racing the Seas, the Autobiography of A. Walter, as told to T. Olsen and Recorded by Him.* London: Hurst & Blackett, 1935.

Notes

1. Immigrants and Children

1 Mary Mehegan, "The Story of 'Grandma Carson,' Al's Mother" (unpublished memoir), 2002, 1.
2 Ibid.
3 Ibid.
4 Lisa Bier, *Fighting the Current: The Rise of American Women's Swimming, 1870–1926* (Jefferson, N.C.: McFarland, 2011), 37.
5 Elaine Haite, "Good old days: high diving in Vaudeville" (Riverside, Calif.: *Press-Enterprise*, 1983), B-3.
6 Livingston Wright, "Boston's Star Girl Swimmers," *Physical Culture* (New York: Physical Culture Publishing Co.), June 1910, 540. The others include Rose Pitonof, who went on to fame as a long-distance swimmer. Her 1913 seventeen-mile swim from East 26th Street, Manhattan, to Steeplechase Pier in Coney Island is commemorated annually with a women's race, the Rose Pitonof Swim.
7 Mehegan, 2002, 1.
8 Emily Gibson with Barbara Firth, *The Original Million Dollar Mermaid: The Annette Kellerman Story* (Crow's Nest, NSW, Australia: Allen & Unwin), 2005, 62.
9 Richard K. Fox, editor and publisher of the popular national magazine *Police Gazette*, offered prizes for various sports, including boxing, rowing, and swimming. That this would make Esther "the American champion diver and swimmer" was ballyhoo.
10 Haite, 1983, B-3.
11 Joe McKennon, *A Pictorial History of the American Carnival* (Sarasota, Fla.: Carnival Publishers), vol. 2, 1972, 128.
12 McKennon, 1972, vol. 1, 76–77.
13 Certain of these details are taken from a 1987 letter from Elizabeth Byars.

14 Mehegan, 2002, 2.

15 Andrew D. Carson, *My Time in Hell: Memoir of an American Soldier Imprisoned by the Japanese in World War II* (Jefferson, N.C.: McFarland & Co.), 1997, 95.

2.   Boyhood

1 Mary Mehegan, *As I Remember It* (unpublished autobiography), 1989, 107.

2 Ibid., 109.

3 I tried to gain access to his Perry School records but was told brusquely by the school department records manager that I could not see them unless I was the official heir of my father's estate. I explained that my father died fifty years ago, his spouse had died, and that there was no estate, all to no avail. Later, however, I received a copy of his Boston Latin School records from the Latin School archivist, who was eager to help and rolled her eyes (if that is possible to detect over the phone) at the records manager's position. It's the difference between a bureaucrat and an archivist.

4 Ibid., 107

5 Ibid.

6 Mary Mehegan, "Some Notes About Al's father — Charles Mehegan" (unpublished one-page memoir), 2000. At a corner of the page, she noted "So late to be writing this — Jan. 2000. Just for the family record."

3.   No Excuse for Deviation

1 *Catalogue of the Public Latin School in Boston* (Boston: Jamaica Press), November 1925, 14.

2 "The Ethan Allen Patriot" (Vermont: Fort Ethan Allen), 1929, 23.

3 Ibid., 24.

4 Ibid., 22.

5 The engine, a historic mechanical relic, was saved from the scrap yard and today is displayed at the American Merchant Marine Museum in Kings Point, New York.

6 *The Bulletin*, vol. 25, no. 11, December 1974, 2–11.

7 "When I was a boy of fourteen, my father was so ignorant I could hardly stand to have the old man around. But when I got to be twenty-one, I was

astonished at how much the old man had learned in seven years." The line is attributed to Twain, with various wordings.

4. Down to the Sea

1 This situation would be wholly reversed with the coming of World War II, with barely qualified young men rushed into command. The captain of Alfred's first U.S. Navy ship was a twenty-three-year-old 1940 graduate of the U.S. Merchant Marine Academy at Kings Point, New York.
2 A Hog Island, sometimes called a Hog Islander, was one of more than a hundred ships built in a crash program during World War I at the Hog Island shipyard near Philadelphia. The program was a forerunner of the mass-production shipbuilding methods perfected in World War II.
3 Mary Mehegan, a typed note, c. 1980s, in Alfred's merchant marine records.
4 Ibid.
5 Mehegan, 1989, 108–9.
6 Ahto Walter, *Racing the Seas, the Autobiography of A. Walter, as told to T. Olsen and Recorded by Him* (London: Hurst & Blackett), 1935.

5. Love and Law

1 I found it on YouTube: http://www.youtube.com/watch?v=j8qXtA2bDCE.
2 Mehegan, 1989, 99.
3 Mehegan, 1989, 112.
4 Ibid., 104. The 1940 law school commencement roster includes the name Muriel Cecilia MacDonald.
5 Ibid., 104–05.
6 Ibid., 105.
7 Ibid., 109.
8 Clearly these green receipts had a multitude of uses. This one, alas, has not been located.
9 He did refer to his father as "Dad" to his sister, and in writing. In addition to the journal entry quoted in "Youth," above, two 1944 letters from his ship in the Pacific are addressed "Dear Dad" and end with "Love, Alfred." It seems, however, that he did not speak the name "Dad" directly to his father, or at least so my mother thought.
10 Charlie did not get custody at that time; see p. 18.

11 Ibid., 106.
12 Ibid.
13 Ibid., 108. The age difference was actually about four months: Her birthday was March 29.
14 Ibid.
15 Ibid., 108.
16 Ibid. "Tom" is Tom Sheehan, the law school friend who had shared the memorable double date at the yacht club.
17 Ibid., 112.
18 Ibid.
19 Ibid., 117.
20 Ibid., 118.

6.   Dark Horizon

1 Ibid., 108.
2 Ibid., 112.
3 Ibid., 119–20, and small handwritten note attached to Feb. 17, 1943, ACM letter to Mallard.
4 Ibid., 120.
5 Socony Vacuum Oil in 1963 became Mobil Oil Corporation.
6 Ibid., 122.
7 Ibid.
8 *Portsmouth Herald*, January 8, 1942.
9 Mehegan, 1989, 123.

7.   Secret Agent

1 Mehegan, 1989, 127; also handwritten notes by her, stapled to his discharge card.
2 Handwritten notes.
3 Mehegan, 1989, 128.
4 Ibid., 133.
5 Ibid., 130.
6 This must have been 1943, not 1942, since she wrote below that Peter, born April 1942, was "a little over a year old."
7 Mehegan, 2002, 2.
8 Carson, 1997, 1.

9 "I think that, as life is action and passion, it is required of a man that he should share the passion and action of his time at peril of being judged not to have lived." Oliver Wendell Holmes Jr., Memorial Day address, Keene, N.H., May 30, 1884.

10 Mehegan, 1989, 133.

8.   For the Duration

1 Ibid., 135.

2 Ibid., 135.

3 Mehegan, 2002, 2.

4 J. W. Clark, *SSS* (Kings Point, N.Y: American Merchant Marine Museum, United States Merchant Marine Academy), 2000, 385.

5 Mehegan, 1989, 144.

6 "Standard Operating Procedure of the Transport of Troops: Navy Transport Service, SS *Young America*," undated, 5.

7 Clark, 395.

8 *Princess O'Rourke*, a 1943 Warner Bros romantic comedy starring Olivia de Havilland, Robert Cummings, Jane Wyman, and Charles Coburn.

9 Mehegan, 1989, 145.

10 Carson, 1997, 140–74.

11 Clark, 402.

12 Ibid., 404.

13 Landon's memoir is found at www.georgefamily.net/HJLWWII.html.

14 Clark, 435.

9.   "My Private War"

1 Mehegan, 1989, 142.

2 Ibid., 143. By a strange coincidence, when my son Owen, who lives in San Francisco, read a draft of this section, he recalled an Ed Dullea, a retired firefighter, who is a fellow member of his rowing club. When he saw him next, he asked him if his father had served in the navy in World War II: "Yes." Was he a lawyer? "Yes." Grandfather the chief of police? "Yes." Owen told him, to his amazement, "Your father and my grandfather were shipmates."

3 Ibid.

4 Ibid.

5 Ibid., 146.
6 Ibid., 145.
7 Ibid., 147.
8 Carson, 1997, back cover copy.
9 Mehegan, 1989, 147.

10. Peace

1 Ibid., 147.
2 Ibid., 150.
3 Ibid.
4 Ibid., 154.
5 Ibid.
6 Ibid., 162.
7 Ibid., 164.
8 Ibid., 162.
9 Ibid.
10 Ibid., 157.
11 Ibid., 163.
12 Ibid., 163.
13 Ibid., 164.

11. The Townies

1 Ibid., 144.
2 Ibid., 167.
3 George Orwell, *Animal Farm* (New York: Harcourt Brace & Company), 34.
4 John McGahern, *All Will Be Well* (New York: Alfred A. Knopf, 2007).
5 Mehegan, 1989, 177.
6 Gordon W. Allport, *The Nature of Prejudice* (Boston: Addison-Wesley Publishing Company), 1954.
7 Mehegan, 1989, 174.
8 Ibid., 175.
9 Ibid., 176.
10 Ibid., 179.

12.   Sweet and Bitter

1 Ibid., 181.
2 *Margaret C. Belger vs. Robert E. Arnot,* 344 Mass. 679.
3 Mehegan, 2002, 2.
4 Ibid., 4.
5 Ibid., 6.
6 Ibid., 3.
7 Ibid.,7.
8 Mehegan, 1989, 181.
9 W. Hugh Missildine, *Your Inner Child of the Past* (New York: Simon & Schuster, 1963).

13.   On His Own

1 Mehegan, 2002, 7.
2 Ibid.
3 Ibid.
4 Ibid., 8.

14.   What He Was Like

1 Mehegan, 1989, 181.
2 Ibid.
3 Mary Mehegan, *Memories of My Mother. Memories of My Father* (unpublished), 1983, 6.
4 Mehegan, 1989, 182.
5 Ibid., 180.
6 Ibid., 118.
7 Ibid., 180.
8 Ibid., 181.

15.   Sickness

1 Mehegan, 1983, 21.
2 Mehegan, 1989, 182.

16.   The End of Time

1 Robert Freeman, *The Land I Live In and Other Verse* (Pasadena, California: privately published by author), 1921. Also available from Amazon.com's CreateSpace Independent Publishing Platform.

Index

(**Abbreviations:** Esther Carson, EC; Alfred Mehegan, AM; Charles Mehegan, CM; Mary Humphreys Mehegan, MHM. Family relationships noted are to AM. Page numbers in bold refer to illustrations.)